PERIODIC
TABLE

30	P	E	R	I
Zn				
65.38				

		45	73	81
42		Rh	Ta	Tl
Mo				
95.94		102.90	180.94	204.38

	82	43		9
	Pb	Tc	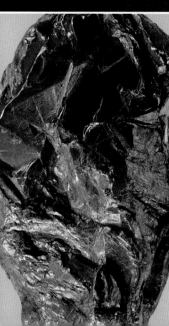	F
	207.2	[98]		18.998

ODIC TABLE

Sean Callery and
Miranda Smith

■ SCHOLASTIC

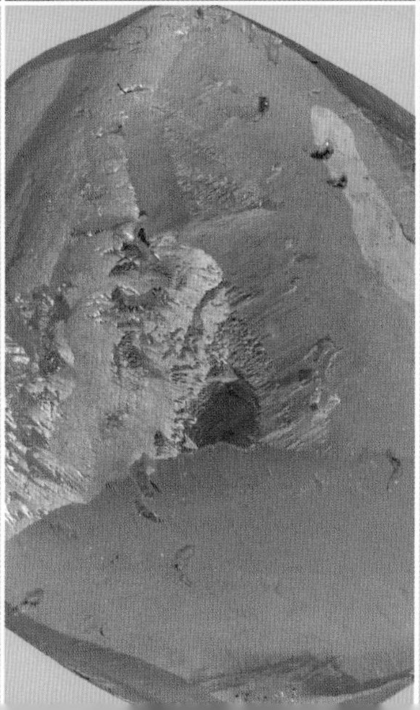

54

Xe

131.29

101

Md

[258]

■■SCHOLASTIC

Art director: Bryn Walls
Managing editor: Miranda Smith
Consultants:
Professor James D. Webster, American Museum
of Natural History, New York
David Ellington BSc, Head of Chemistry,
Seven Kings School, London, England

ISBN 978-1-338-18503-4

10 9 8 7 6 5 4 3 2   17 18 19 20 21

Printed in China   38
First edition, September 2017

CONTENTS

FOREWORD

This book will take you on a journey to the center of the Earth, around its crust, into its atmosphere, and out into space. On the way you will meet the building blocks—the elements—that make you, our world, and the Universe.

Over the centuries, our understanding of elements has grown through experience, observation, and scientific experimentation. It took scientists a long time to work out how to present the elements in a way that showed their relationship to each other. Dmitri Mendeleev's periodic table, published in 1869, does just that, organizing a wealth of data into rows and columns that help us make sense of our world and the Universe we inhabit.

There is so much we still don't know. Elemental matter makes up about 5 percent of the Universe. About 22 percent is dark matter, and 73 percent is dark energy, but we do not know exactly what dark matter and energy are made of. Maybe someone reading this book will find out!

PROFESSOR JAMES D. WEBSTER

DEPARTMENT OF EARTH AND PLANETARY SCIENCES,
AMERICAN MUSEUM OF NATURAL HISTORY

Extraordinary elements create great icons—the Statue of Liberty's coating of copper has reacted over time with water and gases in the air to become blue-green copper carbonate.

WHAT IS AN ELEMENT?

The building blocks of elements—and therefore of all matter—are atoms. Atoms are so tiny that there are many quintillions of them in a grain of sand. Yet, amazingly, they are made of smaller particles—protons, neutrons, electrons—and lots of empty space. If an atom was as big as a stadium, its protons and neutrons would take up the space of a pea.

INSIDE AN ATOM

The core of the atom, and about 99.9 percent of its mass, is the nucleus. This contains protons, which have a positive electric charge, as well as neutrons, which have no charge. Around them spin electrons, whose negative electric charge attracts them to the protons in the middle. This attraction, electromagnetic force, holds the atom together.

ATOMS AND ELEMENTS

An element is a substance that is made entirely from one type of atom. Every element is given an atomic number, which reflects how many protons there are in one atom. Hydrogen atoms have one proton, carbon atoms have six protons, and all gold atoms contain 79 protons, so 1, 6, and 79 are those atoms' atomic numbers.

MOLECULES

Two or more atoms can join together chemically to form a molecule. When atoms do this, they share some of their outermost electrons to make a covalent bond. Molecules have very different

HOW MANY?

Throughout this book, there are diagrams that show the number of protons, neutrons, and electrons that there are in particular elements.

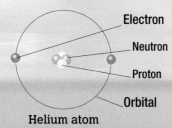

- Electron
- Neutron
- Proton
- Orbital

Helium atom

Mobile molecules

Water molecules contain two hydrogen atoms for every oxygen atom. They are present as a liquid, a solid, and a gas, depending on the temperature. Heat causes the water molecules to move faster until they turn to gas, while cold slows the movement of water molecules until ice is formed.

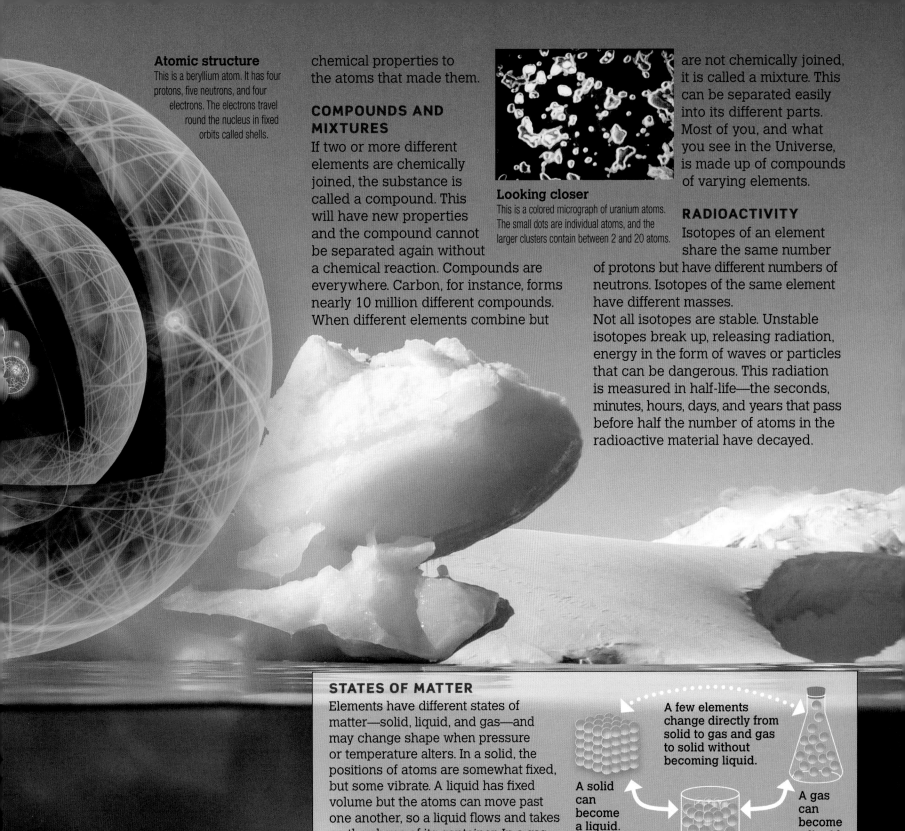

Atomic structure
This is a beryllium atom. It has four protons, five neutrons, and four electrons. The electrons travel round the nucleus in fixed orbits called shells.

chemical properties to the atoms that made them.

COMPOUNDS AND MIXTURES

If two or more different elements are chemically joined, the substance is called a compound. This will have new properties and the compound cannot be separated again without a chemical reaction. Compounds are everywhere. Carbon, for instance, forms nearly 10 million different compounds. When different elements combine but

Looking closer
This is a colored micrograph of uranium atoms. The small dots are individual atoms, and the larger clusters contain between 2 and 20 atoms.

are not chemically joined, it is called a mixture. This can be separated easily into its different parts. Most of you, and what you see in the Universe, is made up of compounds of varying elements.

RADIOACTIVITY

Isotopes of an element share the same number of protons but have different numbers of neutrons. Isotopes of the same element have different masses.

Not all isotopes are stable. Unstable isotopes break up, releasing radiation, energy in the form of waves or particles that can be dangerous. This radiation is measured in half-life—the seconds, minutes, hours, days, and years that pass before half the number of atoms in the radioactive material have decayed.

STATES OF MATTER

Elements have different states of matter—solid, liquid, and gas—and may change shape when pressure or temperature alters. In a solid, the positions of atoms are somewhat fixed, but some vibrate. A liquid has fixed volume but the atoms can move past one another, so a liquid flows and takes on the shape of its container. In a gas, the atoms are randomly arranged and move freely. Gas has no fixed volume or shape, so expands to fill a container.

A few elements change directly from solid to gas and gas to solid without becoming liquid.

A solid can become a liquid.

A gas can become a liquid.

A liquid can become a solid or a gas.

MAKING ELEMENTS

The first elements emerged from the boiling mass of the very early Universe. Others were born in the nuclear furnaces inside stars as they grew and died. The light of the stars that twinkle in the night sky is energy, energy released by violent nuclear reactions like those that created the ingredients that became new stars and planets, and in our case, life itself.

THE FIRST ELEMENTS

The first elements were forged in incredibly high temperatures, around 13.7 billion years ago. Newly formed protons and neutrons cooled and combined into nuclei. These created the gases hydrogen and helium, then the metal, lithium. A little later another metal, beryllium, and a metalloid, boron, appeared. These are the lightest elements on the periodic table. All the remaining, heavier elements we know of were created in blazing nuclear reactions in the hot gases of stars, from around 200 million years later.

A STAR IS BORN . . .

Stars begin as vast clouds of gas and dust hundreds of light years across, known as nebulas. Areas of these clouds knot and collapse under gravity, becoming spinning disks with a core so hot and dense

that it creates its own energy as a star. Small- to medium-size stars like our Sun convert hydrogen and helium into various elements, but nothing heavier than iron. Stars known as red giants (which can be thousands of times bigger than the Sun) make most of the other elements, including those such as copper, zinc, and selenium that the human body needs. The heaviest elements such as iodine (also vital for life) are produced in even more massive stars at the end of their lives called supernovae.

ELEMENTS ON EARTH

Planets such as Earth formed when gravity forced dust and gas into small particles that grew as more matter reached them. The solar wind blew away the lighter elements, such as hydrogen

Mining elements
Many elements can be dug out of the earth, either by hard rock mining deep underground or from open-pit mines like this gold mine in Kalgoorlie, Australia.

and helium, leaving only heavy, rocky materials that eventually became small worlds. Here, the dense material was pulled to the center, leaving lighter materials to make the crust. The elements that made Earth are still here inside our planet, or dissolved in the oceans, or floating in the air, or settled in the crust that forms the land. We can dig them up from under the ground, or drill down to pump out gases and liquids (for example, oil and gas) from deep in the earth below us.

Space rocks
Many elements have blasted into Earth's atmosphere from space on board meteorites. Meteorites are meteoroids that fall to the planet's surface. The largest meteorites leave enormous impact craters.

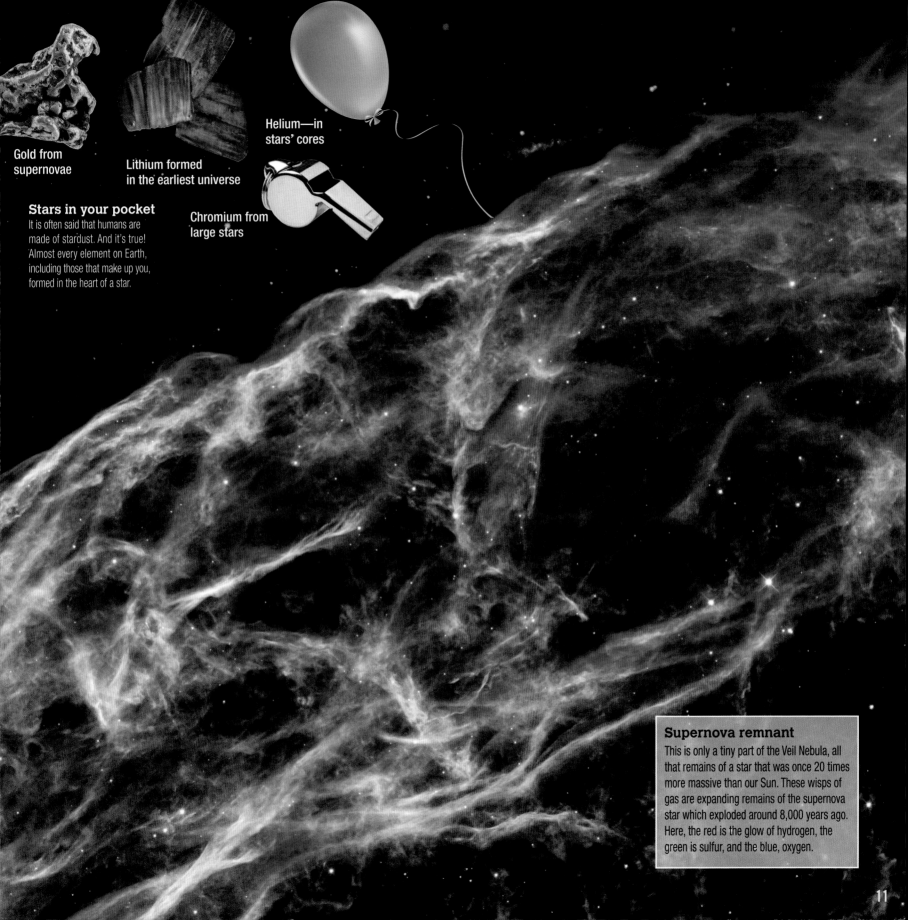

Gold from supernovae

Lithium formed in the earliest universe

Helium—in stars' cores

Chromium from large stars

Stars in your pocket
It is often said that humans are made of stardust. And it's true! Almost every element on Earth, including those that make up you, formed in the heart of a star.

Supernova remnant
This is only a tiny part of the Veil Nebula, all that remains of a star that was once 20 times more massive than our Sun. These wisps of gas are expanding remains of the supernova star which exploded around 8,000 years ago. Here, the red is the glow of hydrogen, the green is sulfur, and the blue, oxygen.

DISCOVERY

Some have worked unnoticed, some have poisoned themselves, some have famously invented things that improved millions of lives. Throughout human history, people have tried to understand elements and what can be done with them. It has been a long journey, and it is far from over.

THE FOUR ELEMENTS

Early civilizations believed that all matter on Earth is made up of mixtures of four "elements"—earth, air, fire, and water. It was thought that materials behaved according to how much of each "element" they contained. People have always valued some materials more than others—gold, for example, has long been prized for its beauty and brightness. Over centuries, people have experimented by tasting, heating, cooling, dissolving in water or acid, grinding to powder, and many other methods. Some were glassmakers wanting to make more highly colored glass; some were doctors looking for new treatments; others were alchemists trying to turn lead into gold.

SCIENTIFIC TESTS

Gradually, these experimenters learned more, such as that air is a mixture of gases and that water is a molecule, showing that neither could be an element in itself. They also developed methods of testing, and theories to prove or disprove. In 1789, French

A fly whisk from the tomb of Tutankhamun

Silicon
Early humans were using rocks to make the first tools at least 2.6 million years ago, during the Stone Age.

Stone Age ax head

Iron
Short swords and daggers were the weapons of choice from the 8th century BCE, during the Iron Age.

Iron Age blade

Gold
Thousands of gold objects were discovered in the tomb of pharaoh Tutankhamun (died ca.1323 BCE).

Copper
Copper coins were used to trade for goods during the Byzantine Empire (330–1453 CE).

Byzantine coins

Bronze Age ax head

Roman pipework

Lead
During the Roman empire (753 BCE—476 CE) lead pipes carried water through the cities.

Copper and tin
By 3500 BCE, copper and tin were being smelted and cast to make bronze.

chemist Antoine Lavoisier showed that an element was a substance that could not be broken down into another substance.

THE PERIODIC TABLE

By 1869, scientists knew of 62 elements, but they struggled to find a way to show how they were related to each other. That year, Dmitri Mendeleev found a way to list elements by their properties, ordering them by their atomic mass (the total number of neutrons and protons in the nucleus) and using columns to show similar properties.

THE NUCLEAR AGE

In 1898, Marie Curie, who, with her husband Pierre, had discovered the elements radium and polonium, coined the term "radioactive," and so began a new age. During the 20th century, nuclear chemists were able to split a nucleus to release huge amounts of energy, which was used to make bombs, and to produce electricity. They also began to make synthetic elements that do not occur in nature but whose existence had been predicted. A team led by Glenn Seaborg discovered 11 synthetic elements and extended the table beyond uranium. In the future, new elements are likely to be discovered and the periodic table will need to be extended further.

Medieval alchemists at work

Dmitri Mendeleev

Marie Curie

Industrial Revolution

Gunpowder

Glenn Seaborg

Computer bank and microchip

Lead and gold
In 13th-century Europe, alchemists worked hard to try and turn lead into gold.

Carbon and sulfur
In 16th-century Europe, gunpowder was used widely in firearms.

Carbon and iron
During the 19th century, new manufacturing processes, industries, and methods of travel became possible.

Silicon
In the 20th century, the development of information technology produced a revolution in communication.

The Large Hadron Collider, the most powerful particle accelerator

New elements
Scientists have made new synthetic elements by colliding particles in particle accelerators.

THE PERIODIC TABLE

Scientists struggled to find a way to display what they knew about the elements until Dmitri Mendeleev put information onto cards that he laid out in rows and columns in 1869. The table was so accurate that he was able to predict the later discovery of unknown elements where there were gaps. The strip of actinoids across the bottom of the table was added by Glenn Seaborg in 1944.

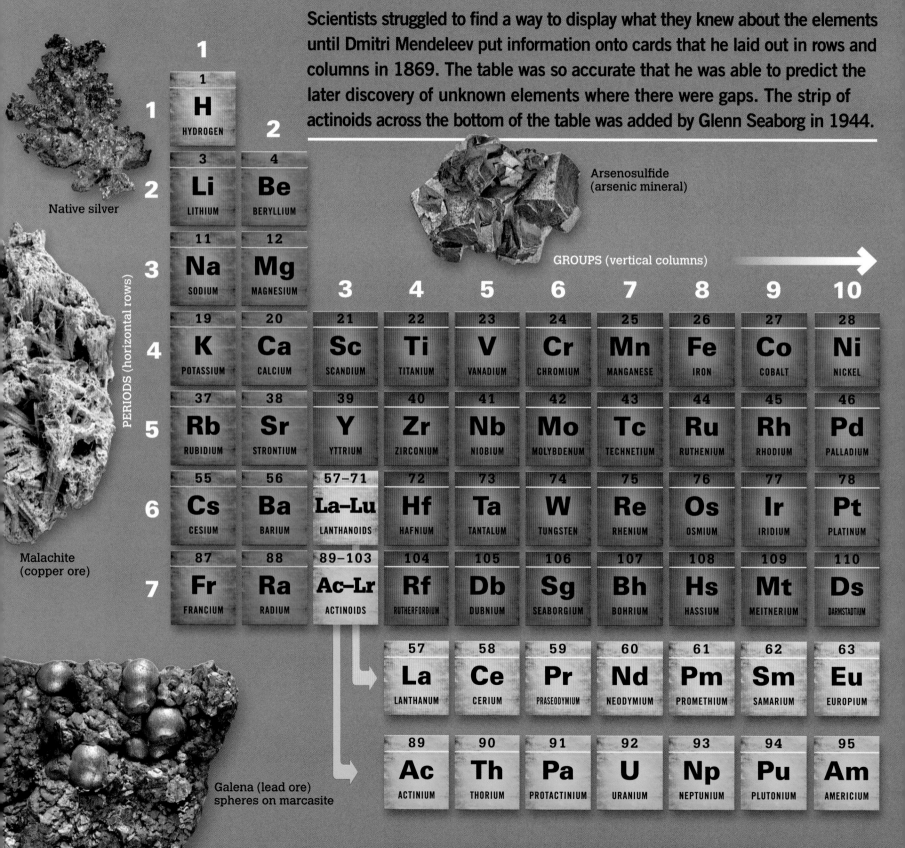

Native silver

Malachite (copper ore)

Arsenosulfide (arsenic mineral)

Galena (lead ore) spheres on marcasite

GROUPS (vertical columns)

PERIODS (horizontal rows)

1	2	3	4	5	6	7	8	9	10
1 **H** HYDROGEN									
3 **Li** LITHIUM	**4** **Be** BERYLLIUM								
11 **Na** SODIUM	**12** **Mg** MAGNESIUM								
19 **K** POTASSIUM	**20** **Ca** CALCIUM	**21** **Sc** SCANDIUM	**22** **Ti** TITANIUM	**23** **V** VANADIUM	**24** **Cr** CHROMIUM	**25** **Mn** MANGANESE	**26** **Fe** IRON	**27** **Co** COBALT	**28** **Ni** NICKEL
37 **Rb** RUBIDIUM	**38** **Sr** STRONTIUM	**39** **Y** YTTRIUM	**40** **Zr** ZIRCONIUM	**41** **Nb** NIOBIUM	**42** **Mo** MOLYBDENUM	**43** **Tc** TECHNETIUM	**44** **Ru** RUTHENIUM	**45** **Rh** RHODIUM	**46** **Pd** PALLADIUM
55 **Cs** CESIUM	**56** **Ba** BARIUM	**57–71** **La-Lu** LANTHANOIDS	**72** **Hf** HAFNIUM	**73** **Ta** TANTALUM	**74** **W** TUNGSTEN	**75** **Re** RHENIUM	**76** **Os** OSMIUM	**77** **Ir** IRIDIUM	**78** **Pt** PLATINUM
87 **Fr** FRANCIUM	**88** **Ra** RADIUM	**89–103** **Ac-Lr** ACTINOIDS	**104** **Rf** RUTHERFORDIUM	**105** **Db** DUBNIUM	**106** **Sg** SEABORGIUM	**107** **Bh** BOHRIUM	**108** **Hs** HASSIUM	**109** **Mt** MEITNERIUM	**110** **Ds** DARMSTADTIUM

57	58	59	60	61	62	63
La LANTHANUM	**Ce** CERIUM	**Pr** PRASEODYMIUM	**Nd** NEODYMIUM	**Pm** PROMETHIUM	**Sm** SAMARIUM	**Eu** EUROPIUM

89	90	91	92	93	94	95
Ac ACTINIUM	**Th** THORIUM	**Pa** PROTACTINIUM	**U** URANIUM	**Np** NEPTUNIUM	**Pu** PLUTONIUM	**Am** AMERICIUM

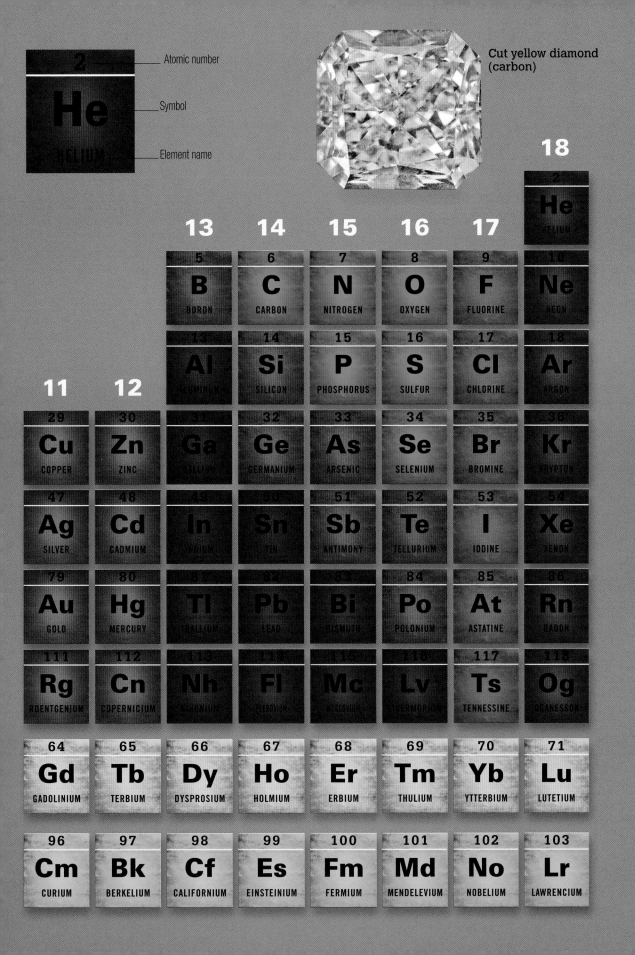

2

He
HELIUM

Atomic number

Symbol

Element name

Cut yellow diamond
(carbon)

18

13 **14** **15** **16** **17**

2
He
HELIUM

5	6	7	8	9	10
B	**C**	**N**	**O**	**F**	**Ne**
BORON	CARBON	NITROGEN	OXYGEN	FLUORINE	NEON

13	14	15	16	17	18
Al	**Si**	**P**	**S**	**Cl**	**Ar**
ALUMINUM	SILICON	PHOSPHORUS	SULFUR	CHLORINE	ARGON

11 **12**

29	30	31	32	33	34	35	36
Cu	**Zn**	**Ga**	**Ge**	**As**	**Se**	**Br**	**Kr**
COPPER	ZINC	GALLIUM	GERMANIUM	ARSENIC	SELENIUM	BROMINE	KRYPTON

47	48	49	50	51	52	53	54
Ag	**Cd**	**In**	**Sn**	**Sb**	**Te**	**I**	**Xe**
SILVER	CADMIUM	INDIUM	TIN	ANTIMONY	TELLURIUM	IODINE	XENON

79	80	81	82	83	84	85	86
Au	**Hg**	**Tl**	**Pb**	**Bi**	**Po**	**At**	**Rn**
GOLD	MERCURY	THALLIUM	LEAD	BISMUTH	POLONIUM	ASTATINE	RADON

111	112	113	114	115	116	117	118
Rg	**Cn**	**Nh**	**Fl**	**Mc**	**Lv**	**Ts**	**Og**
ROENTGENIUM	COPERNICIUM	NIHONIUM	FLEROVIUM	MOSCOVIUM	LIVERMORIUM	TENNESSINE	OGANESSON

64	65	66	67	68	69	70	71
Gd	**Tb**	**Dy**	**Ho**	**Er**	**Tm**	**Yb**	**Lu**
GADOLINIUM	TERBIUM	DYSPROSIUM	HOLMIUM	ERBIUM	THULIUM	YTTERBIUM	LUTETIUM

96	97	98	99	100	101	102	103
Cm	**Bk**	**Cf**	**Es**	**Fm**	**Md**	**No**	**Lr**
CURIUM	BERKELIUM	CALIFORNIUM	EINSTEINIUM	FERMIUM	MENDELEVIUM	NOBELIUM	LAWRENCIUM

Team talk

The groups, or vertical columns, are families of elements that react in similar ways. Three-quarters of all known elements are metals. Some properties are shared across neighboring groups, forming larger teams of related elements.

Alkali metals
Soft, shiny, and extremely reactive metals.

Alkaline earth metals
Silvery-white reactive metals that form minerals.

Transition metals
Tough, versatile metals that are easy to shape.

Poor metals
Soft metals with some nonmetal characteristics.

Metalloids
These have both metal and nonmetal characteristics.

Nonmetals
Gases and solids with differing chemistry.

Halogens
A group of reactive elements, also called salt-formers.

Noble gases
Generally unreactive, colorless, and odorless.

Lanthanoids
Reactive metals with a similar chemistry.

Actinoids
Many of these are made in nuclear reactors.

FIERY

ELEMENTS

THE WILD BUNCH

Do not mess with these elements! They are the fizzy, excitable elements on the left side of the periodic table. These are the most reactive elements, so are rarely found in their pure state because they are always mixing with other elements to form compounds, as in many of these examples. Fiery elements love a party, and as ingredients for fireworks, they are perfect for making a big display.

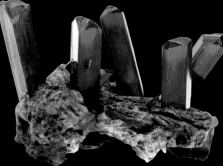

Potassium-ferricyanide (potassium)

The Sun (hydrogen)

Lithium

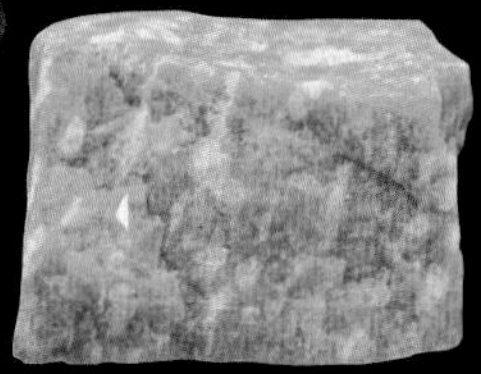

Microcline (potassium)

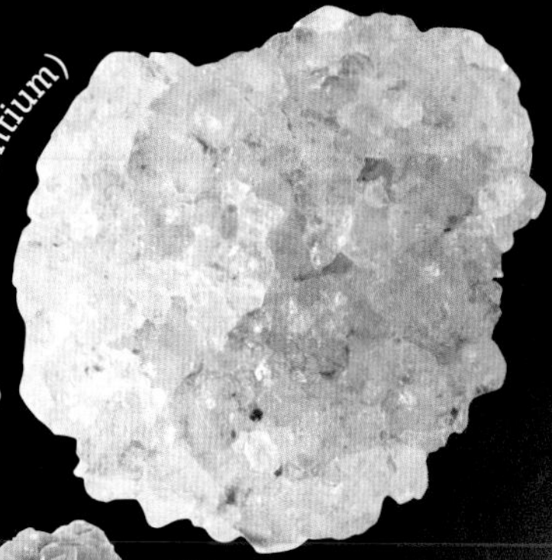

Celestine (strontium)

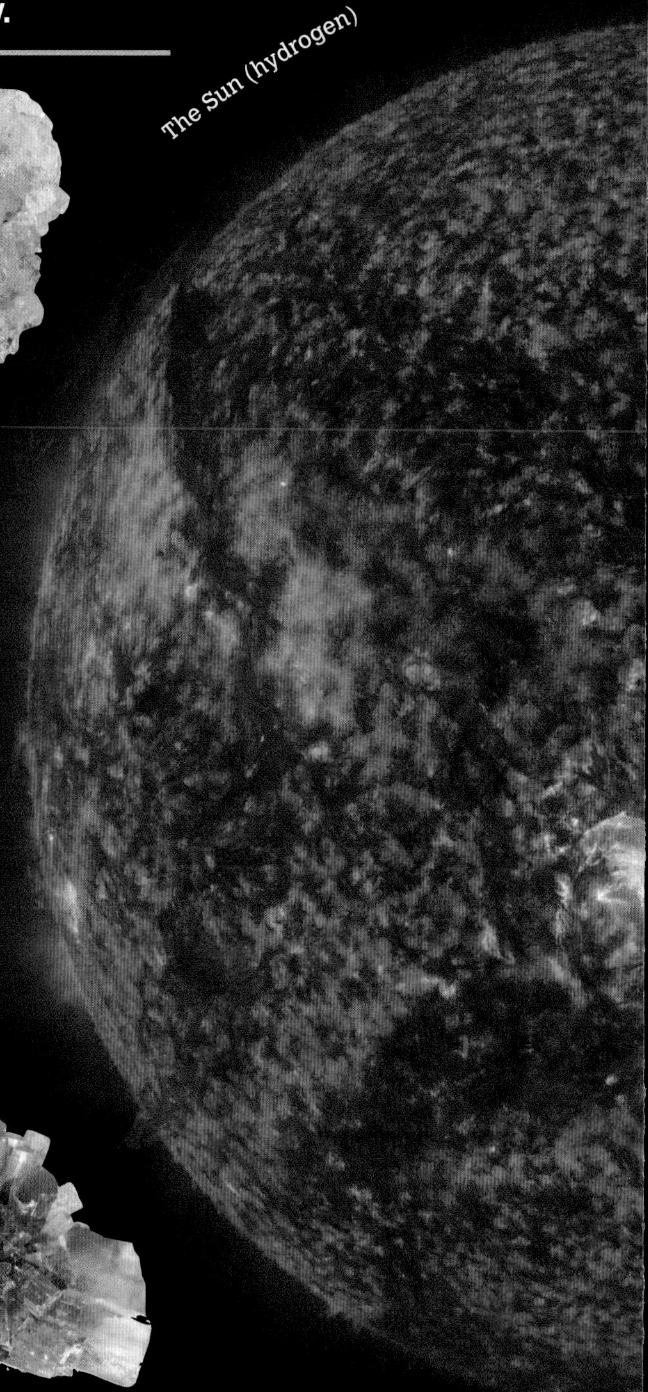

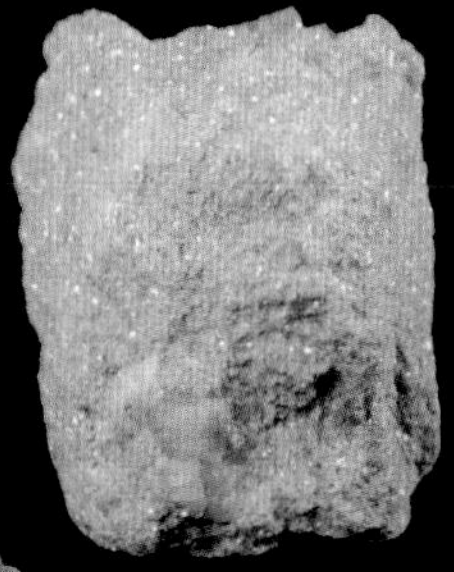

Lepidolite (lithium)

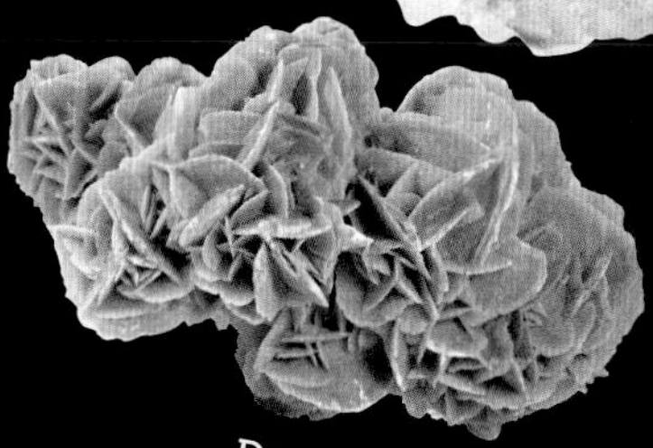

Desert rose (calcium)

Magnesium

Pollucite (rubidium)

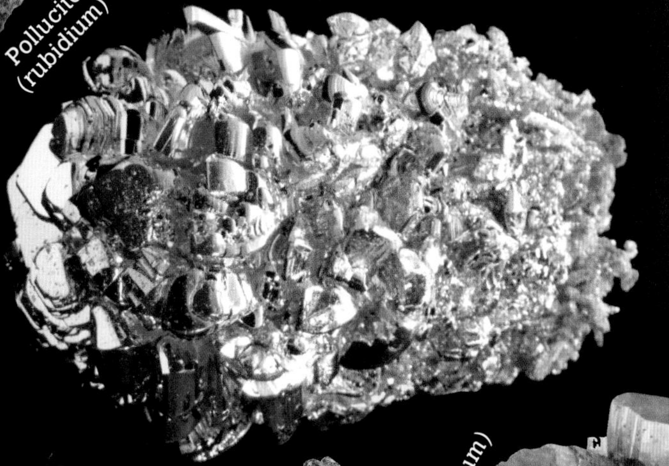

Aragonite (calcium)

Emerald (beryllium)

Water (hydrogen)

Phlogopite (magnesium)

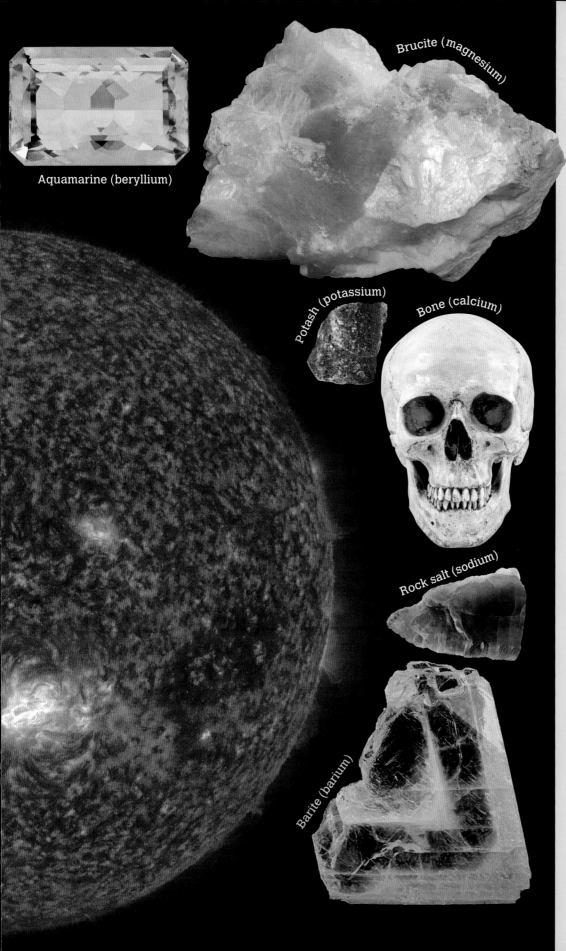

Aquamarine (beryllium)

Brucite (magnesium)

Potash (potassium)

Bone (calcium)

Rock salt (sodium)

Barite (barium)

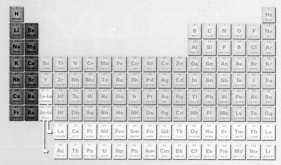

On the left
To the left of the periodic table, hydrogen is in a class of its own, not belonging to any family of elements. It sits at the top of a group of reactive, soft alkali metals, which are followed by the harder but less reactive alkaline earth metals.

HYDROGEN, THE SPECIAL ONE
Every element has its own properties, but hydrogen is a true one-off. It is made up of one proton and one electron and, unlike any other element, it has no neutrons. Although it is a gas, it is different from the other gases, which are mainly non-reactive. Hydrogen could also be considered as a reactive alkali metal since it sometimes reacts with atoms that attract electrons. Indeed, some scientists say they have managed to make it into a metal by squeezing it at incredible pressure between pieces of diamond.

ALKALI AND ALKALINE METALS
Alkali metals have only one electron in their outer shell of electrons, and they really want to lose it by bonding with other elements. This makes them so reactive they can explode if they even touch water, and change color when they reach air. Alkaline earth metals are less lively because their atoms have two electrons in their outer shell, making them more stable—but they are still never found in a pure form on Earth.

HYDROGEN

FIRST ELEMENT

We owe everything to hydrogen. It was among the first elements formed, and it fuels the Sun that warms our planet. It is so light in weight that much of it escapes from Earth's atmosphere. What is left behind binds with other elements to form water, as well as hydrocarbons, acids, and hydroxides. At very low temperatures and high pressures this clear, odorless gas becomes a liquid and even a liquid metal.

1

H

1.008

Atomic number: 1

Formula: H

Atomic weight: 1.00794

State at 68°F (20°C): gas

Boiling point: –423.182°F (–252.879°C)

Melting point: –434.49°F (–259.16°C)

% in the Universe: 73

% in Earth's crust: 0.15

% in Earth's oceans: 11

% in humans: 9.5

Uses: for nuclear fusion reactors; to make ammonia for fertilizers; to remove sulfur from fuels during oil refining; to hydrogenate oils to form fats (ie for margarine); in the glass industry as a protective atmosphere; manufacture of silicon chips; in welding; as a coolant; as a clean fuel; rocket fuel; in the reduction of metallic ores

e1 | p1 | n0

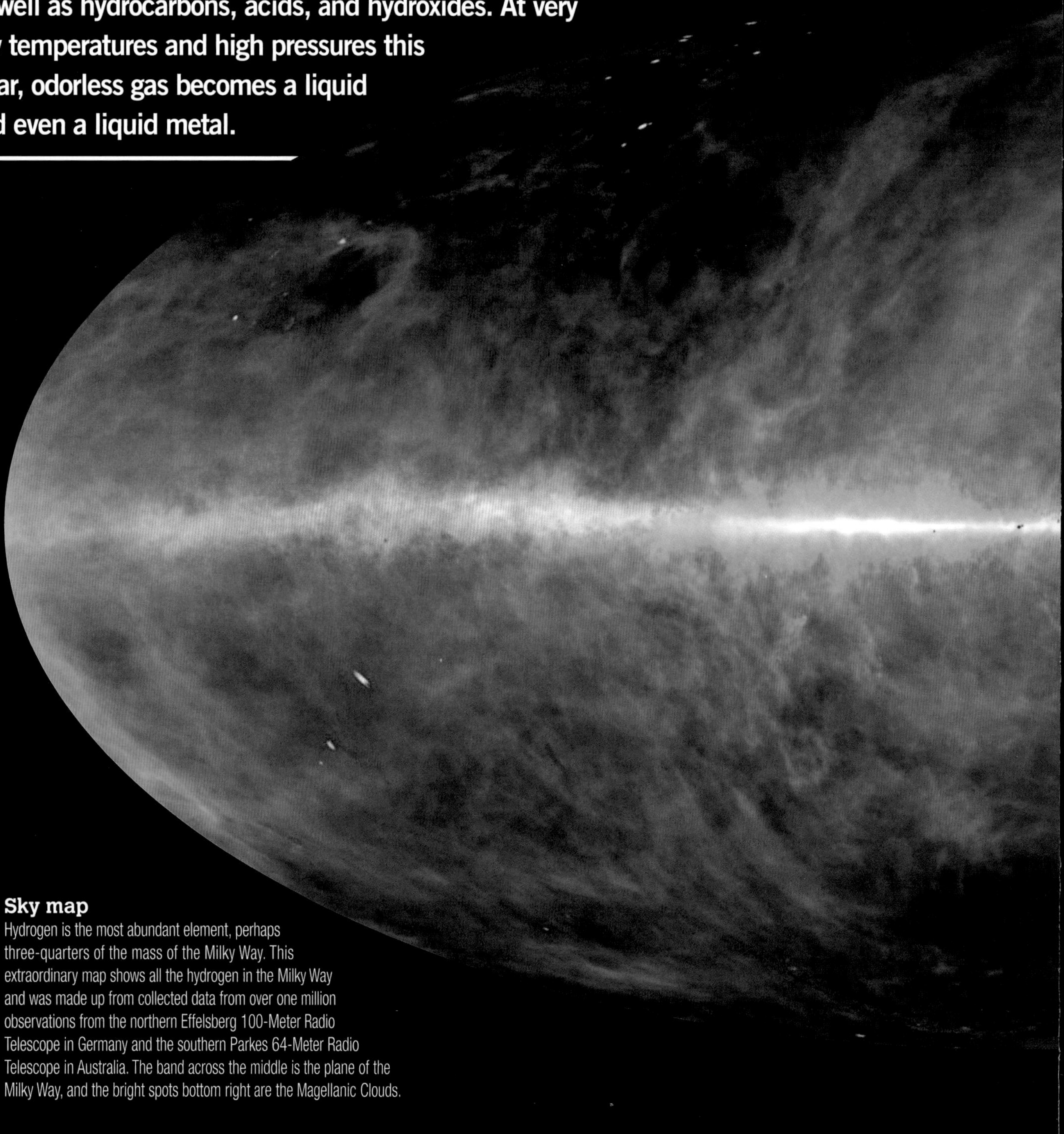

Sky map

Hydrogen is the most abundant element, perhaps three-quarters of the mass of the Milky Way. This extraordinary map shows all the hydrogen in the Milky Way and was made up from collected data from over one million observations from the northern Effelsberg 100-Meter Radio Telescope in Germany and the southern Parkes 64-Meter Radio Telescope in Australia. The band across the middle is the plane of the Milky Way, and the bright spots bottom right are the Magellanic Clouds.

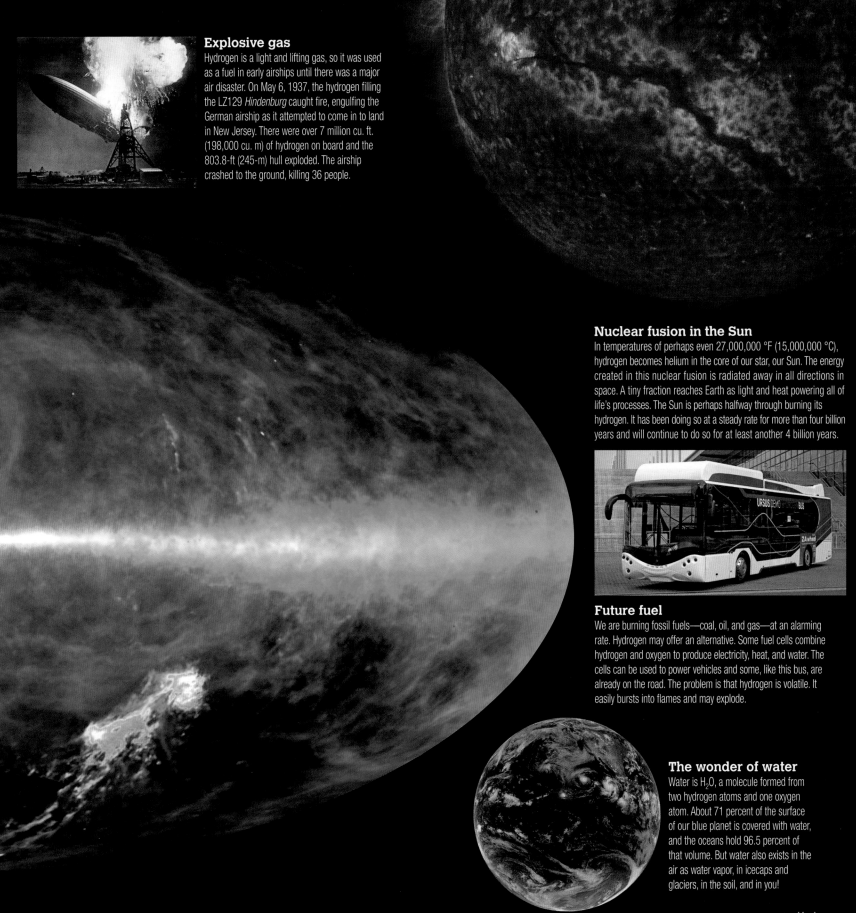

Explosive gas

Hydrogen is a light and lifting gas, so it was used as a fuel in early airships until there was a major air disaster. On May 6, 1937, the hydrogen filling the LZ129 *Hindenburg* caught fire, engulfing the German airship as it attempted to come in to land in New Jersey. There were over 7 million cu. ft. (198,000 cu. m) of hydrogen on board and the 803.8-ft (245-m) hull exploded. The airship crashed to the ground, killing 36 people.

Nuclear fusion in the Sun

In temperatures of perhaps even 27,000,000 °F (15,000,000 °C), hydrogen becomes helium in the core of our star, our Sun. The energy created in this nuclear fusion is radiated away in all directions in space. A tiny fraction reaches Earth as light and heat powering all of life's processes. The Sun is perhaps halfway through burning its hydrogen. It has been doing so at a steady rate for more than four billion years and will continue to do so for at least another 4 billion years.

Future fuel

We are burning fossil fuels—coal, oil, and gas—at an alarming rate. Hydrogen may offer an alternative. Some fuel cells combine hydrogen and oxygen to produce electricity, heat, and water. The cells can be used to power vehicles and some, like this bus, are already on the road. The problem is that hydrogen is volatile. It easily bursts into flames and may explode.

The wonder of water

Water is H_2O, a molecule formed from two hydrogen atoms and one oxygen atom. About 71 percent of the surface of our blue planet is covered with water, and the oceans hold 96.5 percent of that volume. But water also exists in the air as water vapor, in icecaps and glaciers, in the soil, and in you!

Hydrogen in the stars

This giant pillar of dust and gas is part of the Cone Nebula, a turbulent incubator for new stars 2,500 light-years away from Earth in the constellation Monoceros. Ultraviolet light heats the edges of the cloud, releasing hydrogen gas into space, seen here as a red halo.

GASES IN THE UNIVERSE

About 13.7 billion years ago, the gases hydrogen and helium were the first elements to appear. Our Universe is still made up of roughly 73 percent hydrogen and 25 percent helium by mass. The other gases and elements that are forged from the heat of the stars are only present in tiny quantities. But a lot of them are present on Earth, including the gases and elements that support life.

Identifying gases in space

Every element on the periodic table gives off its own unique pattern of colors—a kind of personal fingerprint. To find out what gases are out there in space, most astronomers use some variation of an instrument called a spectrometer. This machine takes the light coming directly from, or reflected by, an object in space, and separates the light out into its unique color pattern or spectrum. This allows astronomers to determine which gases or other elements they are looking at.

Hydrogen emission spectrum

Helium emission spectrum

Mauna Kea observatory, Hawaii

Gas giants

In the outer part of our solar system, there are four gas giants, large planets with solid cores, but that are composed mainly of gases. They include the largest planet in the solar system, Jupiter, as well as Saturn, Uranus, and Neptune.

Jupiter—89.8% hydrogen, 10.2% helium

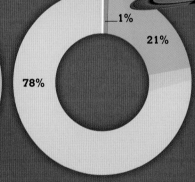

Saturn—96.3% hydrogen, 3.2% helium, trace amounts of methane and ammonia

Uranus—82.5% hydrogen, 15.2% helium, 2.3% methane

Neptune—80% hydrogen, 19% helium, 1% methane

Earth's gases

The layer of gases that surrounds Earth, held to it by gravity, is known as the atmosphere. Scientists say that oxygen was first produced in the atmosphere around 2.7 billion years ago, but it took another billion years for oxidation to take place and enable life to flourish on the planet.

Changing the atmosphere

The air we breathe today came from tiny blue-green algae (above) that started a process called photosynthesis. Plants use energy from sunlight to produce glucose from carbon dioxide and water, and pump oxygen into the atmosphere.

0.8%
3.3%
95.9%

Early composition of air

Earth's early atmosphere was mostly carbon dioxide, similar to that of Mars and Venus today.

1%
21%
78%

Modern composition of air

For the last 200 million years, nitrogen and oxygen have been our planet's main gases.

KEY   ● Nitrogen   ● Carbon dioxide   ● Others in trace amounts,
       ● Oxygen   ● Argon   including carbon dioxide

ALKALI
METALS

Explosive encounter

Alkali metals are so ready to lose the one electron in their shell that, for safety, they must normally be kept in oil or jelly to avoid contact with water or the air. When sodium is added to water (right), the sodium melts to form a ball that moves rapidly around on the surface. The sodium fizzes and the hydrogen gas it produces burns with an orange flame.

These metals want to bond with other elements to get rid of the one electron in their outer shell. But don't be fooled into thinking this is a calm bunch: they are so unstable they can explode in water and will change color as soon as they hit air.

Soft and shiny
This family of six elements is solid and bendable, shiny and light in weight. They are sometimes soft enough to be cut with a dull knife.

ALKALI METALS TIMELINE

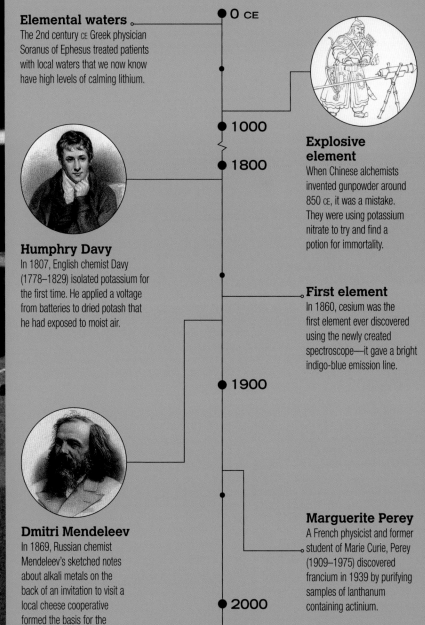

Elemental waters
The 2nd century CE Greek physician Soranus of Ephesus treated patients with local waters that we now know have high levels of calming lithium.

● 0 CE

● 1000

● 1800

Humphry Davy
In 1807, English chemist Davy (1778–1829) isolated potassium for the first time. He applied a voltage from batteries to dried potash that he had exposed to moist air.

Explosive element
When Chinese alchemists invented gunpowder around 850 CE, it was a mistake. They were using potassium nitrate to try and find a potion for immortality.

First element
In 1860, cesium was the first element ever discovered using the newly created spectroscope—it gave a bright indigo-blue emission line.

● 1900

Dmitri Mendeleev
In 1869, Russian chemist Mendeleev's sketched notes about alkali metals on the back of an invitation to visit a local cheese cooperative formed the basis for the periodic table.

● 2000

Marguerite Perey
A French physicist and former student of Marie Curie, Perey (1909–1975) discovered francium in 1939 by purifying samples of lanthanum containing actinium.

LITHIUM

3

Li

6.941

ALKALI METAL

Lithium is a high flier. As the lightest metal, it can be alloyed with other lightweights such as aluminum to make plane parts, and it helps astronauts by absorbing the CO_2 they breathe out. Back on Earth, it is terrific at storing electricity in batteries and, increasingly, cars. Although this silvery metal reacts vigorously with water, it is the least reactive of all the alkali metals.

Atomic number: 3

Formula: Li

Atomic weight: 6.941

State at 68°F (20°C): solid

Melting point: 356.90°F (180.50°C)

Boiling point: 2448°F (1342°C)

% in the Universe: 0.00000060

% in Earth's crust: 0.0017

% in Earth's oceans: 0.000018

% in humans: 0.0000030

Uses: batteries for e.g. cell phones, laptops, digital cameras, electric cars, pacemakers, toys, clocks; armor plating; aircraft; bicycle frames; high-speed trains; special glass; glass ceramics; air-conditioning; as a high-temperature lubricant; for storing hydrogen for use as a fuel

e3 ǀ p3 ǀ n4

Active metal
Lithium is soft and the lightest metal of them all. In its pure form it is silver-white, but it turns gray in the air. It burns white, with a hint of crimson, something that helped separate it from other elements in the 19th century.

Energy source
Many electronic devices use batteries that contain lithium metal or lithium compounds. Lithium is ideal for rechargeable batteries for laptops.

Salty crust
Bolivia's Salar de Uyuni is the largest salt flat in world. Stretching over 4,086 sq. miles (10,582 sq. km), it contains more lithium carbonate reserves than anywhere else, maybe as much as 70 percent of the world's reserves.

Lithium-rich
The mineral lepidolite is the most abundant source of lithium. Lepidolite is not a common ore, and is mainly mined in Afghanistan, Brazil, Sweden, Portugal, and the US. The violet to pink color is a characteristic that helps to identify it.

RUBIDIUM
ALKALI METAL

This silvery metal has such a low melting point that it could turn to liquid in your hand. Each atom gives off radiation at exactly 6,834,682,610.904324 cycles per second, so reliably that rubidium is used in super-accurate atomic clocks.

Atomic number: 37
Formula: Rb
Atomic weight: 85.4678
Melting point: 102.74°F (39.30°C)
Boiling point: 1279°F (688°C)
% in Earth's oceans: 0.000012
% in humans: 0.00046
Uses: only tiny amounts are made, mainly for use in research; also photocells; in devices that control cell phones and sat navs; atomic clocks; in fireworks

Purple fire
This element plays its part in firework displays. Rubidium nitrate is used to give a brilliant violet-red color.

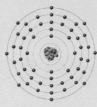

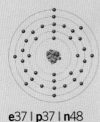

Energy source
Rubidium can be extracted from various minerals, including zinnwaldite (above), lepidolite, and pollucite. Most of it is produced as a byproduct of refined lithium.

Rubidium is as **abundant as zinc** and **about** as **common** as **copper**.

e37 | p37 | n48

CESIUM
ALKALI METAL

Watch out! Cesium is so reactive it explodes in water, so it must be stored in oil and only handled in an inert atmosphere. Still, we all have time for cesium—it is used to keep clocks so accurate that two of them would only be a second apart after 100 million years. Its name is Latin for "sky blue."

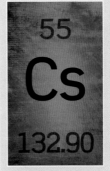

Atomic number: 55
Formula: Cs
Atomic weight: 132.90545
Melting point: 83.3°F (28.5°C)
Boiling point: 1240°F (671°C)
% in the Universe: 0.000000080
% in humans: 0.0000020
Uses: clocks; oil drilling; photoelectric cells; vacuum tubes; in magnetometers; in nuclear reactors

Discovery
German chemists Robert Bunsen (top) and Gustav Kirchhoff discovered cesium in 1860 in mineral water from Dürkheim, in Germany.

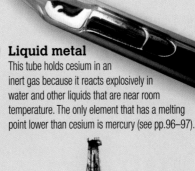

Liquid metal
This tube holds cesium in an inert gas because it reacts explosively in water and other liquids that are near room temperature. The only element that has a melting point lower than cesium is mercury (see pp.96–97).

Oil wells
Cesium hydroxide is made to react with formic acid to make cesium formate fluid. This is used to control well pressures when drilling oil or gas wells.

e55 | p55 | n78

FRANCIUM
ALKALI METAL

Francium is the rarest element on Earth. How rare? Well, every billion billion atoms of uranium ore contains just one atom of francium. The heaviest of the alkali metals, it was discovered in 1939 by French chemist Marguerite Perey, who named it after her home country.

Atomic number: 87
Formula: Fr
Atomic weight: [223]
Half-life: 22 minutes
Uses: no practical applications because of the high-speed rate of decay

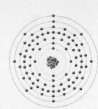

e87 | p87 | n136

SODIUM

ALKALI METAL

11
Na
22.990

Sodium helps our food taste good and lights our cities. This soft, silvery metal is so light that it floats on water, and it reacts quickly with other elements in useful ways. With chlorine, it forms table salt to add to our food. As a solid, it lights our streets because it vaporizes when electricity is run through it, producing an orange glow.

Atomic number: 11
Formula: Na
Atomic weight: 22.989770
State at 68°F (20°C): solid
Boiling point: 1621.292°F (882.940°C)
Melting point: 208.029°F (97.794°C)
% in the Universe: 0.002
% in Earth's crust: 2.3
% in Earth's oceans: 1.1
% in humans: 0.2

Uses: as a heat exchanger in some nuclear reactors; solar farms; as a reagent in the chemicals industry; as sodium chloride: added to food; to de-ice roads in winter; as sodium salts: soaps; glazes, porcelain enamel; manufacture of baking soda, caustic soda, chlorine, and other chemicals

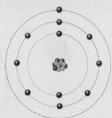

e11 | p11 | n12

Salt in humans
The human body contains many salts, but sodium chloride (rock salt or halite) is the major one. The average human has around 8.8oz (250g) of salt in their body, which is needed to help transmit nerve signals (left) and regulate water levels in tissues and blood. Since salt is lost from the body whenever we sweat, the sodium chloride must be continually replaced.

Halite or rock salt

Maricite

Albite

Tourmaline

Salt mining
Sodium chloride is the only family of rocks to be regularly eaten by humans. Some is mined. Some is produced by evaporation of seawater, or from special ponds of brine, as in the mountains of Peru (above).

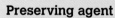

Preserving agent
In ancient Egypt, embalmers carried out a mummification process that could take up to 70 days. This was intended to ensure the survival of a dead person for all eternity. Natron salt crystals collected from the edges of desert lakes were used to dehydrate, or dry out, the dead bodies.

Labradorite
This beautiful mineral is abundant in Earth's crust. It is one of the plagioclase feldspars that are the first to crystallize from high-temperature molten rock. They are calcium- and sodium-rich. As the rock cools, the sodium becomes concentrated and there can be anything from 30 to 50 percent in a sample.

Farming the beaches

At Doc Let Beach, Hon Khoi, in Vietnam, mounds of natural salt are harvested from shallow salt fields. From March to July every year, salt is collected by workers wearing protective clothing. The salt is left to evaporate for about 10 days, then it is collected and covered by canvas for five months to improve its quality. This is one of the largest salt fields in the country. Vietnam has a long coastline, and commercial salt production along its beaches by this and other more complicated methods generates around 810,000 tons a year.

Crystals
Sylvite, also called
sylvine, is very valuable
commercially because it is
mined for potassium. Sylvite forms
crystals that are similar to rock salt
(halite) and they are often found together.
The coarse-grained ore in this sample is
a mixture of sylvite (potassium chloride)
and halite (sodium chloride).

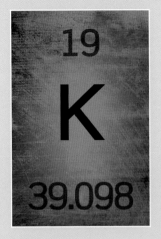

19

K

39.098

POTASSIUM

ALKALI METAL

This soft metal loves color. It burns with a bright lilac flame when it touches water, turns black in the open air, and is found inside all sorts of foods, including vividly colored fruits such as bananas and melons. It helps feed many of us since it is in the powerful fertilizers used by farmers, and it allows your brain to contract your muscles.

FOUND IN

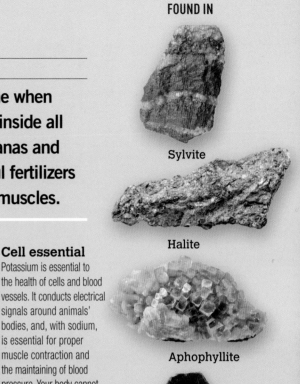

Sylvite

Halite

Aphophyllite

Muscovite

Atomic number: 19

Formula: K

Atomic weight: 39.098

State at 68°F (20°C): solid

Boiling point: 1398°F (759°C)

Melting point: 146.3°F (63.5°C)

% in the Universe: 0.0003

% in Earth's crust: 1.5

% in Earth's oceans: 0.042

% in humans: 0.4

Uses: in fertilizers; in glass production to toughen the glass; dyes; in detergent and liquid soap; in drain cleaners; in alkaline batteries; pharmaceuticals and saline drips; deodorants; textile and leather production; gold mining; photography; as a healthy alternative to table salt; in gunpowder; for fireworks; in nuclear reactors; as a heat exchange medium; bleaching textiles; enamels; ceramics; photographic film

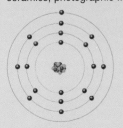

e19 | p19 | n20

Cell essential

Potassium is essential to the health of cells and blood vessels. It conducts electrical signals around animals' bodies, and, with sodium, is essential for proper muscle contraction and the maintaining of blood pressure. Your body cannot make potassium, so it must be obtained from foods. Most of the 85 percent of the potassium your body absorbs is taken in through the cells of the small intestine (left).

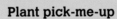

Plant pick-me-up

Potassium is vital for the health of plant cells. Crops quickly deplete potassium, so farmers spread their land with potash-rich fertilizers (potash is a term for any salt that contains water-soluble potassium).

Potassium was the **first elemental metal** to be found using an **electric** current.

Soft metal

If you cut pure potassium—you can do this easily with a knife because it is so soft—it is bright silver. However, it quickly tarnishes to a gray-black when exposed to air. It also reacts instantly with water to release hydrogen that burns with a lilac flame. Potassium is the seventh most abundant element in Earth's crust.

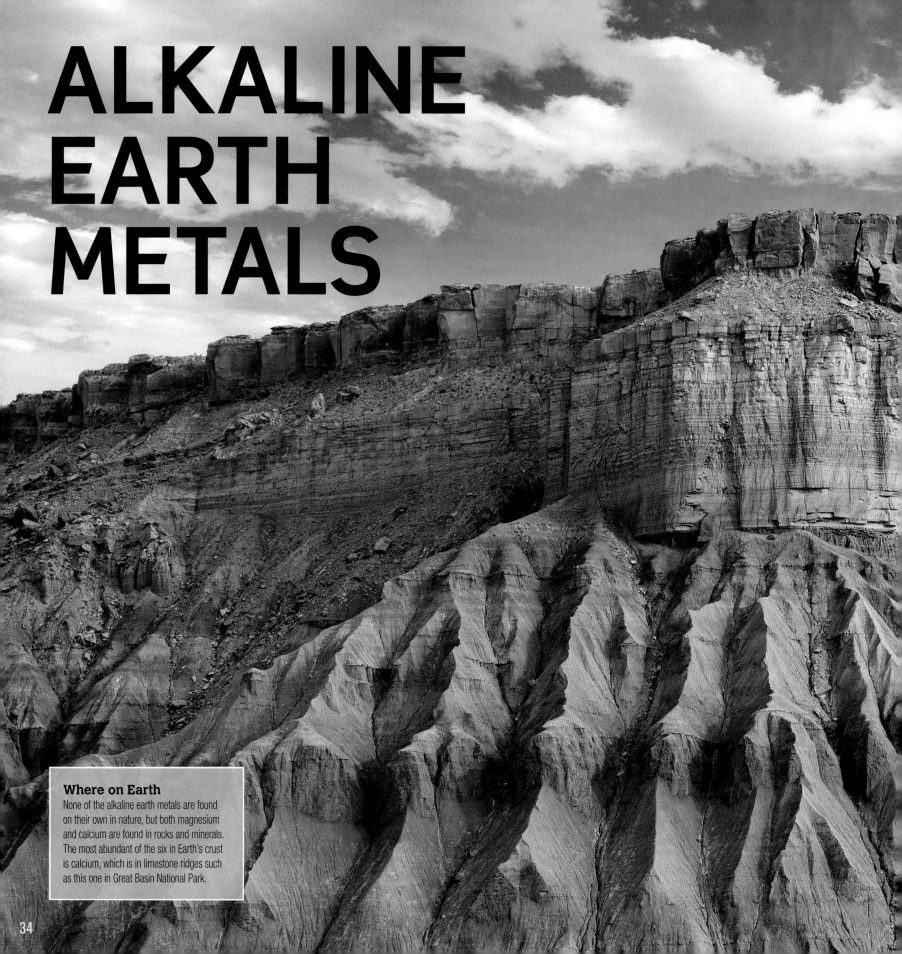

ALKALINE EARTH METALS

Where on Earth
None of the alkaline earth metals are found on their own in nature, but both magnesium and calcium are found in rocks and minerals. The most abundant of the six in Earth's crust is calcium, which is in limestone ridges such as this one in Great Basin National Park.

These soft metals are the less lively cousins of the alkali metals. They are more stable because their atoms have two electrons in the outer shell. They combine easily with oxygen, forming minerals that are found in Earth's crust.

Strong metals
These shiny, silvery-gray metals are very lightweight but also strong, so they are often added to alloys. The six elements are excellent conductors of heat and electricity.

ALKALINE EARTH METALS TIMELINE

● 1700

Limestone

Separating barium
Swedish chemist Carl Wilhelm Scheele (1742–1786) distinguished barium from lime in 1774. He called it "terra ponderosa," meaning "heavy earth."

Joseph Black
In 1775, Scottish chemist Joseph Black (1728–1799) was investigating magnesia alba (magnesium oxide) as a possible cure for indigestion when he recognized that magnesium was actually an element in its own right.

Louis Nicolas Vauquelin
In 1798, French chemist Vauquelin (1763–1829) announced that he had found an element that was later called beryllium.

First isolation
In 1808, British chemist Humphry Davy (1778–1829) isolated magnesium as an element for the first time. In the same year, he isolated strontium and barium.

● 1800

Marie and Pierre Curie
In 1898, the married scientists first identified a new element from a sample of pitchblende. They called it radium. In the same year, they discovered polonium.

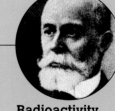

Radioactivity
In 1896, French physicist Antoine Henri Becquerel (1852–1908) found the first evidence of radioactivity when he investigated the X-rays newly discovered by a German professor of physics, Wilhelm Röntgen (1845–1923).

● 1900

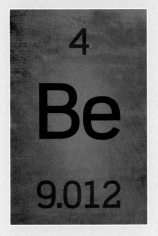

4

Be

9.012

BERYLLIUM

Beryllium is a gem of an element—literally, for it is a key ingredient in gemstones such as emeralds and aquamarine. It is light and strong and does not burn easily when solid, so is used in rockets. And it should feel at home in space because this element is generated during supernova explosions, when stars break up, and by cosmic rays. It should be handled with care, however, because it can be highly toxic.

Atomic number: 4

Formula: Be

Atomic weight: 9.012182

State at 68°F (20°C): solid

Boiling point: 4474°F (2468°C)

Melting point: 2349°F (1287°C)

% in the Universe: 0.0000001

% in Earth's crust: 0.00019

% in Earth's oceans: 0.000000000060

% in humans: 0.000000040

Uses: in alloys with copper or nickel for gyroscopes, computer parts, electrical contacts, spot-welding, and non-sparking tools; for high-speed aircraft, missiles, spacecraft, and communication satellites; for X-ray lithography; in nuclear reactors

e4 | p4 | n5

Gem source
In 1798, French chemist Louis Nicolas Vauquelin found beryllium in the mineral beryl and the green-colored variety of beryl, the emerald (above). Beryl is the source of two other precious gems, aquamarine and morganite.

Silver metal
At room temperature and pressure, beryllium forms a brittle silvery metal. When alloyed with other elements, such as copper and nickel, the element enhances the strength, wear-resistance, and conductivity of the alloy.

Raw form
Today, beryllium is usually extracted from beryl, seen here in its raw form, and another mineral called bertrandite, although it is found in up to 100 different minerals.

Copper specimen
Beryllium's excellent conductivity makes it perfect for use in sensors in communication and observation satellites, such as Jason-2 (right).

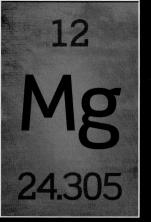

12
Mg
24.305

Atomic number: 12

Formula: Mg

Atomic weight: 24.305

State at 68°F (20°C): solid

Boiling point: 1994°F (1090°C)

Melting point: 1202°F (650°C)

% in the Universe: 0.060

% in Earth's crust: 2.9

% in Earth's oceans: 0.13

% in humans: 0.1

Uses: as an alloy in airplane and car construction; to make lightweight car seats, luggage, laptops, cameras, and power tools; in photographic flashbulbs; in cell phones; in pyrotechnics including fireworks, sparklers flares, incendiary bombs, and signals; to help fix dyes; added to plastics to make fire retardant; to make heat-resistant bricks for furnaces; in medicine; to prepare malleable cast iron

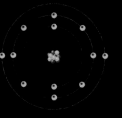

e12 | p12 | n12

MAGNESIUM
ALKALINE EARTH METALS

Magnesium loves parties. When the candles on a birthday cake keep relighting themselves, it is because magnesium in the candle wick reignites as it reacts with oxygen. This element is a good mixer, making friends with almost anything it meets. It also helps plants make their own food, and aids digestion.

Magnesium is the third most abundant element in seawater.

Essential element
This bright silver metal is present in all the cells of living organisms. It is vital for more than 300 functions in the human body alone, including muscle movement and a healthy heart rhythm. Its alloys are very lightweight and are used where weight reduction is important, for example in the building of airplanes and rockets.

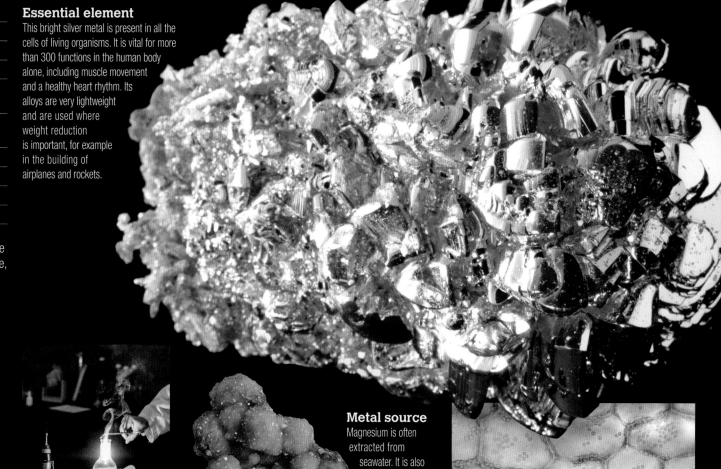

White light
When magnesium in its metal form is heated, it reacts with oxygen in the air to produce magnesium oxide. It reacts very vigorously and burns with an intense white flame.

Metal source
Magnesium is often extracted from seawater. It is also found in more than 60 minerals, including boracite, a green-colored mineral (left).

Sun-catcher
The green chloroplasts inside plant cells (above) are responsible for photosynthesis—the capturing of energy from sunlight using the green pigment chlorophyll. Magnesium is required for chlorophyll production. Without it, most life on Earth as we know it would not exist.

Battlefield illumination

This long-exposure photograph was taken in 1917. It shows artillery shelling over the trenches in northern France. A "star shell' was a form of artillery that was used to light up a battlefield. The shell contained a fuse that would burst when it reached a given height. This would ignite a magnesium flare that burned brightly while the shell gradually fell to earth on a parachute. The flare lit up "no man's land," the area between the frontline trenches of the opposing armies, and exposed to view any activities by enemy patrols.

CALCIUM

ALKALINE EARTH METALS

20		
Ca		
40.078		

Atomic number: 20

Formula: Ca

Atomic mass: 40.078

State at 68°F (20°C): solid

Boiling point: 2703°F (1484°C)

Melting point: 1548°F (842°C)

% in the Universe: 0.0070

% in Earth's crust: 5.0

% in Earth's oceans: 0.00042

% in humans: 1.5

Uses: in building stone, cement, and mortar; as lime in steel-making; as a reducing agent for other metals including uranium; as calcium sulfate (gypsum) for setting bones; as an alloying agent; in insecticides; in food preservatives and additives; for fireworks and flares; in cosmetics; in paints; in fluorescent lights; in animal feed and fertilizers; wax crayons; cosmetics; plastics; paints; toothpaste

e20 | p20 | n20

Calcium has often been called "the scaffolder" because it holds things together—everything from your bones to the bricks of a Roman viaduct. There is lots of calcium on Earth, and it is so reactive that it forms compounds that become rocks such as marble, limestone, and chalk, as well as our skeletons and teeth. Its ions dissolve in water and become hard, forming limescale in kettles and stopping detergents from foaming.

Nautilus shell

Shells such as this hard, coiled one that was originally home to a nautilus, are made from calcium carbonate. Unlike a snail shell, the nautilus has chambers inside. The animal lives only in the outermost part, while it changes the gas content of the inner chambers to control its buoyancy.

Cliffs

These chalk cliffs (left) are also made of calcium carbonate, which is a pure form of limestone. The rock has a very fine-grained texture (above) and was formed from the skeletal remains of minute marine algae, called coccoliths, that lived in the ancient seas. Their shells were made of the mineral calcite.

99% of the body's calcium is stored in the bones and teeth.

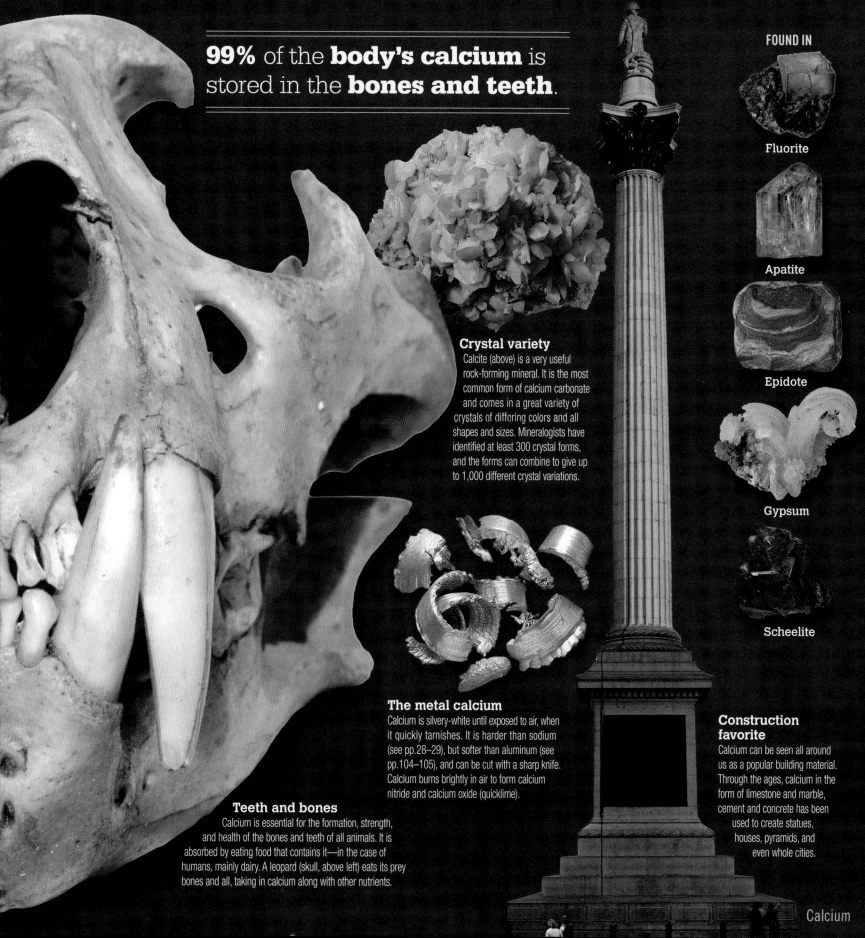

Fluorite

Apatite

Epidote

Gypsum

Scheelite

Crystal variety
Calcite (above) is a very useful rock-forming mineral. It is the most common form of calcium carbonate and comes in a great variety of crystals of differing colors and all shapes and sizes. Mineralogists have identified at least 300 crystal forms, and the forms can combine to give up to 1,000 different crystal variations.

The metal calcium
Calcium is silvery-white until exposed to air, when it quickly tarnishes. It is harder than sodium (see pp.28–29), but softer than aluminum (see pp.104–105), and can be cut with a sharp knife. Calcium burns brightly in air to form calcium nitride and calcium oxide (quicklime).

Construction favorite
Calcium can be seen all around us as a popular building material. Through the ages, calcium in the form of limestone and marble, cement and concrete has been used to create statues, houses, pyramids, and even whole cities.

Teeth and bones
Calcium is essential for the formation, strength, and health of the bones and teeth of all animals. It is absorbed by eating food that contains it—in the case of humans, mainly dairy. A leopard (skull, above left) eats its prey bones and all, taking in calcium along with other nutrients.

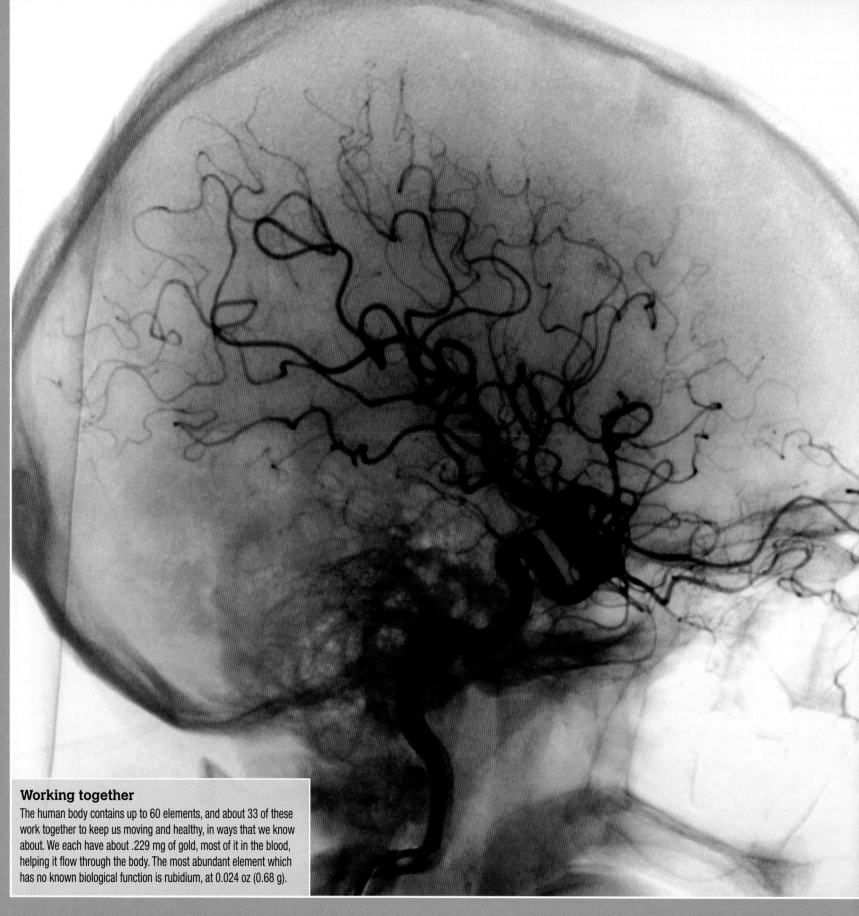

Working together
The human body contains up to 60 elements, and about 33 of these work together to keep us moving and healthy, in ways that we know about. We each have about .229 mg of gold, most of it in the blood, helping it flow through the body. The most abundant element which has no known biological function is rubidium, at 0.024 oz (0.68 g).

ESSENTIAL FOR LIFE

Five elements are key for the human body—oxygen and hydrogen (often bound together as water), carbon, nitrogen, and sulfur. Six others form the main structures and provide the atoms and molecules that flow inside us and make our bodies work. This "inside team" consists of sodium, magnesium, potassium, calcium, chlorine, and phosphorus. However, our bodies contain traces of many more helpful elements.

Extreme living
From the tiniest bacteria to the largest whale, everything alive is made from the same basic building blocks. Recently, scientists have discovered just how adaptable organisms can be to extreme physical and chemical environments.

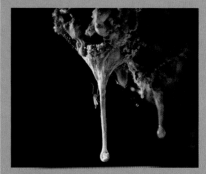

Snottites
The most microscopic lifeforms can be the most adaptable. Snottites are colonies of bacteria. They hang from the walls of caves like soft, dribbly stalactites. They use hydrogen sulfide for energy, producing highly acidic sulfuric acid.

Red-hot vents
Entire ecosystems flourish on the ocean floor around hydrothermal vents. Like snottites, bacteria there don't rely on sunlight for photosynthesis. They create energy from the chemical soup, heated by volcanic activity, that bubbles up from under the seabed, absorbing hydrogen sulfide, carbon dioxide, and oxygen to release energy, grow, and reproduce. They are eaten by a strange array of other animals, from shrimp to giant tubeworms.

Sulfur 0.3%
This is in two of the twenty amino acids which build protein molecules in the body.

Potassium 0.4%
Keeps the body chemistry in balance, sends signals between nerve cells, and regulates heartbeat.

Phosphorus 1.0%
A key ingredient of bones and teeth, and drives chemical reactions in cells.

Sodium 0.2%
An element that is important for nerves and muscles to function.

Calcium 1.5%
Forms bones and teeth, helps muscles to grow, blood to clot, and regulates blood pressure.

Chlorine 0.2%
Used to make hydrochloric acid, which is found in the stomach and digests food.

Nitrogen 3.2%
In essential body chemicals, such as proteins and amino acids. Makes enzymes that help to digest food.

Magnesium 0.1%
Helps flex muscles, regulates heartbeats, aids growth, and builds healthy teeth and bones.

Hydrogen 9.5%
Mostly found in water molecules that keep the body hydrated, and in almost all of the molecules that make up our bodies.

What are we made of?
In an average adult, oxygen, carbon, hydrogen, and nitrogen make up more than 96% of body weight. Of the trace elements, vanadium, at 0.000004 oz (0.11 mg), is the human body's least abundant element that has a known role—it helps bone growth.

Trace elements less than 0.1%
Perhaps the most important trace element, iron, is found in hemoglobin, a protein in red blood cells that carries oxygen from the lungs to the tissues to give them energy to function.

Oxygen 65%
Fuels the body's chemical reactions when breathed in, keeping the body healthy and alive.

Carbon 18.5%
Everywhere in the body, this element is the backbone of all our bodies' cells, including DNA molecules.

STRONTIUM

38

Sr

87.62

ALKALINE EARTH METAL

This element makes flares burn red for danger, which is good since it is toxic and large quantities would kill you. But tiny amounts in toothpaste stop teeth from hurting, and it is used in computer monitors.

Glow in the dark
Many glow-in-the-dark plastics and paints contain strontium aluminate. Toys like this plastic alien absorb light during the day and then release it slowly for hours afterward. Paints containing strontium might be off-white during the day and then glow orange, blue, or green at night.

Atomic number: 38

Formula: Sr

Atomic weight: 87.62

State at 68°F (20°C): solid

Boiling point: 2511°F (1377°C)

Melting point: 1431°F (777°C)

% in the Universe: 0.0000040

% in humans: 0.00046

Uses: fireworks; flares; magnets; in refining zinc; paints and plastics; to generate electricity for space vehicles and navigation buoys

e38 | p38 | n50

Color change
Strontium is silvery-white or yellowish, but turns dark gray when it is exposed to air (above). It is found mainly in the minerals celestite and strontianite. Strontium-90 is a radioactive isotope discovered in the 1940s when developing the nuclear bomb.

It's all in the name
The village of Strontian, in western Scotland, was established in 1724 to house miners. In 1790, French prisoners of war found something there that turned out to be a new element—strontium.

BARIUM

56

Ba

137.327

ALKALINE EARTH METAL

In the early 1600s, an Italian shoemaker who was interested in science found some shiny pebbles and noticed that they glowed when he heated them. He was watching barium in action—just as doctors do today when they use it to check inside the body during a scan.

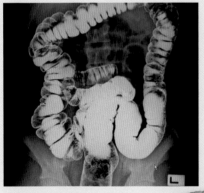

Seeing inside
Barium sulfate glows in X-ray light. Doctors give patients a chalky mixture, called a barium meal, to drink when they need to investigate what is going on in the stomach or intestines.

Barite crystals
The main ores of barium are barite (left) and witherite. The name barium is taken from the Greek barys, which means "heavy." The element can only be found combined with other elements, mainly as a sulfate and carbonate.

Atomic number: 56

Formula: Ba

Atomic weight: 137.327

State at 68°F (20°C): solid

Boiling point: 3353°F (1845°C)

Melting point: 1341°F (727°C)

% in the Universe: 0.0000010

% in humans: 0.000030

Uses: playing cards; car bodies; oil-drilling fluids; paint; glassmaking, paper and rubber; in fireworks to give a green color; for barium meals to see in X-rays; to remove gases from vacuum tubes

e56 | p56 | n81

RADIUM
ALKALINE EARTH METAL

88

Ra

[226]

In the early 20th century, radium was seen as a wonderful drug that would help people feel healthy. It was put into water, soap, and baby clothes. It was even used to treat cancer, when in fact, its radioactivity caused the illness! Today, radium is considered too dangerous to be let out of the laboratory.

Radium waters
Radium Hot Springs in the Canadian Rockies were named after the element when analysis in 1923 showed that the waters contained minute traces of radon, a product of the decay of radium.

Atomic number: 88

Formula: Ra

Atomic weight: [226]

State at 68°F: solid

Boiling point: 2732°F (1500°C)

Melting point: 1285°F (696°C)

Half-life: 1599 years

% in the Universe: almost none

% in Earth's crust: 0.0000000000099

% in Earth's oceans: 0.0000000000000010

% in humans: 0.00000000000010

Uses: today only in research as it is highly radioactive; formerly it was used as luminous paint for dials in aircrafts and on clocks and watches; as a neutron source; as radium needles for medical use

e88 | p88 | n138

Radium was called the **wonder metal** because it gave off **heat** and **light**.

Gray source
Uraninite, formerly called pitchblende, is a uranium-rich mineral that is a very radioactive mineral and therefore should be treated with great care. Three chemical elements were first discovered in pitchblende: uranium (*see pp.*144–145), polonium (*see pp.*123), and radium.

Reading in the dark
Radium gives off a blue light as it reacts to air. This made it perfect for luminous glow-in-the-dark dials in planes, and on watches and clocks. Its powerful radioactivity killed some of the workers who painted it on.

Dangerous power
Uranium is mined mainly to be used as a fuel for nuclear reactors (left). Nuclear power plants produce electricity through a heat-generating process called fission. In nature, uranium-238 decays to form radium-226, which decays in turn to become a gas called radon-222. Inside the core of a reactor, uranium-238 decays to neptunium-239, which in turn decays to plutonium-239.

Destructive force

In 1946, the United States conducted a series of nuclear tests called Operation Crossroads at Bikini Atoll in the Marshall Islands. A total of 167 people living there were evacuated. They were finally allowed to return in the early 1970s, but were evacuated again in 1978 because of the high levels of radiation. Today, only scientists visit the island.

NUCLEAR REACTIONS

There is a tremendous struggle going on in some elements. Their nuclei are unstable, break up, and emit particles and rays as radiation. For humankind, radioactivity can be harmful to living cells but also useful, for example in killing cancer cells. We have learned to control splitting atoms artificially for use in the nuclear power industry but also in the most destructive of all weapons—the atomic bomb.

Radioactive discovery

Polish-born Marie Curie and her French husband Pierre took the work of French scientist Henri Becquerel—the discovery that uranium salts gave out a strong radiation—a stage further. In 1897, they found out how to make precise radiation measurements. Marie Curie called the radiation "radioactivity." In 1898, the Curies isolated the radioactive elements polonium and radium.

Pierre and Marie Curie

Half-life

The half-life of an isotope is the time it takes for half of the atoms in a sample to split, or decay. An isotope with a half-life of 1 hour will decay by 50% in 1 hour, by 75% in 2 hours, and so on.

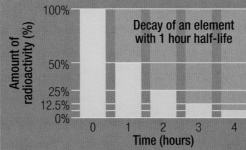

Decay of an element with 1 hour half-life

Amount of radioactivity (%) — 100%, 50%, 25%, 12.5%, 0%
Time (hours) — 0, 1, 2, 3, 4

Chain reaction

The process of a nucleus splitting is called nuclear fission. Uranium (and plutonium) isotopes have largish nuclei that split relatively easily. In a nuclear power station, scientists control how uranium nuclei break up, releasing neutrons which hit other uranium atoms, which also split, releasing neutrons of their own. The chain reaction is especially controlled to stop it going too fast. The tremendous heat produced by fission is used to create electricity.

Power generation (uranium and plutonium)

Uranium-235 is used in nuclear fission.

Nuclear explosion

Scientists load nuclear bombs with a "super critical mass" of uranium. When detonated, the chain reaction releases enormous amounts of heat, with temperatures of several million degrees in the exploding bomb itself, a fireball that can flatten a city, shockwaves that destroy buildings miles from the bomb, and large amounts of lethal, radioactive debris, called fallout.

Types of radiation

Radioactive materials give out radiation all the time. There are three types of nuclear radiation.

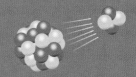

Alpha particles are given off by an atom. They consist of two protons and two neutrons. They only travel less than 1 in. (1–2 cm) in air and can usually be absorbed or stopped by a thin piece of paper.

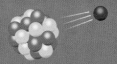

High-energy beta particles are electrons or positrons (like electrons with a positive charge). They can travel a distance of up to 6 ft. (2 m) or more in air and can be stopped by a thin sheet of aluminum.

Gamma rays are waves of energy from the unstable nucleus that travel at the speed of light. These rays can travel much farther than alpha or beta particles. They can be blocked by sheets of lead or large pieces of concrete.

Some **fungi thrive** by using **radioactivity** as an **energy** source.

DOMINANT

METALS

MIGHTY METALS

Almost three-quarters of elements are metals, and there is a key difference between them and their partners in the periodic table. If you heat and hit them, they can change shape without losing strength or falling apart. When early people discovered this, they started to use metals such as the examples here to make tools, and over thousands of years this has helped to form the world we live in today.

Helmet (iron)

Copper

Iron ore

Mercury

Palladium

Zircon crystal (zirconium)

Vanadanite (vanadium) crystals on barite

Molybdenite (molybdenum)

Rhodonite (manganese)

Perovskite (titanium)

Malachite (copper)

Zinc

Pyrite (iron)

Bulb filament (tungsten)

Gold

Silver

Chromite (chromium)

Skudderite (cobalt)

Meteorite (nickel and iron)

Coin (gold)

Leopard ore (chromium)

Nickel

Hematite (iron)

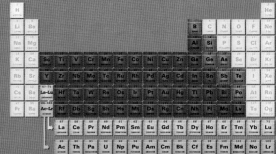

Mainstream metals

Transition metals are strong and hard. Poor metals, or post-transition metals, have lower melting points and are softer. Lanthanoids and actinoids are similar chemically, but less is known about them so they are grouped together. Metalloids have both metallic and non-metallic properties.

KEY CHARACTERISTICS

This is a fascinating bunch, both attractive and useful. The metals are shiny when they are cut or polished—something we are drawn to and explains why gold (which is not the rarest or top-performing metal) is so highly valued. Metals also conduct heat and electricity well, and you can stretch some metals incredibly thin, which is why we use wires to carry electricity. Most metals are also very reactive, easily mixing or forming compounds with other elements—so, for example, iron exposed to oxygen forms iron oxide, which is also known as rust.

BETTER TOGETHER

Metals combine easily with each other to form alloys. This is important because the result can be more useful than the metals in their pure form. An ancient example of this is bronze, formed from copper (which is easily shaped but soft) and tin (which can be too brittle to use on its own). A later example is steel—a mixture of iron, carbon, and other elements—a material that has revolutionized modern life.

Octahedral magnetite (iron)

TRANSITION METALS

In the foundry
Steel foundries are full of dramatic fire and heat. Here, iron is being melted in a shower of sparks to alloy with carbon and make carbon steel. Transition metals such as iron can change shape and exist in many different states because of their strength, density, and high melting and boiling points. They mix well to make all sorts of alloys.

Most of the most commonly used metals are in this group, including iron, copper, gold, silver, and chromium. The transition metals form alloys easily and have high melting points. Many are excellent conductors of heat and electricity.

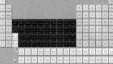

Large group
In the center of the periodic table is a large group of elemental metals. They are mostly shiny, hard, and dense, but are less reactive than the alkali metals.

TRANSITION METALS TIMELINE

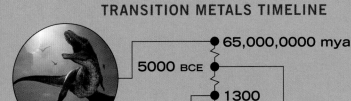

● 65,000,0000 mya

5000 BCE ●

● 1300

● 1700

Early jewelry
Copper beads have been found that are more than 10,000 years old, made from copper nuggets that formed naturally. Copper smelting began in about 5000 BCE.

From space
Traces of iridium have been found in the layer of rocks present 65 million years ago when a giant meteor may have wiped out the dinosaurs.

Sharp metal
The blades of some Japanese swords from the 1300s have been found to contain molybdenum, which was not even recognized as a metal until the 1700s.

● 1800
Ilmenite

Black sand
In 1791, English vicar William Gregor noticed a strange black, sandlike substance. It was the first time a mineral containing titanium had been found.

● 1900

Armor plating
In 1885, the first commercial nickel-steel armor plate was made in a French steelworks Soon after, nickel steels were being forged into naval gun barrels.

Scandium
The first piece of scandium metal was made in 1937, although traces of the element had been found after its discovery 58 years before.

American Eagle
In 1997, the American Eagle, a platinum coin, was released. This is the first and only investment-grade platinum coin guaranteed by the US government.

● 2000

SCANDIUM

TRANSITION METAL

21

Sc

44.956

Scandium loves sport. Its light weight and strength are great for baseball bats, lacrosse sticks, and in high-performance bicycle frames. It also softens the glare of powerful stadium lights. Its name is taken from the Latin for Scandinavia.

Atomic number: 21

Formula: Sc

Atomic weight: 44.955910

State at 68°F (20°C): solid

Boiling point: 5137°F (2836°C)

Melting point: 2806°F (1541°C)

Uses: in planes, bikes, and baseball bats; TV cameras; oil refining

Mig-29 fighter plane

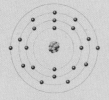
e21 | p21 | n24

Toughener
When scandium is added to aluminum alloys, the scandium significantly increases the strength of the metal. It also has a good resistance to heat. An aluminum-scandium alloy was used in the former Soviet Union for missiles and MiG fighter planes. The alloy is also used in hi-end bicycle frames and baseball bats.

Aluminum-scandium baseball bat

VANADIUM

TRANSITION METAL

23

V

50.942

Vanadium changed transport and warfare forever. Henry Ford said "there would be no automobiles" without vanadium in 1905. And from WW1 on, it allowed fighter planes to carry heavy cannons and toughened soldiers' steel helmets.

Atomic number: 23

Formula: V

Atomic weight: 50.9415

State at 68°F (20°C): solid

Boiling point: 6165°F (3407°C)

Melting point: 3470°F (1910°C)

Uses: steel additive: armor plates; tools; cars; nuclear reactors

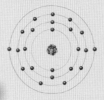
e23 | p23 | n28

Vanadanite
Named after the Scandinavian goddess Vanadis, this element is found in the mineral vanadanite (above) as well as many others.

Vanadium steel
This lightweight and durable alloy revolutionized cars from the beginning of the 20th century. It allowed engineers to make better-performing cars.

MANGANESE

TRANSITION METAL

25

Mn

54.938

In Victorian Britain, manganese was used to cure stinky breath. This was not such a good idea because miners inhaling its dust went crazy with "manganese madness."

Atomic number: 25

Formula: Mn

Atomic weight: 54.938049

State at 68°F (20°C): solid

Boiling point: 3742°F (2061°C)

Melting point: 2275°F (1246°C)

Uses: fungicide; fertilizers; ceramics

e25 | p25 | n30

Tough rails
Steel used for railway tracks relies on the balance of manganese (up to 1.7%) and carbon (up to 0.82%). These two elements help produce hard, wear-resistant rails.

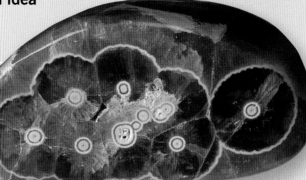

Mineral resource
Rhodochrosite (left) and pyrolusite are the most common ores of manganese. Another source is metal-bearing nodules, some the size of bowling balls, that are found on the ocean floor. They are made up mainly of manganese, but also contain nickel, cobalt, and copper.

TITANIUM

TRANSITION METAL

Titanium is a superstar. Added to toothpaste, it gives us a gleaming "movie star" smile. It is hard, strong, lightweight, and will not corrode. This makes it fantastic for everything from horseshoes to spacecraft parts, as well as artificial bones and the walls of the Guggenheim museum in Bilbao, Spain.

22

Ti

47.867

Atomic number: 22

Formula: Ti

Atomic weight: 47.867

State at 68°F (20°C): solid

Boiling point: 5949°F (3287°C)

Melting point: 3038°F (1670°C)

% in the Universe: 0.00030

% in Earth's crust: 0.66

% in Earth's oceans: 0.00000010

% in humans: none

Uses: principally as an alloy for jet engines; ships; spacecraft; laptops; sports equipment (golf clubs, bikes); replacement hips, other joints, and crutches; dental implants; as pipes in condensers; in desalination plants; in food products; paints; inks; plastics; solar observatories; sunscreens; fireworks; for smokescreens

e22   p22   n26

White paper

Powdered titanium dioxide is the most widely used white pigment. It makes the paper bright white, and gives it high strength. The fact that it is lightweight allows the paper to be very thin while not becoming transparent.

Sport favorite

Titanium is difficult to extract, machine, and fabricate, but it is the material of choice for many serious cyclists. They are attracted by its light weight, super strength, and resistance to stress and wear.

Strong and stable

Titanium does not readily take part in any chemical reaction. This makes it ideal for use in the human body for hip replacements (left) or as a heart pacemaker, as it will not be attacked by bodily fluids.

Flight frame

The ultimate Cold War American spy plane, the Lockheed SR-71 "Blackbird" was in service from 1964 to 1999. It was 92 percent titanium, which helped it to travel at speeds of 2,200 mph (3,540 km/h).

Titanium rich

Perovskite (above) is one of the ores of titanium, as are ilmenite, rutile, and sphene, and many of the iron ores. It does not occur in its pure form in nature. The element is the ninth most abundant in Earth's crust.

A **single supernova** can create **100 Earths'** worth of **titanium-44**.

Rutilated quartz

Rutile (right) is the most common mineral composed of titanium dioxide. This form of the metal is used in the food industry as coloring, in sunscreens, and in cosmetics.

Colorful procession

In the "Great Hall of the Bulls" in the Lascaux cave, in the Dordogne region of southwestern France, there are some extraordinary paintings. Around 20,000 years ago, early people mixed red, brown, and yellow ocher with black manganese dioxide and applied them to the cave walls. In this section, deer and aurochs (huge black bulls) that lived in the region parade across the stone wall. In all, the cave contains 90 paintings of stags, as well as cattle, bison, big cats, a bird, a bear, a rhinoceros, and a human.

CHROMIUM

TRANSITION METAL

24

Cr

51.996

Chromium has a dazzling smile—it is how the bumpers of old cars get that mirrorlike shine. When it is exposed to air, a layer of chromium oxide covers the surface and stops the metal from rusting. This surface will then polish up nicely to a dazzling finish. Our bodies need chromium in tiny amounts because it helps us to use glucose for energy. It comes from foods such as oysters, egg yolks, and nuts.

Atomic number: 24

Formula: Cr

Atomic weight: 51.9961

State at 68°F (20°C): solid

Boiling point: 4840°F (2671°C)

Melting point: 3465°F (1907°C)

% in the Universe: 0.0015

% in Earth's crust: 0.014

% in Earth's oceans: 0.000000060

% in humans: 0.0000030

Uses: ruby lasers; jewelry; glassware; as a compound to produce pigments for artists' paints; in tanning; as a catalyst in steel manufacture, particularly stainless steel; as chromium plating on cars, motorcycles and bikes; in wood preservative; in blast furnaces; in paints; as a superalloy for jet engines; in blast furnaces and molds

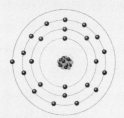

e24 | p24 | n28

Ruby   Emerald

Gem quality

Chromium is nature's bling. It is what makes rubies red and emeralds green. A ruby is a crystal of corundum that has chromium in it as an impurity, making it red. An emerald is a crystal of beryl that also contains chromium, making it green.

Shining metal

This brightest of bright metals not only shines, but it resists rust. In 1913, English metallurgist Harry Brearley discovered that if you add chromium to low carbon steel it gives it stain resistance. Today, stainless steel is part of our everyday lives. Up to 85 percent of chromium produced commercially is used to make alloys, including stainless steel.

Bright colors

Chromium gets its name from the Greek word for color, *chroma*, because the element can form many different colored compounds. School buses were painted "chromium yellow" for years before the realization that the metal was toxic put people off.

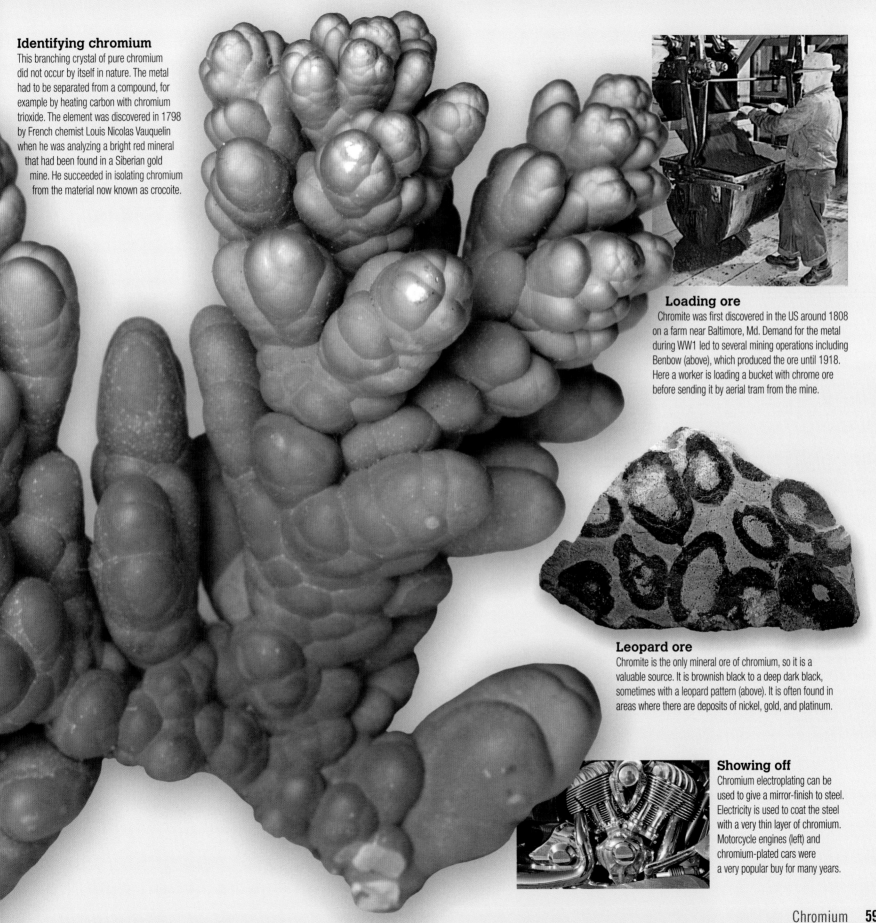

Identifying chromium

This branching crystal of pure chromium did not occur by itself in nature. The metal had to be separated from a compound, for example by heating carbon with chromium trioxide. The element was discovered in 1798 by French chemist Louis Nicolas Vauquelin when he was analyzing a bright red mineral that had been found in a Siberian gold mine. He succeeded in isolating chromium from the material now known as crocoite.

Loading ore

Chromite was first discovered in the US around 1808 on a farm near Baltimore, Md. Demand for the metal during WW1 led to several mining operations including Benbow (above), which produced the ore until 1918. Here a worker is loading a bucket with chrome ore before sending it by aerial tram from the mine.

Leopard ore

Chromite is the only mineral ore of chromium, so it is a valuable source. It is brownish black to a deep dark black, sometimes with a leopard pattern (above). It is often found in areas where there are deposits of nickel, gold, and platinum.

Showing off

Chromium electroplating can be used to give a mirror-finish to steel. Electricity is used to coat the steel with a very thin layer of chromium. Motorcycle engines (left) and chromium-plated cars were a very popular buy for many years.

Chromium 59

26
Fe
55.845

IRON

TRANSITIONAL METAL

Our world is, literally, built with iron, for without it many of our structures would collapse. Iron's cubic crystal structure brings great strength, which is increased by heating it to shrink the size of its grains. When mixed with carbon, iron makes the most important metal in the world, steel. Iron is at the center of our planet, in the core, and it also flows in the blood through our bodies, making oxygen-carrying red blood cells.

Atomic number: 26

Formula: Fe

Atomic weight: 55.845

State at 68°F (20°C): solid

Boiling point: 5182°F (2861°C)

Melting point: 2800°F (1538°C)

% in the Universe: 0.11

% in Earth's crust: 6.3

% in Earth's oceans: 0.00000030

% in humans: 0.0060

Uses: steel from iron ore used for lintels, cutlery, furniture, cooking pans, reinforced concrete, pylons, girders, bridges, cutting tools, rifle barrels, surgical instruments, bicycle chains; iron in our bodies; powerful magnets for use in computers, cell phones, medical equipment, toys, motors, wind turbines

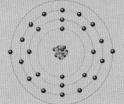

e26 | p26 | n30

FOUND IN

Space iron
Iron meteorites came from the broken cores of ancient planets that were destroyed some 4.5 billion years ago when our solar system was formed. The meteorites are made up of alloys of iron and nickel. Millions of chunks of material travel through Earth's atmosphere every day. Meteorites are the ones that survive the journey.

Hematite

Magnetite

Iron meteorite

Fool's gold
Iron pyrite, or iron sulfide, is a mineral that is also known as "fool's gold" because its yellow color and shine caused many prospectors to think they had struck gold. Some were not disappointed because iron pyrite is often found near a source of gold. One easy way to tell the difference is that pyrite has hard edges, while gold has rounder edges.

Ironstone

About **90 percent** of all the **metal** refined in the world **today** is **iron**.

Iron core

Earth could be called the iron planet. A third of its mass, including the core, is iron, making this the most common element, ahead of oxygen. Earth's magnetic field (see pp.62–63) is generated by the movement of liquid iron in the outer core.

Rocky crust

Liquid magma mantle

Liquid iron and nickel outer core

Solid iron and nickel inner core

An age of iron

Ironworking first began in what is now Turkey around 3,500 years ago and then spread throughout Europe. People learned how to separate the iron by heating its ores with charcoal, coal, or coke. Iron then gradually replaced bronze for tools and weapons.

Iron Age spearheads

Iron Age hill fort, Santa Tecla, in Galicia, Spain

Rusty surface

When Earth was formed, most of the heavy iron sank to the core of the young planet. Mars is smaller than Earth and, although some iron has formed the core, much of it exists in the upper layers too. The "Red Planet" gets its name from the iron oxide—or rust—on its surface. Rust appears when iron is exposed to oxygen. Scientists have many theories about how Mars got "rusty"—a color that is visible from millions of miles away—but no one knows for sure.

Iron for health

The human body needs iron to work properly. Iron helps hemoglobin in red blood cells to carry oxygen around the body. This in turn helps both the brain and the muscles work well and gives us energy. Good sources of iron in food include red meat, shellfish, and beans, as well as green, leafy vegetables.

Building high

When iron is mixed with carbon to make steel (see pp.112–113), the resulting metal can be cast, machined, and welded into many forms, to create everything from paper clips to skyscrapers. Steel beams set in concrete are used to frame most tall buildings, from the early skyscrapers in New York to today's tallest building, the 2,717-ft. (828-m) Burj Khalifa in Dubai.

Light display

When fast-moving electrons rain into Earth's atmosphere from the magnetosphere, they collide with oxygen and nitrogen and transfer their energy into light. In the Arctic and Antarctic circles we see beautiful colored ripples in the sky. Oxygen emits a greenish-yellow or red light, while nitrogen usually gives off a blue light.

MAGNETIC ELEMENTS

Magnetism is created by the motion of electrons within an atom, and iron is especially magnetic. The area into which a magnetic force reaches is called a magnetic field. The field is polarized—strongest at the two extremities or poles; opposite poles are attracted to each other, the same poles repel each other. The Ancient Greeks used magnets, and compasses were invented in China in about 200 BCE.

World magnet

Earth is one big magnet. The mostly iron inner core is solid. The liquid metal outer core is constantly on the move and produces a magnetic field, with magnetic north and south poles. Earth's magnetic field, or magnetosphere, extends out from the planet up to 3,900,000 miles (6,300,000 km) into space. This protects Earth from both space radiation and the traveling particles of the solar wind.

Magnetic compass

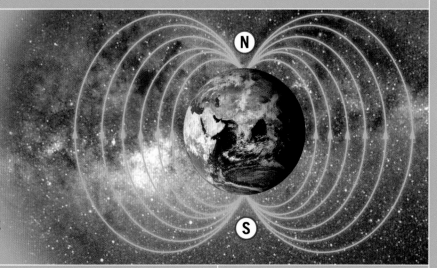

Types of magnetism

All matter is magnetic, but some materials are more magnetic than others. These are three of the different types of magnetism.

Diamagnetism

This very weak form is not normally noticed, but most substances are diamagnetic. Examples include copper, mercury, gold, bismuth, boron, carbon, and nitrogen.

Bismuth

Paramagnetism

In this type of magnetism, materials become magnetized in a magnetic field. However, the magnetism disappears when there is no field. Examples include aluminum, platinum, magnesium, lithium, molybdenum, tantalum, and oxygen.

Platinum

Ferromagnetism

This is the strongest type. The ferromagnets all have some magnetic force on their own. There are four main ferromagnetic elements: iron, cobalt, nickel, and gadolinium.

Iron

Magnetism in use

Very strong electromagnets, such as those used to move metal in garbage tips (right), work when an electric current produces a magnetic field. Even more powerful superconducting electromagnets are used in the Large Hadron Collider near Geneva, Switzerland. These electromagnets help trillions of particles to circle the 16.8-mile (27-km) tunnel 11,245 times per second.

Large Hadron Collider

Electromagnet

Strong magnetism

Magnetite, at 72 percent, has the highest iron content and is the most strongly magnetic mineral. Many animals, including dolphins, have been found to have magnetite in their brains, which allows them to navigate enormous distances.

Magnetite

Dolphin

Superconducting magnets

Trillions of particles circle the tunnel of the Large Hadron Collider particle accelerator (see p.63). More than 50 types of magnets are needed to keep the particles moving without losing speed or drifting. All the magnets are electromagnets—they have soft metal iron cores that are made into magnets by passing an electric current through coils surrounding them. The magnets include eight huge superconducting magnets (the gray tubes in this picture). These allow the high currents of electricity to flow without losing any energy.

COBALT

TRANSITION METAL

Cobalt can be a show off, but is also sneaky. The "ta-da" side is in the rich, deep blue it brings to pottery and glass, including beads found in the tomb of Tutankhamun. The secret part came in the 17th century when cobalt was mixed with water to make invisible ink that showed up only when it was heated. Today, the element keeps turbine blades turning inside jet engines.

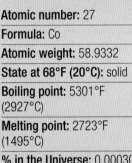

27

Co

58.933

Atomic number: 27

Formula: Co

Atomic weight: 58.9332

State at 68°F (20°C): solid

Boiling point: 5301°F (2927°C)

Melting point: 2723°F (1495°C)

% in the Universe: 0.00030

% in Earth's crust: 0.0030

% in Earth's oceans: 0.0000000080

% in humans: 0.0000020

Uses: powerful magnets; jet turbines and gas turbine generators; rechargeable batteries; for high-temperature cutting tools; for electroplating; as cobalt salts for paint, porcelain, glass, pottery, and enamels; as cobalt-60, a radioactive isotope used as a tracer for cancer and other treatments; sterilizing medicine and foods

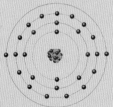

e27 I p27 I n32

Colorful cobalt
Cobaltoan dolomite is a rare variety of the mineral dolomite that contains cobalt. The color of the cobalt crystals can range from a pink to bright fuschia to purple.

Artists' choice
Cobalt-based pigments are used to give a rich blue color to glassware. The artist Vincent van Gogh wrote about Cobalt blue that ". . . there is nothing so beautiful for putting atmosphere around things . . ."

Cobalt ores
Cobalt is not found on its own in nature, it is found in mineral ores. The main ores are cobaltite, erythrite (above), glaucodot, and skutterudite (opposite).

It's in the name
The name of this element comes from the German *kobald*, which means "goblin." Goblins were often blamed by miners for leading them astray because cobalt could be mistaken for silver.

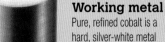

Working metal
Pure, refined cobalt is a hard, silver-white metal that can be used to make magnets, pigments, diamond cutting tools, and battery electrodes.

Prospecting for silver
Work crews building the Temiskaming and Northern Ontario Railway in 1903 found silver nuggets on the shore of Long Lake. A mining industry grew up and the town of Cobalt was named in 1907 for the cobalt that prospectors found in the silver ore.

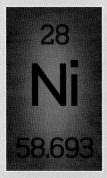

NICKEL

TRANSITION METAL

German copper miners thought nickel looked like copper, so they called it *kupfernickel*, or "copper devil." Now it is used in a tough alloy for corrosion-resistant steel, and has many uses from armor plating to guitar strings.

Atomic number: 28

Formula: Ni

Atomic weight: 58.6934

State at 68°F (20°C): solid

Boiling point: 5275°F (2913°C)

Melting point: 2651°F (1455°C)

% in the Universe: 0.0060

% in humans: 0.000010

Uses: stainless steel and other corrosion-resistant alloys; desalination plants; coins; vaults; toasters; ovens; armor plating; propeller shafts; turbine blades; rechargeable batteries

From space
Much of the nickel that we can use on our planet arrived as space dust and on meteorites. Iron meteorites (left) may contain as much as 20 percent nickel. Lots more nickel is trapped in Earth's core.

Nickel ores
The element is extracted from ores that include limonite, millerite, and pentlandite. It is found with sulfur, iron, and oxygen in these minerals as a more or less pure metal. It is also readily recycled after many of its uses.

Limonite

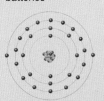

e28 | p28 | n31

Skutterudite

About **1,540,000 tons** of **nickel** are **produced** and used **annually** worldwide compared with **1,600,000,000** tons of steel.

Metal content
The five-cent "nickel," is in fact an alloy with copper. Issued in 1866, the coin is composed of 75 percent copper and only 25 percent nickel. From 1942 to 1945, silver and manganese were used instead.

ZINC

TRANSITION METAL

Zinc gets in the way—and that's a good thing. It galvanizes steel to stop water and oxygen from rusting it, and it blocks ultraviolet light in sunscreen creams. For thousands of years, it has been alloyed with copper to make brass.

Atomic number: 30

Formula: Zn

Atomic weight: 65.38

State at 68°F (20°C): solid

Boiling point: 1665°F (907°C)

Melting point: 787.149°F (419.527°C)

% in the Universe: 0.000030

% in humans: 0.0033

Uses: solder; paints; rubber; cosmetics; in alloys such as brass, and nickel silver; inks; soaps; batteries; textiles; as a coating

Protective coating
Screws, nuts, bolts, and brackets can be galvanized, or zinc-plated, to protect them from rust. The zinc is electroplated onto the surface of metals that contain iron.

Main ores
Zinc is often found with lead in sulfide ores. The most common zinc ore is the mineral sphalerite (right), also known as zinc blende. Zinc is also found in smithsonite and hemimorphite.

e30 | p30 | n35

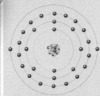

Power source
Zinc batteries have been used for decades. Zinc-carbon batteries are used in remote controls, flashlights, toys, and electronics.

Shaping metal
Zinc, like other metals, is cast into ingots first before it is used in another process. The zinc is heated and poured into a mold to be frozen and to solidify. The metal is cast like this because it is a convenient form for storing, shaping, remelting, or refining.

Mining for zinc

Zinc usually occurs naturally with lead, and often copper or silver are found in the same place. One area in southeast Missouri is even called "the Lead Belt." In 1873, a farmer there named John C. Webb discovered lead in one of his cornfields. He took on a partner and began to mine lead and zinc. By 1875, he had established Webb City (now a suburb of Joplin) to house the miners flooding into the area. Between 1894 and 1904, they produced 23 million dollars' worth of lead and zinc, and continued to mine until after the end of WWII.

COPPER

TRANSITIONAL METAL

29
Cu
63.546

Copper is almost perfect! It is beautiful on its own, and even better when mixed with other metals to make bronze or brass. It is easily shaped, so is great as a pipe to carry water and, as it can be stretched really thin and is a good electrical conductor, ideal for use in the wires we need to power electrical equipment.

Atomic number: 29

Formula: Cu

Atomic weight: 63.546

State at 68°F (20°C): solid

Boiling point: 4640°F (2560°C)

Melting point: 1984.32°F (1084.62°C)

% in the Universe: 0.0000060

% in Earth's crust: 0.0068

% in Earth's oceans: 0.00000030

% in humans: 0.0001

Uses: copper pipes to carry water; in superconductors e.g. maglevs; coins; electricity wires, telecommunication cables, and electronics; cooking pots; tools; jewelry; to give antimicrobial surfaces in hospitals; wiring in motors; photovoltaic cells; boat propellers; magnetrons in microwaves; welding electrodes; vacuum tubes; heat sinks; fuel gas distribution pipes

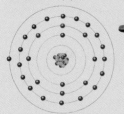

e29 | p29 | n35

FOUND IN

Azurite with malachite

Malachite

Chalcopyrite

Lightning strike on church

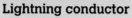

Lightning rod

Lightning conductor

About 100 cloud-to-ground lightning bolts hit somewhere in the world every single second. They are one of the most common causes of building fires, so copper conductors provide much-needed protection.

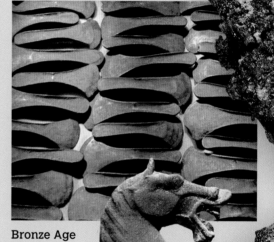

Bronze Age axe heads

Chinese Bronze Age horse and chariot

Old bronze

Copper was one of the first metals to be used by people, mainly because it occurs naturally in pure forms. Some tools date back to 9000 BCE, but it was probably in early Mesopotamia, around 5,500 years ago, that people began to mine and work copper, alloying it with tin to make bronze. This horse and chariot is a superb example of ancient Chinese art during the Bronze Age.

Native metal
Native copper is found in the earth not as a compound (mixed with other substances) but in its pure form. It is one of the few metals like this—others include gold, silver, copper, and platinum. These metals are called "native metals." Native copper is most commonly found in small quantities in volcanic basalt rocks, often as distorted masses like this one.

Golden orb-weaver spider

Cuttlefish

Horseshoe crab

Burgundy snail

Wonder wire
Copper has the best electrical conductivity of any metal except silver. Copper wires allow electric current to flow easily without much loss of energy, so are used in mains cables in houses and offices.

Blue bloods
Some spiders, crustaceans, squid, octopuses, and mollusks have blue blood. They do not have iron-rich hemoglobin to turn their blood red. Instead, the copper-based protein hemocyanin transports oxygen to their cells and turns their blood blue.

The **Statue of Liberty** is made of **179,000 lbs. (81,193 kg)** of copper.

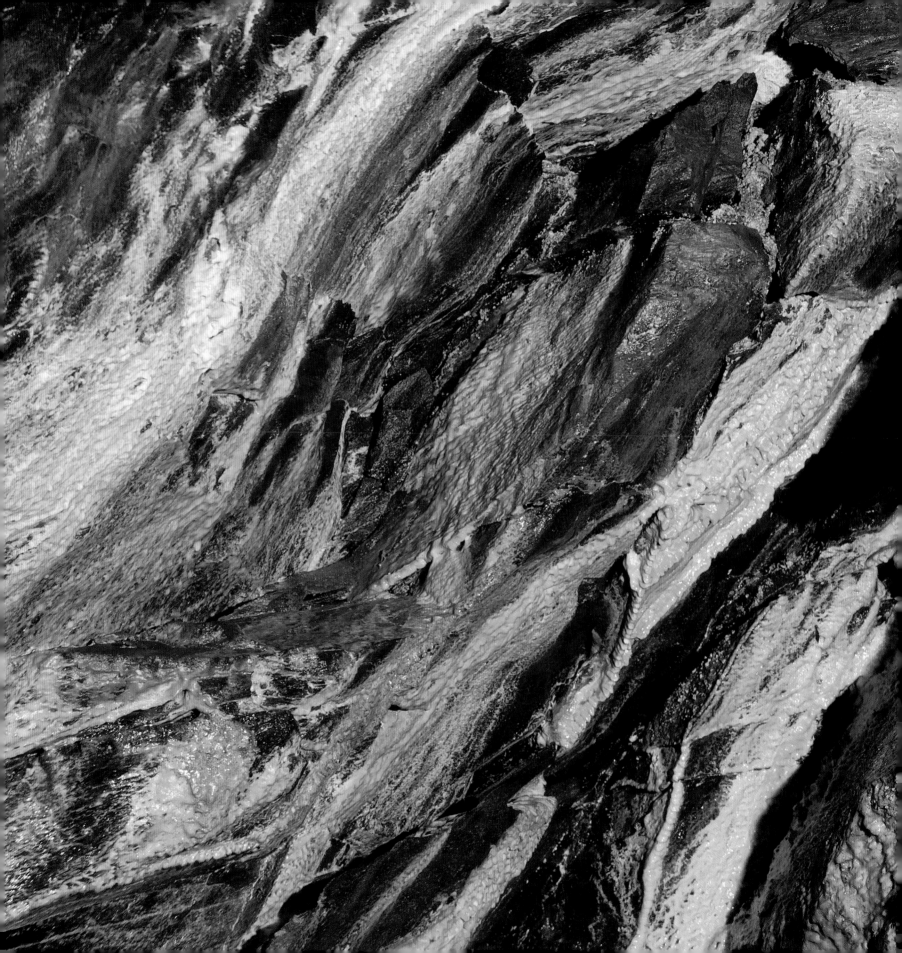

Rich blue copper seam

For 333 years, until 1977, mines near Røros, in Sør-Trøndelag county in Norway, produced copper and zinc from sulfide deposits. It has been calculated that total production from the district over that time was 6,600,000 tons of raw ore producing 130,000 tons of copper. Copper ore was found in the Røros mountains in 1644, and the following year, a furnace for smelting was built near a waterfall in the Hitterelva River. The rich copper seams are still visible and the mining town was declared a World Heritage Site in 1980.

YTTRIUM

TRANSITION METAL

39 Y 88.906

This element has special powers. It fights cancer cells and makes fake diamonds. It was discovered by a Finnish chemist, Johan Gadolin, in 1794, when he was examining an unusual black rock from Ytterby, in Sweden.

Atomic number: 39

Formula: Y

Atomic weight: 88.90585

State at 68°F (20°C): solid

Boiling point: 6053°F (3345°C)

Melting point: 2772°F (1522°C)

Uses: radar; lasers; additive in alloys; white LED lights; camera lenses; superconductors

Key mine
This plaque in the Swedish town of Ytterby records the finding of seven new elements in the 1790s and 1800s. The elements were in minerals from a local mine.

Born in the stars
Samples of rock and dust brought back from the Apollo Moon landings show a high yttrium content. However, most of the yttrium in the solar system was created in red giant stars (right).

e39 | p39 | n50

Silver luster
Silver-gray yttrium metal was first isolated in 1828 in Berlin by Friedrich Wöhler. It never occurs in its pure form in nature, but it is 400 times more common than silver on Earth. It is soft and ignites in air when it is heated.

ZIRCONIUM

TRANSITION METAL

40 Zr 91.224

Zirconium is so heat-resistant that it is used to carry and mold molten metal. It is also so corrosion-resistant that it is prized by the chemical industries. It is lighter than steel, but hard and brilliant enough, as cubic zirconia, to be a substitute for diamonds in jewelry.

Atomic number: 40

Formula: Zr

Atomic weight: 91.224

State at 68°F (20°C): solid

Boiling point: 7963°F (4406°C)

Melting point: 3369°F (1854°C)

Uses: fireworks; pigments; furnaces; magnets; abrasives; glass and ceramics; antiperspirants; food packaging; cosmetics

Protective layers
More than 90 percent of the zirconium metal production is used in nuclear reactors. Its resistance to heat and chemical corrosion make it perfect for the cladding, or outer covering, of the fuel rods that power the nuclear reaction.

Bright jewel
Cubic zirconia is a manufactured material that is colorless, hard, and flawless. It is used as a cheaper substitute for diamonds. Powdered zirconium is melted with zirconium dioxide to form cubic zirconia.

Medical uses
Zirconium's characteristics give it a vital role in today's medicine. Zirconia is widely used today for anti-corrosive dental implants, and its light weight makes it a great choice for artificial joints and limbs.

e40 | p40 | n51

Cute crystal
The main ores of zirconium are zircon (below) and baddeleyite. The pyramid-shaped crystals of zircon may be brown or clear, but when heated, become many different colors. Zircon crystals were used as gemstones by the ancient Egyptians.

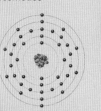

NIOBIUM

41	
Nb	
92.906	

TRANSITION METAL

This silvery metal is very resistant to corrosion because it has a layer of oxide on its surface. This makes it hypoallergenic—not likely to cause an allergic reaction—and therefore perfect for use as jewelry.

Atomic number: 41
Formula: Nb
Atomic weight: 92.90638
State at 68°F (20°C): solid
Boiling point: 8566°F (4741°C)
Melting point: 4491°F (2477°C)
Uses: planes and space planes; in particle accelerators; MRI scanners; jewelry; for spectacles

e41 | p41 | n52

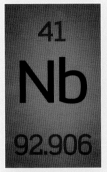

Blue-gray ore
More than 90 percent of the world's niobium ores, such as niobite (left) are mined in Brazil. It is much sought-after since it is used in steel products. It is also a "superalloy," because it functions well in high temperatures, for example in the turbines of jet engines.

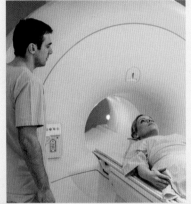

Crystal structure
This strip of niobium shows the cubic shape of its crystals. The atoms are packed together tightly in the crystals to form a strong bond. The metal was named for a Greek goddess who became the symbol of a tragic mourning mother.

Super magnet
Alloys such as niobium-tin and niobium-titanium are used to make the coils for superconducting magnets. These signal-receiving coils surround the part of the body being imaged in an MRI scan.

MOLYBDENUM

42	
Mo	
95.94	

TRANSITION METAL

Molybdenum strengthens steel, although it was not recognized as a metal until the 1700s. Today, most of it is used to make alloys such as "moly steel" to increase the steel's hardness and resistance to corrosion.

Atomic number: 42
Formula: Mo
Atomic weight: 95.94
State at 68°F (20°C): solid
Boiling point: 8382°F (4639°C)
Melting point: 4752°F (2622°C)
Uses: in alloys for engines, drills, saws; in lubricants; in the petroleum industry; pigments; fertilizers; inks; electrodes

e42 | p42 | n54

Identifying the element
The mineral molybdenite, seen here as gray crystals on this dark-colored rock, is the main ore of molybdenum. In 1778, Swedish chemist Carl Wilhelm Scheele was studying molybdenite when he realized he was looking at a new element.

In the heat of battle
Big Bertha was the name given to a WW1 German 43-ton gun that could fire shells over a distance of 9 miles (14.5 km). Molybdenum alloyed to its steel could withstand heat of up to 4,750°F (2,620°C).

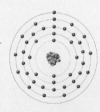

New element
Molybdenum is mainly extracted from molybdenite, but it is also found in wulfenite (left). The element was finally isolated in 1781 by Swedish scientist Peter Hjelm.

TECHNETIUM

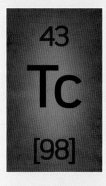

43

Tc

[98]

TRANSITION METAL

Once technetium was thought to exist only in the laboratory, but it has now been seen by astronomers in red giant stars. Today, this radioactive metal is extracted as a waste product from nuclear reactors.

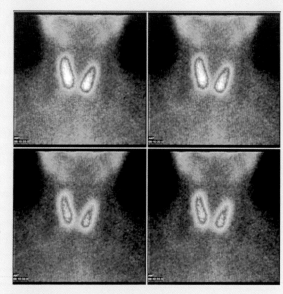

Atomic number: 43

Formula: Tc

Atomic weight: [98]

State at 68°F (20°C): solid

Boiling point: 7704°F (4262°C)

Melting point: 3915°F (2157°C)

Uses: anti-corrosive; medical imaging

e43 | p43 | n55

Imaging element

Millions of people are grateful for technetium because it is used to find diseases in the human body. Gamma-ray emitting Technetium-99 is used in imaging called scintigraphy. It acts as a radioactive tracer to help spot problems, such as these nodules on a thyroid gland.

Atomic number: 44

Formula: Ru

Atomic weight: 101.07

State at 68°F (20°C): solid

Boiling point: 7497°F (4147°C)

Melting point: 4231°F (2333°C)

Uses: as a hardener; for electrical contacts; solar cells; jewelry; fingerprinting

e44 | p44 | n57

Flaming stone

At Yanartas ("Flaming stone") in the mountains of southwestern Turkey, there are fires that have been burning for thousands of years and inspired Homer's fire-breathing monster, Chimera. The flames are caused by ruthenium in the rocks acting as a catalyst to burn methane.

RUTHENIUM

44

Ru

101.07

TRANSITION METAL

Unlike most metals, this rare element does not react with air, water, or acids. It is added to platinum or palladium to make super-hard alloys that can take the wear and tear of life. The alloys are used as microchips, in jewelry, for electrical contacts; and to form the tips of gold fountain-pen nibs.

RHODIUM

45

Rh

102.906

TRANSITION METAL

Rhodium is named after the Greek word for "rose" because it was first extracted from a rose-colored liquid in 1803. It is the world's most expensive metal and used as a hardener for platinum and palladium. Most white gold jewelry is rhodium-plated because it gives a white and mirror-like finish.

Atomic number: 45

Formula: Rh

Atomic weight: 102.90550

State at 68°F (20°C): solid

Boiling point: 6683°F (3695°C)

Melting point: 3565°F (1963°C)

Uses: in catalytic converters; as a catalyst; optic mirrors; optic fiber coating

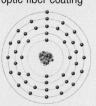

e45 | p45 | n58

Discovery

English chemist William Hyde Wollaston (1766–1828) was the first person to produce pure platinum. His work led him to the discovery of palladium and rhodium in 1803.

Shining cleaner

This metal's resistance to corrosion makes it perfect for use in headlight reflectors. It is also put in catalytic converters to reduce nitrogen oxide so the cars give out less dangerous fumes.

PALLADIUM

46

Pd

106.42

TRANSITION METAL

Palladium has an unusual chemical trick. No one knows exactly how, but at room temperature this solid metal can absorb more than 900 times its own volume of hydrogen gas. It is therefore used in industry to purify the gas.

Atomic number: 46

Formula: Pd

Atomic weight: 106.42

State at 68°F (20°C): solid

Boiling point: 5365°F (2963°C)

Melting point: 2830.6°F (1554.8°C)

Uses: in catalytic converters; jewelry; dentistry; watch-making; surgical instruments

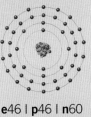

e46 | p46 | n60

Close-up
This picture, taken by a scanning electron microscope (SEM), shows clearly the typical close-packed and complicated cubic shapes of silver-white palladium crystals. The metal itself can be hammered into shape without cracking.

Cleaner air
When exhaust gases flow through a car's catalytic converter, they pass through a ceramic honeycomb that is coated with palladium. The metal acts as a catalyst, allowing poisonous carbon monoxide to react with oxygen to produce the less harmful carbon dioxide.

Future energy
The efficiency of solar cells may be massively improved in years to come. Makers of experimental cells made from cadmium telluride are claiming that they are much better than silicon-based solar panels.

CADMIUM

48

Cd

112.41

TRANSITION METAL

Cadmium compounds make great paints because, when its atoms combine with other atoms and molecules, they produce brilliant colors that do not fade. For example, cadmium sulfide was a favorite yellow used by French impressionist painter Claude Monet.

Key ore
Dark gray sphalerite (left), the chief zinc mineral, is also the main ore of cadmium. The name comes from the ancient name for calamine, or zinc carbonate, because it was thought similar to zinc. Cadmium is a soft, blue-white metal that can be easily cut with a knife.

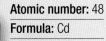

Charged
The nickel-cadmium rechargeable battery was first used on a large scale in 1917 to light subway trains in Paris, France. Today, this type of battery is in common use.

Atomic number: 48

Formula: Cd

Atomic weight: 112.411

State at 68°F (20°C): solid

Boiling point: 1413°F (767°C)

Melting point: 609.92°F (321.07°C)

Uses: to coat parts of aeroplanes and oil platforms; in nuclear reactors; rechargeable batteries; solar cells; in nanotechnology

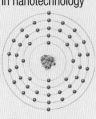

e48 | p48 | n64

SILVER

TRANSITION METAL

47

Ag

107.87

Silver is the stuff of champions. It can be stretched or hammered to become incredibly long and thin. When it needs to be harder, it makes alloys with other metals. It also has the highest thermal and electrical conductivity of any metal. It seems unfair that those who come second in sports events get silver medals, when it out-performs gold in so many ways.

Atomic number: 47

Formula: Ag

Atomic weight: 107.8682

State at 68°F (20°C): solid

Boiling point: 3924°F (2162°C)

Melting point: 1763.2°F (961.78°C)

% in the Universe: 0.000000060

% in Earth's crust: 0.0000079

% in Earth's oceans: 0.00000001

% in humans: none

Uses: defroster in rear windows of cars; coins; photography; jewelry; dental fillings; ornaments; batteries; electronics; silver-infused fabrics to prevent bacteria; in nuclear reactors; silver iodide for cloud seeding; in radiology; to coat prostheses such as knee joints to reduce infection; to purify water on Apollo spacecraft; in railway switch gear; in solar panels; 3D printing; silvering mirrors

Striking silver

In 1857, two brothers struck it lucky in Nevada when they found the Comstock Lode. According to some sources $305,779,612.48 worth of silver was mined there between 1859 and 1992. Most silver is extracted from minerals such as galena, argentite, and chalcopyrite. Pure silver or silver as an alloy is also sometimes found in Earth's crust. Other "native" metals are gold, copper, and platinum.

Chalcopyrite

Native silver

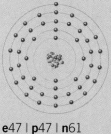

e47 | p47 | n61

Silver mine

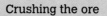
Crushing the ore

Cleaning extracted metals

Through the ages
Silver was probably first mined in Anatolia (modern Turkey) in 3000 BCE. In medieval Europe, there was a "silver rush," and silver was the metal of choice in South America in the 1600s. By the 1900s, there were mines all over the world. Silver ore was first crushed and then smelted—the silver extracted by melting with a flux (a chemical agent) while heating—before being freed from impurities.

Monetary value
The first coins for payment were used in the 7th century BCE, probably minted by the people of Lydia (now Turkey). The coins were electrum, combining silver with gold. Silver coins have been used all over the world since, some made to keep, not spend. The Morgan dollar (left) was minted from 1878–1904, and then in 1921. It is 90 percent silver and 10 percent copper.

Silver is a better **electrical conductor** than **copper**, but its **high cost** makes it **less attractive for electrical wiring.**

18th-century automaton swan

Detailed modeling of the silver wings

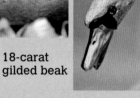

18-carat gilded beak

Elaborate work
Silver has long been a favorite of metalworkers. It is one of the few metals that can be beaten into delicate sheets or pulled out to make a strong wire—0.035 oz (1 g) can be pulled into a piece of wire more than 2 km (1.25 m) long. The silversmith who made this magnificent coffee set displayed all of its possibilities in the intricate working of the leaves and birds.

Swan automaton
Dating from 1773, this swan is the only one of its kind in the world. It is life-size and controlled by three separate clockwork mechanisms made by inventor John Joseph Merlin. It sits on a "stream" complete with silver fish. When it is wound up, the swan twists it head and preens its back before lowering its beak to catch a fish and swallow it.

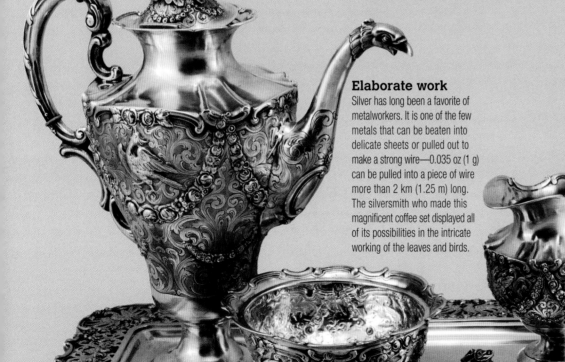

A river runs through

The Río Tinto river ("Red River") in southwestern Spain rises in the Sierra mountains and flows down to the Gulf of Cádiz. The landscape surrounding this unique river is colored red, ocher, violet, blue, orange, and black from 5,000 years of opencast mining. The main ores are those of copper, but silver, gold, iron, and zinc ores are also mined here. The dissolving iron gives the river itself a rusty-red color. There is little free oxygen in the water, and it is very acidic. The only life is the bacteria that live off the iron and minerals in the water.

Mining for elements

Hard rock mining underground is used to excavate minerals at depths of more than 200 ft (60 m). Some mines are enormous. One of the deepest mines in the world is the Mponeng gold mine in South Africa, which is 2.4 miles (3.9 km) deep and has 236 miles (380 km) of tunnels. It is hot down there, up to 140°F (60°C), so icy air is blown through the tunnels.

EXTRACTING ELEMENTS

Single elements, or more often compounds, form minerals that we can use. They are often mixed with other substances and can be hidden deep underground. The process of getting them out is called extraction, and might involve digging or drilling, before various methods are used to isolate prized elements. Increasingly, recycling is proving to be an essential way of preserving and reusing valuable materials.

Found in nature
Gold can be found as both grains and nuggets—around 1200 BCE, the Egyptians used sheepskins to sift gold dust from the sands of the Black Sea. Together with silver, copper, and platinum, gold is found free in nature in abundance, although several other metals also occur in their native state. Prospectors pan for gold or diamonds, and when successful, move upstream to mine rocks from which these precious items come.

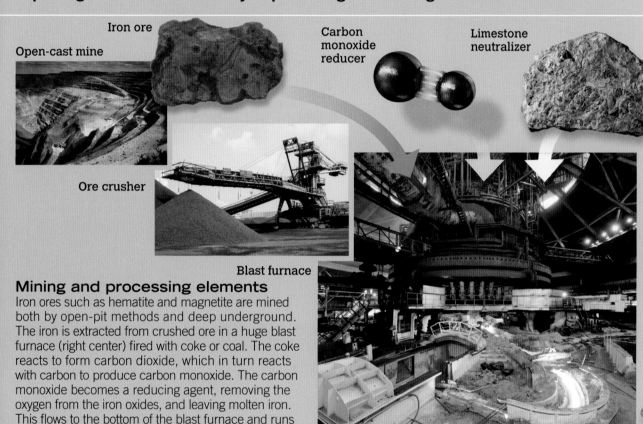

Iron ore

Open-cast mine

Carbon monoxide reducer

Limestone neutralizer

Ore crusher

Blast furnace

Rough diamond

Panning for gold

Gold nugget

Mining and processing elements
Iron ores such as hematite and magnetite are mined both by open-pit methods and deep underground. The iron is extracted from crushed ore in a huge blast furnace (right center) fired with coke or coal. The coke reacts to form carbon dioxide, which in turn reacts with carbon to produce carbon monoxide. The carbon monoxide becomes a reducing agent, removing the oxygen from the iron oxides, and leaving molten iron. This flows to the bottom of the blast furnace and runs off. Limestone is added to convert impurities into slag.

Separating elements
Aluminum is abundant but expensive because the method of extracting it, electrolysis, is costly. Bauxite ore is purified to give a white powder, aluminum oxide. This is dissolved in cryolite, an aluminum compound that has a lower melting point. When an electric current is passed through the mixture, molten aluminum sinks to the bottom of the tank and is poured off into molds.

Aluminum electrolysis units

Recycling
People are increasingly aware of the need to take care of Earth's elements. Farm waste can be recycled as fertilizers, batteries recharged and reused, scrap metal converted into new products, and nuclear fuel reprocessed. For example, recycling aluminum requires only 5 percent of the energy used to make new aluminum.

General metal waste

Aluminum waste blocks

HAFNIUM

72
Hf
178.49

TRANSITION METAL

This shiny metal is chiefly found in ores with zirconium and does not like to be parted from its twin. This means that it usually has zirconium impurities.

Atomic number: 72

Formula: Hf

Atomic weight: 178.49

State at 68°F (20°C): solid

Boiling point: 8312°F (4600°C)

Melting point: 4051°F (2233°C)

Uses: control rods; plasma welding

torches; microchips; wires; gas-filled and incandescent lamps

e72 | p72 | n106

Cutting tool
Plasma cutting torches are tools that can cut most metals. When oxygen is used in the process, hafnium is added to the metal because it lasts a long time.

RHENIUM

TRANSITION AND NOBLE METAL

75
Re
186.207

Rhenium is rarer than gold in Earth's crust, but it has been found in a volcano. The Kudriavy volcano on Iturup island in Russia has been sending out hot gas jets for decades. In 1994, it was found that rhenium minerals crystallize from the jets.

Atomic number: 75

Formula: Re

Atomic weight: 186.207

State at 68°F (20°C): solid

Boiling point: 10094°F (5590°C)

Melting point: 5765°F (3185°C)

Uses: ovens; X-ray

machines; single-crystal turbine blades; in aviation and rocket industries

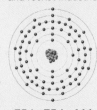

e75 | p75 | n111

Superalloy
Rhenium is used for aero engines and turbine blades in fighter jet engines. It is alloyed with nickel to make a superalloy that can handle very high temperatures.

TANTALUM

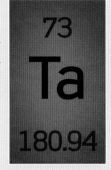

73
Ta
180.94

TRANSITION METAL

This element is a high performer. It allows cell phones and other electronic devices to be smaller, aero engines to work at hotter temperatures, and nuclear reactors to operate more safely. And, because it resists corrosion, it is sometimes hidden away inside the human body, as a bolt that holds broken bones together.

Atomic number: 73

Formula: Ta

Atomic weight: 180.9479

State at 68°F (20°C): solid

Boiling point: 9851°F (5455°C)

Melting point: 5463°F (3017°C)

Uses: surgical implants; wire; neon lights; turbine blades; rocket nozzles; nose caps on supersonic planes

Tough alloy
Its tough nature makes tantalum ideal as part of nickel-based superalloys—alloys that can be used at very high temperatures. The alloys are used for turbine blades in aircraft engines and for industrial gas turbines.

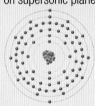

e73 | p73 | n108

Finding the ore
Tantalum does not occur in its pure form in nature. It is often found in minerals, such as tantalite (left) with niobium, thorium, and uranium. The pure element is extracted as a byproduct of industrial mining.

Capacitors
Capacitors store an electric charge and are widely used in televisions, digital cameras, radios, and other electronic devices. About half the tantalum each year is used by the electronics industry, mainly in capacitors.

OSMIUM

76
Os
190.23

TRANSITION AND NOBLE METAL

Osmium was discovered in 1803 by English chemist Smithson Tennant, who also found iridium. Its compound osmium tetroxide was used briefly for fingerprint detection, but it is toxic. However, it still plays a corrosion-resistant role in medical pacemakers and heart valves.

Atomic number: 76

Formula: Os

Atomic weight: 190.23

State at 68°F (20°C): solid

Boiling point: 9046°F (5008°C)

Melting point: 5491°F (3033°C)

Uses: needles; electrical contacts; in medical implants

e76 | p76 | n114

Tough needle
Osmium alloys are found in places where use over and over again would cause wear in less tough materials. Examples are needles for the phonograph, an early form of record player, and ballpoint pen tips.

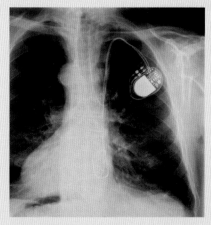

Heart of the matter
Alloyed with other metals in the platinum group, osmium is used for heart pacemakers. These small devices are placed in the chest where they emit electrical pulses to help the heart beat at a normal rate.

IRIDIUM

77
Ir
192.21

TRANSITION AND NOBLE METAL

Iridium is one of the rarest elements in Earth's crust. It is the most corrosion-resistant metal of them all, so it was used to set the international standard weight of the kilogram in 1884. Today, it helps to give the spark that starts a car, strengthens platinum, and is in pen tips.

Atomic number: 77

Formula: Ir

Atomic weight: 192.217

State at 68°F (20°C): solid

Boiling point: 8002°F (4428°C)

Melting point: 4435°F (2446°C)

Uses: pen tips; compass bearings; crucibles; spark plugs; as a hardening agent

e77 | p77 | n115

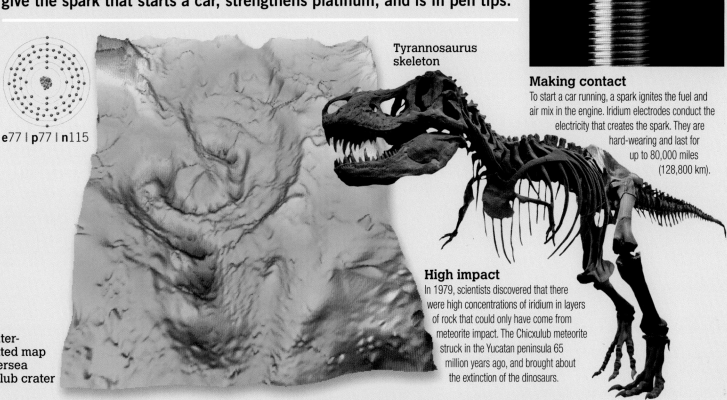

Tyrannosaurus skeleton

Computer-generated map of undersea Chicxulub crater

Making contact
To start a car running, a spark ignites the fuel and air mix in the engine. Iridium electrodes conduct the electricity that creates the spark. They are hard-wearing and last for up to 80,000 miles (128,800 km).

High impact
In 1979, scientists discovered that there were high concentrations of iridium in layers of rock that could only have come from meteorite impact. The Chicxulub meteorite struck in the Yucatan peninsula 65 million years ago, and brought about the extinction of the dinosaurs.

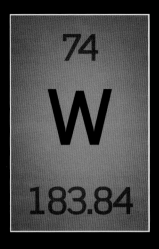

74

W

183.84

Atomic number: 74

Formula: W

Atomic weight: 183.84

State at 68°F (20°C): solid

Boiling point: 10031°F (5555°C)

Melting point: 6177°F (3414°C)

% in the Universe: 0.000000050

% in Earth's crust: 0.00011

% in Earth's oceans: 0.000000012

% in humans: none

Uses: arc-welding electrodes; heating elements in high-temperature furnaces; lightbulbs; metalworking; mining; in the petroleum industry; cutting and drilling tools; fluorescent lighting; manufacture of paints; in smartphones controlling vibration; military weapons

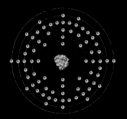

e74 | p74 | n110

TUNGSTEN

TRANSITION METAL

The word tungsten comes from the Swedish for "heavy stone." A tough performer, it has a high melting point and makes an ideal material for rocket engine nozzles. Its high density means small pieces are used to add weight and keep zooming Formula 1 racing cars glued to the track.

Bright arc

Tungsten electrodes are used in some welding processes when metals are heated so that they melt and stick together. In arc welding, an electric arc is directed from a tungsten electrode to the welding point. Tungsten is used because it has such a high melting point.

Extracting the element

Tungsten ores include the dark crystals of wolframite (below), scheelite, ferberite, and hubnerite. Its formula, W, comes from *wolfram*, the German name for tungsten. The metal is produced by heating powdered tungsten oxide in a stream of hydrogen at temperatures up to 1560°F (850°C).

Bright light

A lightbulb is a form of incandescent lighting—it gives off light as a result of being heated. The glass bulb houses a filament, which is a coiled tungsten wire. The filament is heated by an electric current until it gets so hot that it glows white and gives off light. The bulb is filled with a gas such as argon (see p.194) to stop the filament burning out.

Tungsten filament in lightbulb

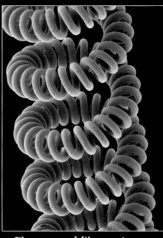

Close-up of filament

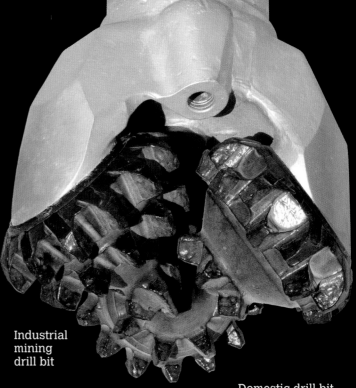

Industrial mining drill bit

Domestic drill bit

Drilling down

Tungsten carbide is the hardest tungsten compound. It is used to make drill bits that can drill through virtually all materials and still hold their edge. They are used for metalworking, mining, and in construction, as well as in the home.

Lead replacement

Fishermen use weights to help them control where their fishing lines land. Although it costs more, tungsten has begun to replace lead for fishing weights because it is more environmentally friendly.

Tungsten has the highest **melting point** of all of the **pure metals**.

Tough coating

Tungsten was used for nozzles on early space rockets, but it is heavy and often cracked. However, tungsten disulfide, a dry lubricant that was developed for NASA, provides a protective heat-resistant coating for new spacecraft.

PLATINUM

TRANSITION AND NOBLE METAL

78
Pt
195.084

Platinum is rarer than gold—and more expensive. It is a stable metal and very useful because it is a brilliant catalyst for chemical reactions. A major use of platinum is in jewelry, both as a setting for gemstones and a decoration in its own right. It is also in car exhausts, where it converts harmful carbon monoxide and hydrocarbons into carbon dioxide and water.

Atomic number: 78

Formula: Pt

Atomic weight: 195.084

State 68°F (20°C): solid

Boiling point: 6917°F (3825°C)

Melting point: 3214.8°F (1768.2°C)

% in the Universe: 0.00000050

% in Earth's crust: 0.0000037

% in Earth's oceans: none

% in humans: none

Uses: jewelry; watches; as a currency as coins, bars, and ingots; oxygen sensors, spark plugs, turbine engines; missile nose cones; hypoallergenic dentistry equipment and dental crowns; magnets; catalytic converters; as a catalyst for fuel cells; laboratory vessels; corrosion-resistant equipment; dentistry; implants in heart pacemakers and replacement valves

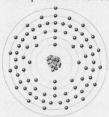

e78 | p78 | n117

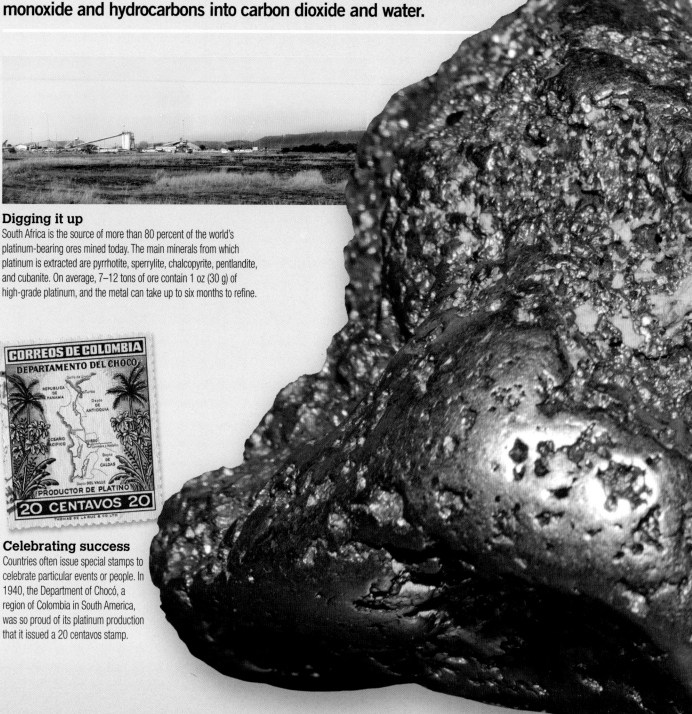

Digging it up
South Africa is the source of more than 80 percent of the world's platinum-bearing ores mined today. The main minerals from which platinum is extracted are pyrrhotite, sperrylite, chalcopyrite, pentlandite, and cubanite. On average, 7–12 tons of ore contain 1 oz (30 g) of high-grade platinum, and the metal can take up to six months to refine.

Celebrating success
Countries often issue special stamps to celebrate particular events or people. In 1940, the Department of Chocó, a region of Colombia in South America, was so proud of its platinum production that it issued a 20 centavos stamp.

Top metal

From the earliest times, platinum was used to make jewelry. The Ancient Egyptians imported gold mixed with platinum from the kingdom of Nubia, and the daughter of the King of Thebes was buried in a sarcophagus decorated with gold and platinum hieroglyphs. Today, platinum sets off the most sparkling of diamonds in many engagement rings.

Standard weight

This is Kilogram 18, the 18th copy of the 1889 international prototype, which established standard weight. This is the United Kingdom's copy and it is kept at the National Physical Laboratory at Teddington in England. This and other copies are checked regularly against the Le Grand K— the International Prototype Kilogram, a cylinder of platinum-iridium alloy kept in Sevres, France.

In **1557** an Italian **doctor** described a **metal** found in **South America** that would not **melt**—it was **platinum**.

Exhaust fumes

Honeycomb cleaner

Untold wealth

Platinum is rare but can be found in its pure form as nuggets (left), flakes, and grains. The name comes from the Spanish word *platina*, which means "little silver," given to it by Spanish conquistadores when they invaded South America in the 1500s. They did not value it, unlike the gold and silver they found there. Platinum is one of the "noble metals" —metals that do not rust or corrode, even at high temperatures.

Top converter

Platinum, rhodium, iridium, and palladium are all used as catalysts in catalytic converters for the exhaust system of vehicles. They convert toxic gases into less dangerous substances. There are 0.1–0.24 oz (3–7 g) of platinum group metals in a standard catalytic converter.

GOLD

TRANSITION AND NOBLE METAL

79

Au

196.967

The golden jewelry made thousands of years ago by shaping this highly malleable metal still shines today because gold does not corrode. Gold has been used for decoration, as money, to repair teeth, and, in the modern world, its conductivity makes it ideal for semiconductor chips. And we still love to wear it—the biggest "bling" metal of them all!

Atomic number: 79

Formula: Au

Atomic weight: 196.967

State at 68°F (20°C): solid

Boiling point: 5137°F (2836°C)

Melting point: 1947.52°F (1064.18°C)

% in the Universe: 0.000000060

% in Earth's crust: 0.00000031

% in Earth's oceans: 0.0000000050

% in humans: 0.000010

Uses: electrical wires; cell phones; computer memory chips; decorative gold leaf; gold bars; dentistry; Chinese medicine; modern medicine; spaceships and space visors to reflect infrared radiation; jewelry; to color glass; medical use for rheumatoid arthritis

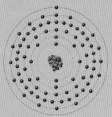

e79 | p79 | n118

Finding gold

In the 19th century there were major gold rushes in the Americas, Australia, and South Africa, with 100,000 prospectors moving into the Klondike region in northwest Canada alone over a period of only three years. Today, enormous open-pit mining operations, such as Australia's Super Pit Gold Mine, prove that the lure of gold is as strong as ever.

Klondike gold rush, northwest Canada, 1896–1899

Today's Super Pit gold mine, Kalgoorlie, Australia

Hidden away

A large proportion of the world's supply of gold is held in reserve at central banks or is in the hands of investors. According to the World Gold Council, the United States' official gold holdings in March 2016 were 8,965.64 tons.

From the ground

Gold is one of the few elements that you can find just lying on the ground. It is also found in veins in rocks underground. It can be fine gold grains, crystals, flakes, or nuggets. The largest nugget ever found was the "Welcome Stranger," discovered in western Victoria, Australia in 1869, which weighed more than 157 lbs. (71 kg).

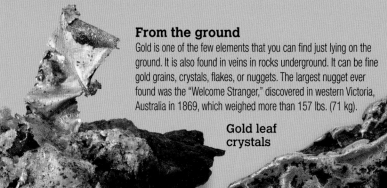

Gold leaf crystals

Gold nugget

1 oz (28 g) of gold can be drawn into a wire 50 miles (80 km) long.

"Sun" shine

Gold was prized by early civilizations because it was so easy to shape. However, it is too soft for weapons and tools. Its bright luster reminded ancient peoples of the Sun. The ancient Egyptian Sun god Ra was called "the mountain of gold," and the Inca of Peru believed that gold was the sweat of their Sun god Inti. Gold was used for jewelry and grave goods, such as this gold leaf mask of a Greek king dating from 1550–1500 BCE.

Koala's gold feast

Traces of gold have been found in the leaves of eucalyptus trees. Australian scientists experimented with trees near gold-mining sites and also by planting them. They discovered that the roots, which dig deep down into the earth more than 130 ft. (40 m) searching for water, send microscopic gold particles up to the leaves. The gold is probably toxic to the plant so it moves the particles to its extremities.

Space gold

Out in space is a large stony asteroid called Eros, from which NASA's Near Earth Asteroid Rendevous (NEAR) Shoemaker spacecraft has collected data as it flew nearby. The 20.5 x 8-mile (33 x 13-km) asteroid is estimated to contain 20 billion tons of gold, as well as similar amounts of other metals, such as platinum and aluminum. Most of the gold on Earth has been mined, but in the future asteroids may offer a golden opportunity!

Silver treasure trove

In 2008, while excavating a Bronze Age tomb, archeologists found a Viking treasure trove near Arlanda airport in Sweden. It included 472 silver coins, mostly from Baghdad and Damascus. The hoard has been dated to about 850 CE, and is a significant find because it is believed that the Vikings had only begun to import eastern coins that century.

PRECIOUS ELEMENTS

Why do we value some materials formed by elements above others? Sometimes it is because we see them as beautiful, and maybe we prize them even more if they are rare and hard to get. But value is not always logical. For example, gold is too soft and heavy for tools, so it is used mostly for decoration. This is a collection of objects that are highly prized, for all sorts of reasons.

Precious metals

Metals described as precious are those that are considered to be the most valuable because they are rare, durable, and do not tarnish. The four most well-known are gold, silver, platinum, and palladium. Historically, silver, gold, and platinum have been used for currency, jewelry, and decoration, as well as in the electronics and technological industries. Palladium is very rare indeed, and its main uses are in medicine and industry.

Precious minerals

The role that elements play in the gems that we love can be complex. While diamonds consist only of carbon, rubies and sapphires are both the mineral corundum. Tiny amounts of iron and titanium create the deep blue of the sapphire, while chromium turns rubies red. Emeralds are a variety of the mineral beryl, and are that color because of vanadium, chromium, and iron.

Diamond (carbon)

Ruby (aluminum oxide)

Sapphire (aluminum oxide)

Emerald (beryllium aluminum silicate with trace amount of chromium)

Platinum and platinum American Eagle coin

English 17th-century James I gold coin and nugget

Global gold

Throughout history, gold has been linked to royalty and immortality. Pharaohs were buried with it and it was stolen from the Aztecs by the Spanish conquistadores. Built in 1577, the Golden Temple of Amritsar in India was gilded with 1,653 lbs. (750 kg) of pure gold.

Tutankhamun gold coffin, Egypt

Aztec gold mask, Mexico

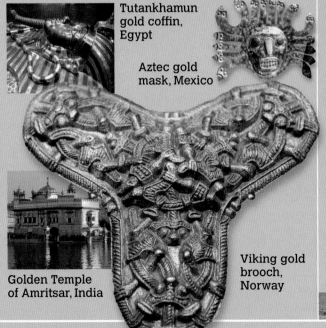

Golden Temple of Amritsar, India

Viking gold brooch, Norway

Pirates and treasure

From the 16th century, Spanish galleons carried silver, platinum, and gold treasure across the Atlantic from the Americas to the Mediterranean. The sea journey was a dangerous one because of the threat from pirates and privateers sent to rob them by enemy governments. The mainland coast round the Caribbean Sea was known as the Spanish Main.

English ship attacking a Spanish galleon, 1743

Spain

Mexico

Spanish galleon

Route of Spanish treasure trade

Spanish gold doubloons

Native silver and Spanish doubloon

A pharaoh's tomb

On November 26, 1922, the best known and most spectacular archeological find in the world happened in the Valley of the Kings, Egypt. Howard Carter made a small hole in a sealed door and inserted a candle to check for poisonous gases. He recorded ". . . strange animals, statues, and gold—everywhere the glint of gold." He was describing the anteroom to the nearly intact tomb of Tutankhamun in the Valley of the Kings. This richly decorated gold and silver inlaid throne, depicting the pharaoh and his wife, was found there.

80
Hg
200.59

MERCURY

TRANSITION METAL

As fast and deadly as a striking snake, heated mercury transforms into a toxic gas that can make people very sick. Also known for years as quicksilver, it is liquid at room temperature, which made it perfect for thermometers and barometers, because it moved as temperature or pressure changed without sticking to its glass container. But today we know it is too dangerous to use.

Atomic number: 80

Formula: Hg

Atomic weight: 200.59

State at 68°F (20°C): liquid

Boiling point: 673.914°F (356.619°C)

Melting point: −37.892°F (−38.829°C)

% in the Universe: 0.000000100

% in Earth's crust: 0.0000067

% in Earth's oceans: 0.0000000050

% in humans: none

Uses: in the past in the making of hats, paints, batteries, fluorescent lights, felt production, thermometers and barometers; today mainly in the chemical industry as a catalyst; in electrical switches; mercury amalgams in dental fillings; fluorescent lamps; for liquid mirrors; as a primer in firearms; in disinfectant and solutions

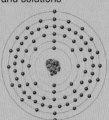

e80 | p80 | n121

Toxic landscape
In the Altai mountains of central Asia there is an area the size of France that has been mined extensively for copper, lead, and zinc ores. About 5,000 tons of metal mercury was produced in this region between 1941 and 1991. The mining activity has left a multi-colored soil that is rich in mercury deposits.

Cinnabar

Mineral source
Liquid mercury is found as very small amounts on top of mercury ores of which cinnabar is the main one. The mercury is lodged in small crevices in the mineral or simply sticks to the surface.

Cinnabar crystals on dolomite

Vermilion pigment mixed with linseed oil

Bright pigment

Cinnabar (mercuric sulfide) is a beautiful red mineral that is one of the sources of mercury. It was also used to make an artist's red pigment called vermilion. This is widely seen in the decorative arts of ancient China and Rome, and in the illustrated manuscripts of monks in the Middle Ages. It became popular with artists such as Titian in Renaissance Europe. Today, it has been replaced by the pigment cadmium red.

Titian's *The Descent of the Holy Ghost*

Liquid metal

The chemical symbol for mercury is Hg, from the Latin for "liquid silver," because this is the only metal that is liquid at room temperature. Early scientists loved it for this and thought it could be turned into gold.

Fluid mirror

Liquid mirror telescopes are used to scan the stars and planets in the night sky. They are made with mercury because the element stays liquid, and the mirror is created by spinning the highly reflective element. These telescopes can be built more cheaply than a conventional glass telescope mirror, but can only look straight up.

Clearing mercury-laden sludge by hand in the 1940s

Dangerous times

Mercury was used for medical treatments for a long time (right). And up to the early 1970s, in mines like this one in California (above), workers handled mercury and their activities contaminated the area around the mines. Finally people realized just how dangerous a substance the element was, and these days it is handled very carefully.

STEEDMAN'S SOOTHING POWDERS

In use over Fifty Years.

For Children Cutting Teeth.

RELIEVE FEVERISH HEAT, PREVENT FITS, CONVULSIONS, &c.

Preserve a healthy state of the constitution during the period of Teething.

CAUTION.—Please observe the EE in Steedman, and the address: Walworth, Surrey.

Victorian teething cream for babies made with mercury

RUTHERFORDIUM

104

Rf

[267]

TRANSITION METAL

Rutherfordium is a synthetic element that is made only in tiny amounts at nuclear research labs. So little is made at a time that it has never been seen with the naked eye, and anyway much of it fades away in just over an hour. It was created by bombarding californium with carbon nuclei, and is named after the physicist Ernest Rutherford, who discovered the atomic nucleus.

Atomic number: 104
Formula: Rf
Atomic weight: [267]
State at 68°F (20°C): solid
Boiling point: unknown
Melting point: unknown
Half-life: 1.3 hours

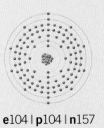

e104 | p104 | n157

Atomic number: 105
Formula: Db
Atomic weight: [268]
State at 68°F (20°C): solid
Boiling point: unknown
Melting point: unknown
Half-life: 1.2 days

e105 | p105 | n163

DUBNIUM

105

Db

[268]

TRANSITION METAL

This superheavy radioactive element has had many names. It has been called eka-tantalum, hahnium, and unnilpentium but is now named dubnium.

Village sign
The element is now named dubnium after the Russian town of Dubna where it was first made by bombarding californium with nitrogen-15 nuclei in 1967.

Atomic number: 106
Formula: Sg
Atomic weight: [269]
State at 68°F (20°C): solid
Boiling point: unknown
Melting point: unknown
Half-life: 2.4 minutes

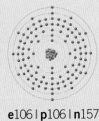

e106 | p106 | n157

SEABORGIUM

TRANSITION METAL

Only half of this synthetic element sticks around after a couple of minutes. It was first made in 1970, but the team led by Albert Ghiorso in California did not think they had enough data. They were finally credited with the discovery in 1997, and named it for Glenn Seaborg.

106

Sg

[269]

In honor of...
This element was named for the Danish atomic physicist Niels Bohr. It was created by bombarding bismuth with chromium nuclei.

Atomic number: 107
Formula: Bh
Atomic weight: [270]
State at 68°F (20°C): solid
Boiling point: unknown
Melting point: unknown
Half-life: 61 seconds

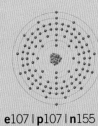

e107 | p107 | n155

BOHRIUM

107

Bh

[270]

TRANSITION METAL

Like the other superheavy synthetics, Bohrium is made by smashing together lighter elements in a particle accelerator. It has a half-life of just over a minute.

HASSIUM

108
Hs
[269]

TRANSITION METAL

Hassium was first made in 1984 in Darmstadt, Germany. There were years of arguments about what to call it. Some scientists suggested hahnium, for a German radiochemist, but eventually is was named after the German state of Hesse, where it was created by bombarding lead with iron nuclei.

Atomic number: 108	Half-life: 22 seconds
Formula: Hs	
Atomic weight: [269]	
State at 68°F (20°C): solid	
Boiling point: unknown	
Melting point: unknown	

e108 | p108 | n157

MEITNERIUM

Atomic number: 109	Half-life: about 8 seconds
Formula: Mt	
Atomic weight: [278]	
State at 68°F (20°C): solid	
Boiling point: unknown	
Melting point: unknown	

e109 | p109 | n157

109
Mt
[278]

TRANSITION METAL

This is a silvery metal that quickly corrodes in air, steam and acids . . . we think. No one has ever investigated it as this synthetic element begins to decay in less than a second and only a few atoms have been made by bombarding bismuth with iron nuclei. It is named for physicist Lise Meitner (*see* p.143), pioneer in nuclear fission.

DARMSTADTIUM

110
Ds
[281]

TRANSITION METAL

This element is named in honor of the German city of Darmstadt, where it was discovered. Its isotopes are extremely unstable and radioactive, which sounds like trouble, but don't worry—most of its atoms disappear faster than you can blink. It is formed by nuclear fusion of nickel and lead atoms in a heavy ion accelerator.

Atomic number: 110	Half-life: 13 seconds
Formula: Ds	
Atomic weight: [281]	
State at 68°F (20°C): solid	
Boiling point: unknown	
Melting point: unknown	

e110 | p110 | n151

ROENTGENIUM

Atomic number: 111	Half-life: 26 seconds
Formula: Rg	
Atomic weight: [280]	
State at 68°F (20°C): solid	
Boiling point: unknown	
Melting point: unknown	

e111 | p111 | n161

111
Rg
[280]

TRANSITION METAL

Named for the German discoverer of X-rays, William Conrad Röntgen, this element is both superheavy, and super rare, with only a few atoms of it ever forming. It decays in just under 26 seconds. It was discovered in Germany by a team led by Peter Armbruster and Gottfried Münzenberg.

COPERNICUM

Atomic number: 112	Half-life: 30 seconds
Formula: Cn	
Atomic weight: [285]	
State at 68°F (20°C): solid	
Boiling point: unknown	
Melting point: unknown	

e112 | p112 | n173

112
Cn
[285]

TRANSITION METAL

In 1996, scientists spent two weeks bombarding lead with a beam of zinc ions traveling at 18,640 miles (30,000 km) per second. The result was a few atoms of element 112, later named for Nicolaus Copernicus (1473–1543), the astronomer who explained how the Sun is at the center of our solar system.

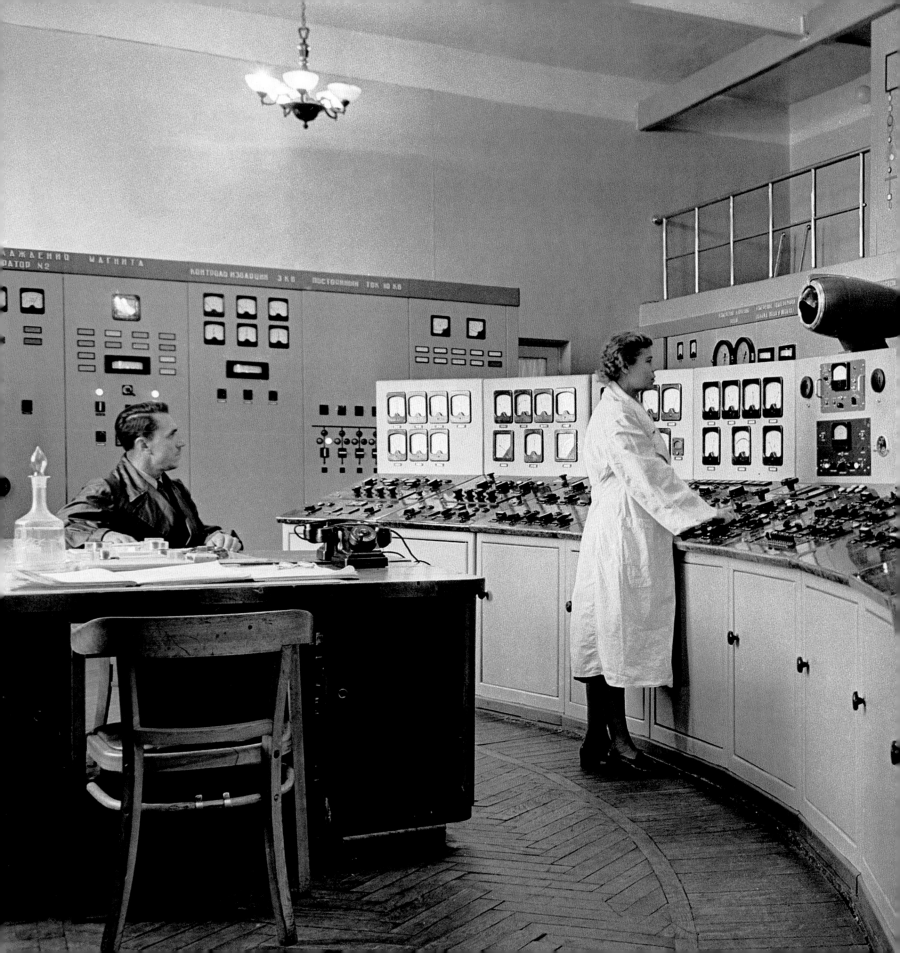

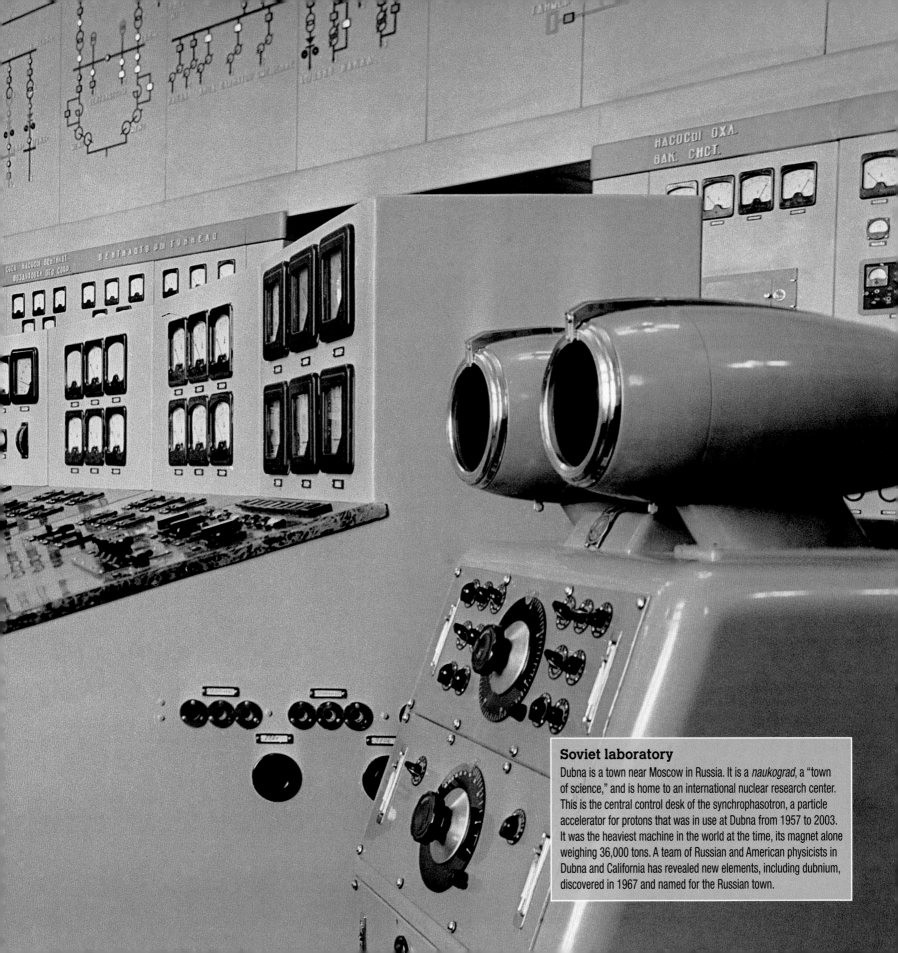

Soviet laboratory

Dubna is a town near Moscow in Russia. It is a *naukograd*, a "town of science," and is home to an international nuclear research center. This is the central control desk of the synchrophasotron, a particle accelerator for protons that was in use at Dubna from 1957 to 2003. It was the heaviest machine in the world at the time, its magnet alone weighing 36,000 tons. A team of Russian and American physicists in Dubna and California has revealed new elements, including dubnium, discovered in 1967 and named for the Russian town.

POOR METALS

Aluminum recycling
The global demand for aluminum is expected to soar even higher than the 60 million tons used today. Scrap metal aluminum is becoming more vital. Recycling one aluminum can, instead of making a new one, saves enough energy to light a 60-watt lightbulb for 20 hours.

These elements, also known as post-transition, are called "poor" because they are softer and have lower melting and boiling points. Although not very strong, they are good conductors of heat and electricity and very easy to shape.

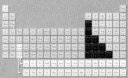

Two extremes
The most abundant of the poor elements on Earth is aluminum. In contrast, so little of elements 113 to 116 has been created that it is impossible to say what their chemical properties are.

POOR METALS TIMELINE

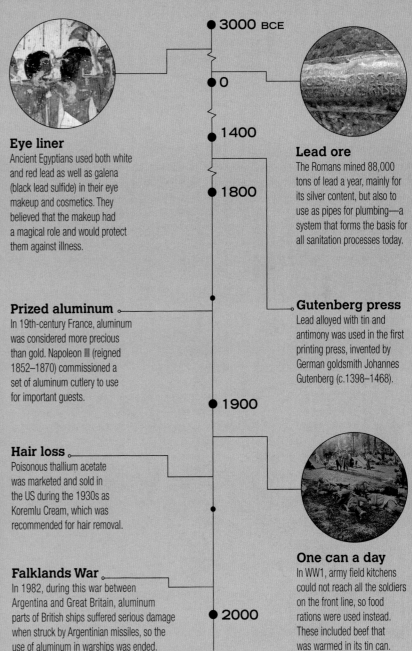

● 3000 BCE

● 0

● 1400

● 1800

● 1900

● 2000

Eye liner
Ancient Egyptians used both white and red lead as well as galena (black lead sulfide) in their eye makeup and cosmetics. They believed that the makeup had a magical role and would protect them against illness.

Lead ore
The Romans mined 88,000 tons of lead a year, mainly for its silver content, but also to use as pipes for plumbing—a system that forms the basis for all sanitation processes today.

Prized aluminum
In 19th-century France, aluminum was considered more precious than gold. Napoleon III (reigned 1852–1870) commissioned a set of aluminum cutlery to use for important guests.

Gutenberg press
Lead alloyed with tin and antimony was used in the first printing press, invented by German goldsmith Johannes Gutenberg (c.1398–1468).

Hair loss
Poisonous thallium acetate was marketed and sold in the US during the 1930s as Koremlu Cream, which was recommended for hair removal.

One can a day
In WW1, army field kitchens could not reach all the soldiers on the front line, so food rations were used instead. These included beef that was warmed in its tin can.

Falklands War
In 1982, during this war between Argentina and Great Britain, aluminum parts of British ships suffered serious damage when struck by Argentinian missiles, so the use of aluminum in warships was ended.

ALUMINUM

POOR METAL

The third most abundant element in the world—after oxygen and silicon—aluminum makes a lightweight, strong metal that conducts electricity well, so it is used for everything from power cables to kitchen foil and compact discs. It is planet-friendly, too, because the metal hardly corrodes and is easy to recycle. Aluminum is second only to iron as our most used metal.

13	
Al	
26.982	

Atomic number: 13

Formula: Al

Atomic weight: 26.98153

State at 68°F (20°C): solid

Boiling point: 4566°F (2519°C)

Melting point: 1220.581°F (660.323°C)

% in the Universe: 0.0050

% in Earth's crust: 8.1

% in Earth's oceans: 0.00000050

% in humans: 0.000090

Uses: as sheet, tube, and castings for transportation: cars, tires, railway cars, marine vessels, bike frames, aircraft fuselages, spacecraft; packaging: foil; drink cans, bottle tops; cooking pans; cutlery; space blankets; computer parts; balloons; ventilation systems; wire; paints; alloys; furnaces; ornaments; industrial abrasives; as cladding in windows, door frames, gutters, roofing for buildings; makeup; medicine packs

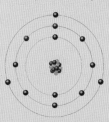

e13 | p13 | n14

Australian bauxite mine

Australian bauxite industry commemorative stamp

Raw material

Not many ores have special stamps issued for them. One of the main sources of aluminum is the ore bauxite, and Australia is the largest producer of bauxite in the world, with 91.9 million tons produced in 2016–17. Of the five Australian bauxite mines, Weipa in Queensland (far left) and Gove in the Northern Territory, produce the most bauxite. The ore is crushed and ground into a paste, heated with steam to remove any silicon, then smelted to produce aluminum oxide.

Bauxite

Precious oxide

A ruby is a deep red crystal, one of the most beautiful of the gemstones. It is aluminum oxide, a mineral called corundum, that has a small amount of chromium in it. This changes the color to red. If tiny amounts of iron and titanium are in the corundum instead, the result is the blue gemstone we call a sapphire.

Raw rubies on matrix

Cut ruby

Early space food

Aluminum played a significant role in the early dining experiences of astronauts. The first astronauts in the 1960s ate bite-sized cubes, freeze-dried foods, and semi-liquids in aluminum toothpaste-type tubes. In 1973, the United States' first space station, Skylab, was launched, and the food became more sophisticated. Meals, such as steak, asparagus, mashed potato, and ice cream, were packed into aluminum cans and rehydratable packages placed in a food warmer tray (left).

Lightweight power

Aluminum is a very light metal when compared with the traditional iron and steel used to build car engines (right), and it can improve performance. Although it can cost more, the metal can be recycled at the end of the car's life.

Recycling **aluminum cans** takes **95 percent less energy** than producing it from its **raw materials**.

Light flight

A single Boeing 747 contains more than 147,000 lbs. (66,000 kg) of high-strength, lightweight aluminum. The plane is assembled from around six million parts, half of which are fasteners or rivets. The outer skin is an aluminum alloy that is just 0.2 ins. (5 mm) thick.

Monumental cap

The top of the 555-ft. (169-m) Washington Monument in Washington D.C. is capped with a 8.9-ins. (22.6-cm) aluminum pyramid. It was originally put there in the 1880s to act as a lightning rod, but it did not work very well, so copper rods were added later on.

GALLIUM

POOR METAL

When Mendeleev created the periodic table in 1869, he predicted an element would be found to fill the space under aluminum. Six years later, French scientist Paul-Émile Lecoq de Boisbaudran spotted a pale violet line coming from the spectrum of some zinc he was studying, and gallium filled the gap. Today it is valuable in medicine and electronics, and brilliant for use in Blu-ray technology and LEDs.

Atomic number: 31

Formula: Ga

Atomic weight: 69.723

State at 68°F (20°C): solid; some alloys are liquid

Boiling point: 4044°F (2229°C)

Melting point: 85.576°F (29.765°C)

% in the Universe: 0.0000010

% in Earth's crust: 0.0019

% in Earth's oceans: 0.0000000030

% in humans: none

Uses: on mirrors, glass, and ceramics; thermostats, switches; barometers; heat transfer systems; thermal cooling and heating devices; as gallium nitride and gallium arsenide in semiconductors and LEDs; solar panels; medical thermometers; laser diodes; solar panels

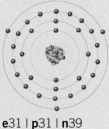

e31 | p31 | n39

Vanishing act
If a chemist offers you a hot drink, watch out, the spoon you stir it with might disappear! Solid gallium (below) is brittle, but this silvery, glass-like metal will turn to liquid in the warmth of your hand. The only other metals to do this are cesium, francium, and mercury. Gallium's main ore is sphalerite, but it is mainly obtained as a by-product of zinc refining and the aluminum industry.

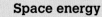

Space energy
Following success with gallium arsenide solar cells for the Mars Pathfinder mission in 1997, the Mars Rovers Opportunity (above) and Spirit explored the surface of Mars with solar cells powered by alloys of gallium, indium, and germanium in 2003.

Prediction
The existence of gallium was predicted by Mendeleev. He identified a gap in the periodic table, naming the missing element (gallium) "ekia-aluminum," because he said it would be like aluminum. It was not discovered until 1875.

New light?
Both gallium and indium (opposite) are used in the LED (light emitting diodes) lighting systems that are energy efficient and very effective. They have in fact been in use for more than 50 years, but they are only recently being used as a replacement for other white light sources.

INDIUM

POOR METAL

Indium was a late developer. For decades after it was found in 1863, the most interesting thing about it was the squeaking sound, or "tin cry," it gave when it was bent! Now it is notable for its use in LCD televisions, touch screens, and computer monitors, as well as fire sprinkler systems, mirror finishes on skyscrapers, and to coat ball bearings in Formula One racing cars.

Atomic number: 49

Formula: In

Atomic weight: 114.818

State at 68°F (20°C): solid

Boiling point: 3681°F (2027°C)

Melting point: 313.88°F (156.60°C)

% in the Universe: 0.000000030

% in Earth's crust: 0.000016

% in Earth's oceans: 0.000000000010

% in humans: none

Uses: for mirrors; semiconductors; glass for buildings; ball bearings for Formula One engines; display and touch screens; flat-screen televisions; solar panels; in germanium transistors; transparent photoconductors; low melting alloys; added to solders; coatings of aircraft parts; optical devices

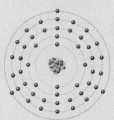

e49 | p49 | n66

Sticky stuff
A thin layer of indium is transparent, sticks to glass, and reflects heat well. This makes it perfect as a protective coating on the goggles of people using welding torches for machinery or in glassmaking.

Safer for use
In many thermometers, a combination of the non-toxic elements indium, gallium, and tin are used instead of toxic mercury.

Soft metal
This soft and silvery-white metal is usually found with zinc minerals and in iron, lead, and copper ores. It was isolated by German chemist Ferdinand Reich in 1863. Reich was color-blind and asked chemist Hieronymous Richter to take a look at the spectrum. Richter noted a bright indigo line, so the element was later named indium.

TIN

POOR METAL

Tin changed the world. When early cultures mixed it with copper, they found a new material that was better than rock or wood for tools and weapons—bronze. If you bend tin it "cries" a crackling sound, and it can melt easily in a flame. Tin is resistant to water, so is ideal for plating other metals to prevent rust, and to use as a solder to "glue" metals together. And most of us come into contact with tin every day—many food cans are made of tin-plated steel.

50

Sn

118.71

Atomic number: 50

Formula: Sn

Atomic weight: 118.710

State at 68°F (20°C): solid

Boiling point: 4687°F (2586°C)

Melting point: 449.47°F (231.928°C)

% in the Universe: 0.00000040

% in Earth's crust: 0.00022

% in Earth's oceans: 0.000000001

% in humans: 0.000020

Uses: to produce window glass; to fix colors when dyeing materials; ceramics; tin cans; fire retardants; mirror frames; roofing material; sheet metal wall coverings; flashing, gutters, and downspouts; as an alloy: soft solder, pewter, bronze, and phosphor bronze; as a niobium-tin alloy for superconducting magnets and wire; to coat harder metals such as iron and steel

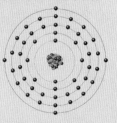

e50 I p50 I n69

Pewter plate

Bronze coin

Allied with the best

Tin has been used for thousands of years, forming partnerships with many other metals. An alloy of copper and tin was so useful that a whole period of history is called the Bronze Age (c. 3500–500 BCE). And in medieval times, pewter, the alloy of tin with lead and other metals, became a vital part of the economies of many European countries.

Success and failure

When Robert Falcon Scott and his team left England in 1910 for their ill-fated attempt to reach the South Pole, they carried tinned Huntley & Palmers biscuits. Tin was also used to store paraffin, but it developed tiny holes and the fuel leaked out.

Early storage

In 1804, French chef Nicolas Appert experimented with meat packed in tin cans. Appert's process was published in 1810, and in the same year the preservation of food in tin cans was patented by Peter Durand in England. Canned food such as oysters, sardines, and tomatoes quickly became popular, although the can opener was not even invented until nearly 50 years later.

Versatile metal

This low-melting metal is very versatile and can be pressed or hammered into shape. Combined with niobium, it makes superconductive wires. And when it is melted, it is used to create the sheets of the flat float glass found in most modern windows.

THALLIUM

POOR METAL

Thallium was sold as a potion to get rid of rats or ants, or even unwanted hair! The trouble is that less than a teaspoon could kill you—and it is colorless, tasteless, and odorless, so you would not know you were eating or drinking it. People in the past used it to get away with murder!

Atomic number: 81

Formula: Tl

Atomic weight: 204.3833

State at 78°F (20°C): solid

Boiling point: 2683°F (1473°C)

Melting point: 579°F (304°C)

Uses: photoresistors; low-temperature thermometers and switches; infrared optical equipment; rodent and ant killer; hair removal cream (not today); thallium salts as a treatment for skin diseases

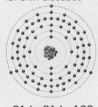

e81 | p81 | n123

Sun collectors

Most thallium is used in photoelectric cells, which generate electricity when light falls on them. These are used in many devices, from small solar panels on calculators and digital watches to houses and enormous solar farms.

Deep-sea source

Thallium is found in minerals such as crooksite, lorandite, and hutchinsonite. It has also been found in the manganese nodules (above) that cover thousands of square miles of the deep-sea floor. The nodules range in size from a potato to a cabbage.

Safer weight

Fishermen use metal sinkers as weights to help lines or nets sink below the surface of the water. In the past lead was used, but now bismuth is a safe alternative.

Sprinkler trigger

In some sprinkler systems, a plug made of a mixture of bismuth, lead, tin, and cadmium melts at a relatively low temperature to release the water.

BISMUTH

POOR METAL

Bismuth is your friend. It can soothe an upset stomach, is used in nail varnishes, and makes the fizzing, crackling sound in firework displays. Bismuth even saves lives. Because it melts quickly to become a liquid at low temperatures, it is used in fire alarms to detect rising temperatures and trigger the alarm bell or set off a sprinkler.

Crystal ore

Bismuth is found in nature and also in ores such as bismuthinite and bismite. Here, silver bismuthinite crystals and pure bismuth are visible in quartz.

Geometric form

Bismuth crystals grow in a distinctive staircase-like formation. This is because the growth rate on the outside edges is faster than that on the inside. As the crystals appear, a layer of oxidation gradually adds rainbow colors.

Atomic number: 83

Formula: Bi

Atomic weight: 208.98038

State at 78°F (20°C): solid

Boiling point: 2847°F (1564°C)

Melting point: 520.531°F (271.406°C)

Uses: fire detectors and extinguishers, electric fuses; solders; yellow pigment in cosmetics and paint; stomach upset aid; in catalysts for making acrylic fibers; in magnets; to make aluminum and copper machineable

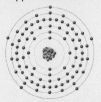

e83 | p83 | n126

LEAD

POOR METALS

82

Pb

207.2

Lead is poisonous to humans and other animals, but despite this, it is extremely useful. It is flexible, so works well on roofs. Lead also protects us by acting as a radiation shield—we could not use X-ray machines without it. And it keeps the traffic moving; about half of all the lead produced today is used in the manufacture of car batteries.

Atomic number: 82

Formula: Pb

Atomic weight: 207.2

State at 68°F (20°C): solid

Boiling point: 3180°F (1749°C)

Melting point: 621.432°F (327.462°C)

% in the Universe: 0.0000010

% in Earth's crust: 0.00099

% in Earth's oceans: 0.0000000030

% in humans: 0.00017

Uses: pipes; pewter; paint; lead glazes for pottery; insecticides; hair dyes; additive for petroleum; lead-acid car storage batteries; pigments; type metal; antifriction metals; solder; lead foil; ammunition; cable sheathing; weights; weight belts for diving; lead crystal; radiation protection in X-rays and nuclear reactors; cable sheathing; in the production of sulfuric acid

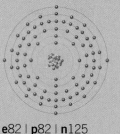

e82 | p82 | n125

Soft metal

Lead can be used for many tasks because it is so flexible, which is why it protects many church roofs. The way stained glass windows are made has hardly changed since the 12th century. Some of the leadwork that holds the colored glass in place has lasted for more than 800 years of exposure to all weather.

Roll of lead sheet

Stained glass windows

Printing revolution

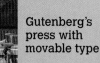

In the middle of the 15th century, something happened that changed the world. Johannes Gutenberg, a stonecutter and goldsmith of Mainz, Germany, invented an alloy of lead, tin, and antimony that made separate pieces of type to use in a printing press. They could be reused and rearranged. In 1452, Gutenberg began work on the famous two-volume Gutenberg Bible.

Movable metal type

Heavy weights

Divers must be weighted against their buoyancy and that of their equipment. These Turkish naval divers, pictured around 1890, are wearing equipment made by a company called Siebe Gorman. The machine in the middle, operated by the handles on the two sides, pumped air into the helmets. There were lead weights hanging from their waists and their boots had lead soles that weighed 34 lbs. (15.4 kg).

Toxic color

The ancient Greeks used white lead for their complexions. This practice was revived in late 16th-century Europe. Elizabeth 1 used Venetian Ceruse for her complexion, which was a mixture of vinegar and lead.

Gutenberg's press with movable type

Heavy ore

Galena (right) is the most important ore of lead, and it is often mined for its silver (see pp.78–79) as well. Soft, blue-gray lead is also found in other minerals such as cerussite and anglesite. About half of the lead used today is produced by mining, while the other half is from recycling, mainly from car batteries.

In **ancient Rome**, "sugar of lead" was added to **wine** as an **artificial sweetener**.

Eye treatment
Today, we know that lead can be toxic, but people through time have believed in its medical as well as everyday uses. Recently, French scientists analyzing samples of ancient Egyptian eye preparations found lead in the kohl (eyeliner) that they used. Ancient manuscripts reveal that the Egyptians also used the lead salts as treatments for eye ailments, scars, and skin discolorations.

Killer lead
These "musketballs" are examples of the lead bullets fired from a variety of guns, including muskets. They help archaeologists because they can determine the type of gun that fired them and so figure out who was where on which part of a battlefield.

Melting heat

Most alloys are made by melting two or more metals, mixing them while they are liquid, pouring them into molds, and then leaving them to cool and turn solid again. To do this, very high temperatures are needed. Here, sparks fly as workers wearing protective clothing pour molten metal from a melt vessel into a mold in an industrial foundry.

ALLOYS

If you combine a pure metal with another metal or a different element, the result is an alloy. Alloys are usually created by melting the elements to form a liquid. When the liquid cools and becomes solid, it is a new material with different properties. The alloy is usually harder than the pure metal, and has become a stronger, more useful material.

Aluminum
This element is typically alloyed with copper, iron, magnesium, silicon, zinc, or manganese, which may make up to 15% of the weight. The alloys are used where high strength and light weight is an advantage. Cast aluminum alloys are used for many Formula 1 racing car engines as well as the heat shields that protect the drivers.

Bronze
The first alloy that we know about was bronze. About 5,000 years ago, people found out that they could strengthen copper by smelting it (90%) with tin (10%) to make bronze. The alloy is tough and easy to shape, and can be given a sharp edge. For centuries, bronze was used for tools and for weapons such as spears, arrows, and swords.

Cast iron
This is an alloy of iron and carbon that was invented in China in the 5th century BCE. At very high temperatures, iron begins to absorb carbon rapidly from the air and starts to melt. The resulting cast iron contains up to 4.5% carbon. Today, ironworkers cast a mixture of iron, carbon, and silicon directly into molds to make stoves, cookware, ornaments, and drainage covers.

Gold
Gold does not exist in nature as a pure metal and the jewelry that you buy today is not pure gold. When the element is found or mined, it is usually alloyed to silver, copper, or zinc. The percentage of gold in jewelry is measured in carats, so the purest is 24 carats, which contains more than 99.7%. 22-carat yellow gold (right) would be 91.67% gold, 5% silver, 2% copper, and 1.33% zinc.

Stainless steel
Easily cleaned stainless steel is created by alloying iron with carbon, and adding at least 10% chromium. Chromium oxide forms in a thin layer on the surface to provide a protective coating.

Brass
Brass is an alloy of copper and zinc. Although the ancient Egyptians, Greeks, and Romans all used it for objects such as coins and helmets, it was not until the 19th century and the industrial revolution that it came into its own.

Pewter
This metal is mainly tin, up to 95%, alloyed to other hardening elements such as copper, bismuth, lead, and antimony, although lead and antimony are not used today. This pewter lidded tankard, or stein, dates from the 17th century. Today, pewter is still used for goblets and tankards.

Silver
Some materials that have silver in their name are not silver at all. They may be nickel silver, also called German silver, which is an alloy of copper, nickel, and zinc. Silver is very soft, so silver alloys are usually used to create jewelry, tableware, and coins.

NIHONIUM

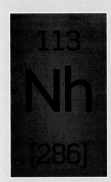

113

Nh

[286]

POOR METAL

Only a few atoms of superheavy nihonium have ever been made. It was created first in 2004, when a Japanese team of scientists, led by Kosuke Morita, collided zinc ions with a bismuth target.

Atomic number: 113
Formula: Nh
Atomic weight: [286]
State at 68°F (20°C): solid
Boiling point: unknown
Melting point: unknown
Half-life: 20 seconds

Uses: only in research

e113 | p113 | n173

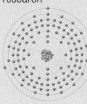

Made in...
In 2016, the scientists named element 113 after *Nihon*, the common name for Japan. They had established their right to choose a name after creating the element three times, in 2004, 2005, and 2012.

Atomic number: 114
Formula: Fl
Atomic weight: [289]
State at 68°F (20°C): solid
Boiling point: unknown
Melting point: unknown

Half-life: 2.6 seconds
Uses: only in research

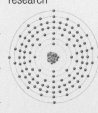

e114 | p114 | n175

114

Fl

[289]

FLEROVIUM

POOR METAL

Flerovium is a synthetic element made from a nuclear reaction between plutonium and calcium. Not enough flerovium has been made to measure its physical or chemical properties, but it is most likely to be a soft, dense metal that changes color when exposed to air.

MOSCOVIUM

115

Mc

[288]

POOR METAL

This element was created in 2003 when Russian and American scientists bombarded atoms of americium with ions of calcium in a cyclotron, a type of particle accelerator.

Atomic number: 115
Formula: Mc
Atomic weight: [288]
State at 68°F (20°C): solid
Boiling point: unknown
Melting point: unknown
Half-life: 220 milliseconds

Uses: only in research

e115 | p115 | n174

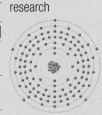

Made in ...
The work of the scientists produced only four atoms of highly radioactive moscovium, which was later named for the Moscow region where it was created.

Named for...
The element was named for the US laboratory that had provided vital target material for the experiment.

Atomic number: 116
Formula: Lv
Atomic weight: [293]
State at 68°F (20°C): solid
Boiling point: unknown
Melting point: unknown

Half-life: 53 milliseconds
Uses: only in research

e116 | p116 | n177

116

Lv

[293]

LIVERMORIUM

POOR METAL

There had been various attempts to make radioactive element 116 before it was finally achieved in Russia in 2000 by bombarding curium atoms with calcium ions.

Neutron scattering

This neutron source is part of the superconducting linear particle accelerator (LINAC) that was built in 2007 for the Spallation Neutron Source (SNS) at Oak Ridge National Laboratory, Tennessee. The unique accelerator generates the most intense pulsed neutron beams in the world for scientific and technological research. A proton beam is fired at a mercury target to release neutrons. By collecting the neutrons and observing their behavior, scientists have been able to better understand the molecular structure of different materials.

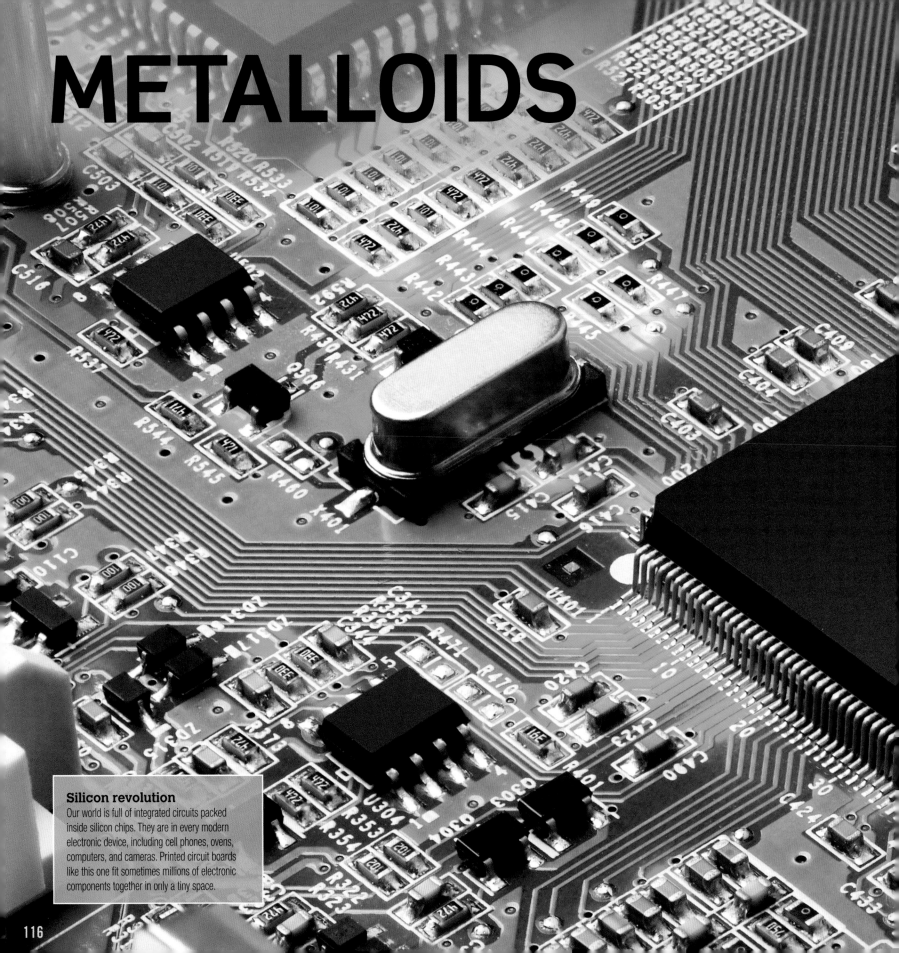

METALLOIDS

Silicon revolution
Our world is full of integrated circuits packed inside silicon chips. They are in every modern electronic device, including cell phones, ovens, computers, and cameras. Printed circuit boards like this one fit sometimes millions of electronic components together in only a tiny space.

Is it a metal or not? Some elements do not fit easily into the metal group, because they look like metals, but are brittle and do not behave like them. These are called metalloids. Some are deadly and some make great semiconductors.

Diagonal set
Metalloids form a diagonal line on the periodic table and have properties of both metals and nonmetals. They usually behave as nonmetals in chemical reactions.

METALLOIDS TIMELINE

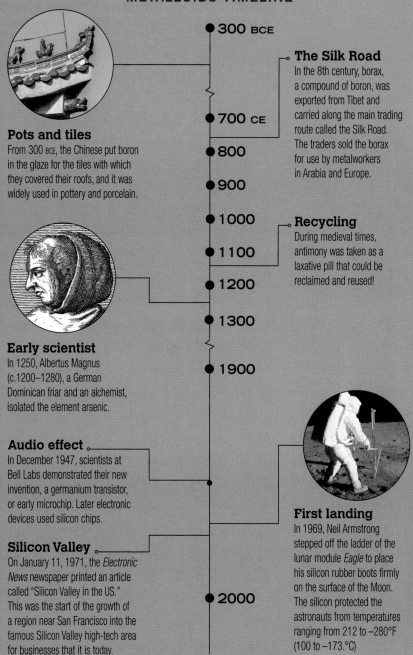

● 300 BCE

● 700 CE

● 800

● 900

● 1000

● 1100

● 1200

● 1300

● 1900

● 2000

The Silk Road
In the 8th century, borax, a compound of boron, was exported from Tibet and carried along the main trading route called the Silk Road. The traders sold the borax for use by metalworkers in Arabia and Europe.

Pots and tiles
From 300 BCE, the Chinese put boron in the glaze for the tiles with which they covered their roofs, and it was widely used in pottery and porcelain.

Recycling
During medieval times, antimony was taken as a laxative pill that could be reclaimed and reused!

Early scientist
In 1250, Albertus Magnus (c.1200–1280), a German Dominican friar and an alchemist, isolated the element arsenic.

Audio effect
In December 1947, scientists at Bell Labs demonstrated their new invention, a germanium transistor, or early microchip. Later electronic devices used silicon chips.

Silicon Valley
On January 11, 1971, the *Electronic News* newspaper printed an article called "Silicon Valley in the US." This was the start of the growth of a region near San Francisco into the famous Silicon Valley high-tech area for businesses that it is today.

First landing
In 1969, Neil Armstrong stepped off the ladder of the lunar module *Eagle* to place his silicon rubber boots firmly on the surface of the Moon. The silicon protected the astronauts from temperatures ranging from 212 to –280°F (100 to –173.°C)

5	
B	
10.81	

BORON

METALLOID

Boron gets things done. It is essential to plant growth, and seed and fruit development. It is a key ingredient in borax, a white powder that was used as a detergent, fungicide, and pesticide for centuries. As the only nonmetal apart from silicon among the metalloids, it is used to make heat-proof glass, eyewash, and bulletproof vests.

Atomic number: 5

Formula: B

Atomic weight: 10.811

State at 68°F (20°C): solid

Boiling point: 7232°F (4000°C)

Melting point: 3771°F (2077°C)

% in the Universe: 0.000000100

% in Earth's crust: 0.00086

% in Earth's oceans: 0.00044

% in humans: 0.000070

Uses: in eye drops, mild antiseptics, and washing powder; soap; tile glazes; ceramics; bulletproof vests; tanks; cosmetics; for pest control; the manufacture of Pyrex (borosilicate glass); rocket fuel igniter; pyrotechnic flares; fiberglass for fast cars, speedboats, and insulation

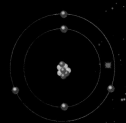

e5 | p5 | n6

Heat loss
The boron compound pentahydrate is used in the manufacture of fiberglass material. The fibreglass insulates the roofs of many houses, providing a barrier that reflects escaping heat back down into the building.

Tough stuff
If boron is heated with carbon to a temperature of 4530°F (2500°C) in an electric arc furnace, it produces the compound boron carbide. This extremely tough ceramic is used in bulletproof vests and tank armor.

Boron ores
This element is not found in nature as a solid. It occurs in a small number of minerals that include ulexite, borax, kernite, and colemanite. It is found as an acid in volcanic springs.

Open-pit boron mine

Boron town sign

Out of the earth
Boron, California, is home to the Rio Tinto Boron Mine, the state's largest open-pit mine. It began as an underground mine in the Mojave Desert in 1927, coming above ground in the late 1950s.

Elemental birth
During a supernova explosion, the heavier elements that formed the star are blown apart, creating a scattering of lighter particles. This is how the rarest three light elements, boron, lithium, and beryllium, are created.

SILICON

METALLOID

14	
Si	
28.085	

Atomic number: 14

Formula: Si

Atomic weight: 28.085

State at 68°F (20°C): solid

Boiling point: 5909°F (3265°C)

Melting point: 2577°F (1414°C)

% in the Universe: 0.070

% in Earth's crust: 27

% in Earth's oceans: 0.0001

% in humans: 0.026

Uses: dynamos; engine blocks; machine tools; lubricant; cosmetics; hair conditioners; waterproof sealants; semiconductors; buildings; glassmaking; pottery, enamels and ceramics; lasers; microelectronics; crystals for computer chips; solar cells; contact lenses; in steel manufacture

e14 | p14 | n14

Silicon hates being on its own. It is everywhere in the Universe but always bound to other elements. With oxygen it forms silica, the raw material for silicate rocks. As a compound, it takes many forms as silicones for thousands of applications, from shampoo to waterproofing. When you open up a new computer, you expect it to be run by microchips made of silicon, but the packaging probably contains silica gel to keep out moisture as well.

Metallic metalloid

There are two physical forms, or allotropes, of silicon at room temperature. Amorphous silicon is a brown powder. Crystalline silicon (above) is a form of silicon that has a highly reflective surface.

Tough nature

A visit to the countryside may cause you silicon pain. The stems and leaves of stinging nettles are covered in trichomes—tiny needles containing silicon—that inject a cocktail of irritating chemicals. And silicon dioxide content is why some blades of grass will cut you like knives.

Silicon ores

Not found in nature, the element is largely in silica-rich rocks such as sandstone (above), quartz sand, granite, diorite, and obsidian. Gemstones such as amethyst, bloodstone, opal, and agate are all forms of silica.

Making computer chips

Silicon is the basis of all computer processors today. It is the most abundant and available of all the semiconductors on Earth and its conductivity increases with temperature. Scientists are able to grow large, near-perfect silicon crystals that are easy to work. These are sliced into thin wafers and chips etched in a grid formation onto the wafers' surface (right).

Hard flint

Flint is almost pure silica that was formed in ancient oceans. It is one of the hardest materials but has a fine crystalline grain that means it fractures like glass when struck. Prehistoric peoples fashioned flint into tools, axes, knife blades (left), spearpoints, and arrowheads.

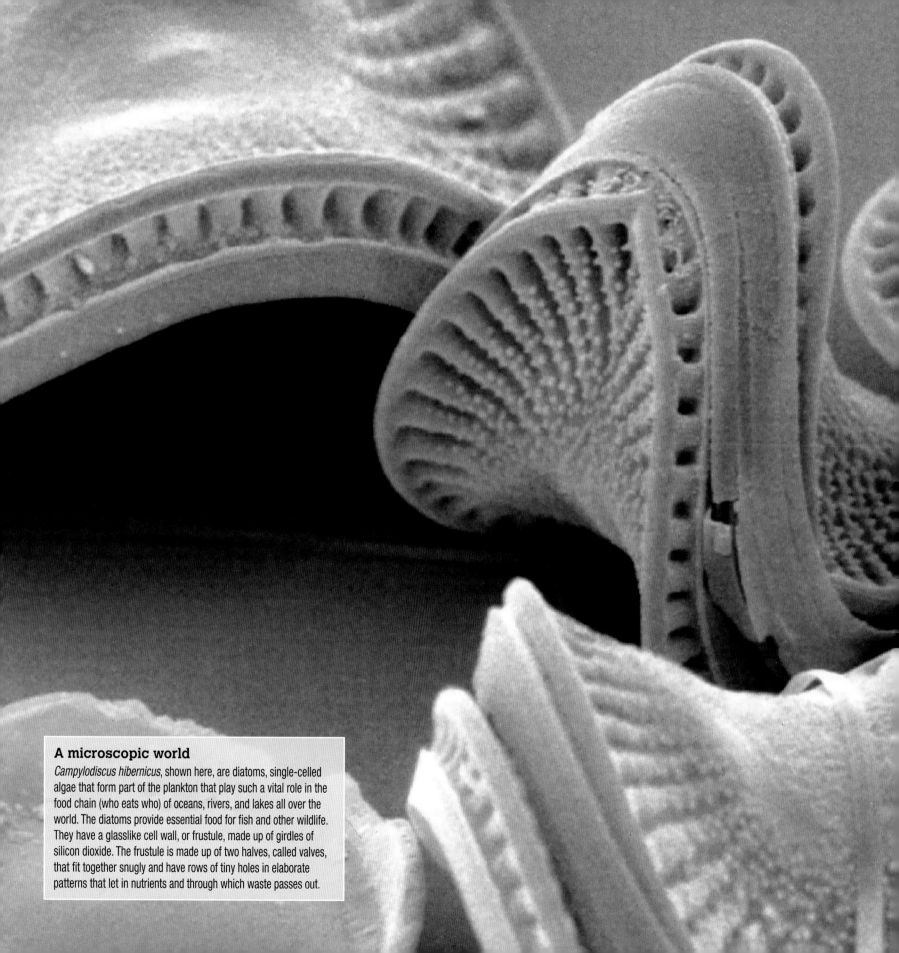

A microscopic world

Campylodiscus hibernicus, shown here, are diatoms, single-celled algae that form part of the plankton that play such a vital role in the food chain (who eats who) of oceans, rivers, and lakes all over the world. The diatoms provide essential food for fish and other wildlife. They have a glasslike cell wall, or frustule, made up of girdles of silicon dioxide. The frustule is made up of two halves, called valves, that fit together snugly and have rows of tiny holes in elaborate patterns that let in nutrients and through which waste passes out.

GERMANIUM

METALLOID

In 1871, Dmitri Mendeleev said there was an element to fill the gap between silicon and tin, and 15 years later it appeared. Germanium was used in the first American semiconductors in WWII, and today in fiber-optic cables.

Atomic number: 32

Formula: Ge

Atomic weight: 72.630

State at 68°F (20°C): solid

Boiling point: 5131°F (2833°C)

Melting point: 1720.85°F (938.25°C)

Uses: WW2 semiconductors; alloying agent; fluorescent lamps; night-vision goggles; camera and microscope lenses; food containers; metallurgy; some pharmaceutical use

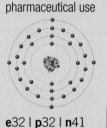

e32 | p32 | n41

Night vision
Germanium allows us to see in the dark because it is transparent at infrared wavelengths. This makes it perfect for thermal night-vision goggles used by soldiers and firefighters.

Country name
Clemens Winkler was the German chemist who discovered germanium in 1886. The element is taken from Germania, the Latin name for Germany.

It's in the air...
The atmospheres of Jupiter (right) and Saturn are mainly composed of hydrogen and helium. Recently, molecules of germane (germanium tetrahydride) have been found in the atmospheres of both planets.

Brittle element
This hard, shiny, gray-white metalloid is brittle in its pure form. Its two most common minerals are argyrodite and germanite. Most, however, is mined from sphalerite, but it is also found with silver, lead, and copper ores.

Black and red
Black antimony trisulfide protects soldiers. It reflects infrared light in the same way as vegetation does, so it is used in military camouflage paint for tanks, munition dumps, and buildings. There is also a red antimony trisulfide that is called antimony vermilion. This is used to color ruby glass.

Antimony was used in **ancient Egypt** as **kohl**, a form of **eyeliner**.

Element-rich mineral
This silvery, brittle metal is not an abundant element, but it is found in small quantities in more than 100 minerals. The most important source is stibnite (below), also called antimonite, which is poisonous.

ANTIMONY

METALLOID

Once used by murderers as a hard-to-spot poison, antimony trioxide protects lives as an ingredient in fire-retardant paints, plastics, and textiles. It also protects soldiers, because antimony trisulfide looks like vegetation in infrared light, so can be used for military camouflage.

Atomic number: 51

Formula: Sb

Atomic weight: 121.76

State at 68°F (20°C): solid

Boiling point: 2889°F (1587°C)

Melting point: 1167°F (630.628°C)

Uses: fire retardant paint, plastics, rubbers, textiles, and paper; infrared detectors and diodes; batteries; type metal in printing; tracer bullets; cable sheathing; enamels; pottery; glassmaking

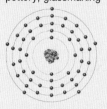

e51 | p51 | n71

TELLURIUM

52

Te

127.6

METALLOID

People who work with tellurium stink of its garliclike smell. It is actually very useful for jobs such as making lead tougher, stainless steel and copper easier to work, and as a coating on rewritable DVD and Blu-ray discs.

Atomic number: 52

Formula: Te

Atomic weight: 127.6

State at 68°F (20°C): solid

Boiling point: 1810°F (988°C)

Melting point: 841.12°F (449.51°C)

Uses: vulcanizing rubber, tinting

glassware and ceramics; in solar cells; oil refining (as a catalyst); as a semiconductor; added to cast iron

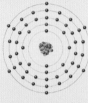

e52 | **p**52 | **n**76

Catalyzing agent
The high purity element is used as a catalyst in the oil industry. It helps to increase the rate of the chemical reaction in the processes leading to the production of oil in refineries.

Easy working
Half of the tellurium produced annually is used in steel and iron alloys. It increases machinability—it can be cut easily and accurately, with little power demand.

Vulcan grip
Tellurium is used in a process called vulcanization. This turns soft rubber into a harder, longer-lasting product that is ideal for making everyday items including tires, shoe soles, bowling balls, and hoses.

Radioactive element
Polonium is found in uranium ores, such as uraninite (left), but it is uneconomical to extract it. Instead, bismuth-209 is bombarded with neutrons to give bismuth-210, which then decays to form polonium. All commercial polonium is made in Russia.

POLONIUM

84

Po

[209]

METALLOID

This is one of the deadliest substances in the world. It is so radioactive that a lump of it in its most common isotope, Po-210, actually glows in the air. It was used to heat equipment in the Russian lunar rovers that explored the Moon in the 1970s.

Trigger element
This atomic bomb devastated the Japanese city of Nagasaki on August 9, 1945. The bomb's polonium-beryllium Urchin initiator kick-started the chain reaction.

Polish name
Polonium was discovered by Marie and Pierre Curie in 1898, when they were trying to find out why uraninite was radioactive. Marie Curie named it for her home country, Poland.

Atomic number: 84

Formula: Po

Atomic weight: [209]

State at 68°F (20°C): solid

Boiling point: 1764°F (962°C)

Melting point: 489°F (254°C)

Uses: heat for space equipment; to remove dust on film; to eliminate static

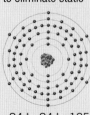

e84 | **p**84 | **n**125

ARSENIC

METALLOID

33	
As	
74.922	

Arsenic is so toxic that it can kill people in less than a day, but it can be hard to detect—so many royals were speedily wiped out that it became known as the "poison of kings." It has been used for centuries and was alloyed with bronze to harden the metal. It came in handy in medicines and yellow paint, and was employed as a wood preservative. This dangerous material is very useful today to speed up semiconductor chips and to add to copper and lead alloys, hardening them and making them easier to work.

Atomic number: 33

Formula: As

Atomic weight: 74.92160

State at 68°F (20°C): solid

Vaporization point: 1141°F (616°C)

% in the Universe: 0.00000080

% in Earth's crust: 0.00021

% in Earth's oceans: 0.00000023

% in humans: 0.0000050

Uses: insecticides; rat poison; poultry feed; pyrotechnics; as a doping agent in semiconductors; bronzing; glass; in preservatives for wood; as gallium arsenide in lasers and LEDs (light-emitting diodes); in lead alloys for ammunition

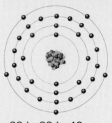

e33 | p33 | n42

Arsenic pills

Napoleon's tomb

Cure or kill?
Although there is no proof, it was believed that Napoleon Bonaparte died in 1821 because he had been fed arsenic by someone in his entourage. In the 19th century, arsenic pills and potions were sold for medical use. Dr. Fowler's Solution, a "cure-all tonic," is one of the potions that was popular—it was even taken by writer Charles Dickens.

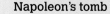

GOLD MEDAL, PARIS, 1889,
and
Seventeen other Gold, Silver, and Bronze Medals.

WM WOOLLAMS & CO.,
Original Makers of

WALL PAPERS,
GUARANTEED
FREE FROM ARSENIC.
Of all Decorators and Contractors.

Manufactory: 110, HIGH STREET,
NEAR MANCHESTER SQUARE,
LONDON, W.

Safe product?
In 1778, the Swedish chemist Carl Scheele used copper arsenite to create a vivid green pigment. Its rich color made it very popular for paint and wallpaper in the home, and also for clothes. By the late 1800s, the dangers of arsenic were beginning to be recognized, as this 1890 advert for wallpaper free from arsenic shows.

Arsenic was known to **Aristotle** as early as the **4th century** BCE—he referred to *sandarach*, or **arsenic trisulfide**.

Ore source

Arsenic is found in water, air, food, and soil. Arsenopyrite (left), also called mispickel, is the main ore of the mineral and element. It is the most common and widespread of the arsenic ores and is often found with gold, silver, and tin. The most stable form of arsenic is gray arsenic, and this is what is used in industry.

FOUND IN

Orpiment

Realgar

Arsenopyrite

Erythrite

Fly catcher

One very effective use of arsenic in the past was in flypapers. This inexpensive way to get rid of annoying insects involved pieces of paper coated with a sweet-smelling substance that was also sticky. When the flies landed they would then get stuck. The papers were further coated with arsenic to kill them more quickly.

Safety first

In the 20th century, many farmers sprayed their fields with insecticides that contained arsenic compounds. When such poisons get into crops such as rice (left), there is a danger of it getting into the food chain. Across the world today, people are working toward removing arsenic from the soil of the rice fields.

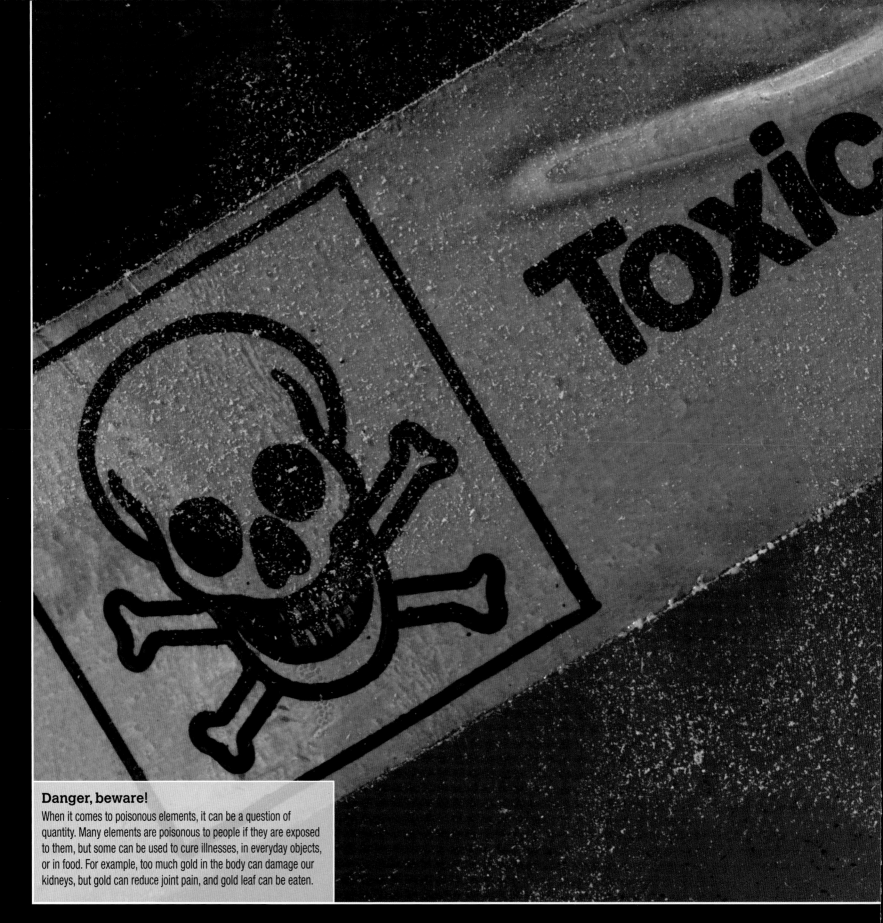

Danger, beware!

When it comes to poisonous elements, it can be a question of quantity. Many elements are poisonous to people if they are exposed to them, but some can be used to cure illnesses, in everyday objects, or in food. For example, too much gold in the body can damage our kidneys, but gold can reduce joint pain, and gold leaf can be eaten.

POISONOUS ELEMENTS

Throughout history, some unlucky people have found out the hard way that elements can kill. This could be because some of them reacted into powerful acids, or attacked airways and lungs until it was impossible to breathe, or released invisible but lethal radioactive particles. From classic poisons such as arsenic to heavily radioactive polonium, we need to be careful how we handle these dangerous elements.

Cyanide
Made famous by many detective stories for its smell of "bitter almonds," cyanide exists in different forms. Breathing in cyanide gas does the most harm, but swallowing it in crystal form, as sodium cyanide or potassium cyanide, can be toxic as well.

Arsenic
This poison has been a favorite of murderers for thousands of years. Often referred to as the "king of poisons," it is difficult to detect because symptoms of arsenic poisoning are similar to food poisoning. A fatal dose of white arsenic (arsenic trioxide) can be a quantity as small as a pea.

Arsenopyrite

The Borgias
This murderous 15th-century Italian family—father Pope Alexander VI, son Cesare, and daughter Lucrezia—lived in Florence. They are said to have poisoned their enemies.

Grigori Rasputin
In 1917, to end his influence over the Russian royal family, a group of nobles gave Rasputin cakes that were laced with cyanide. When this did not work, Rasputin was shot.

Radium
The discovery of radioactive radium in 1898 ushered in a new age of nuclear chemistry, but it was many years before people realized how truly dangerous this material is. Radiation poisoning happens when people are exposed to a large dose of radiation in a short time, for example because of a nuclear accident.

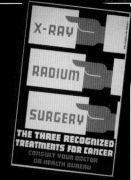

Glowing killer
Many women factory workers died from radiation poisoning from 1917 through the 1920s. They painted watch and clock faces with luminous radium without realizing the danger.

Kill or cure?
For decades, radium and radon were used to help treat cancers. It was finally declared unsafe in 1976, and replaced by cobalt-60.

It is said that if **0.017 oz (0.5 g)** of **plutonium** is released into the atmosphere it **would kill 2 million** people.

Thallium
In 1959, Fidel Castro took power in Cuba, and so began many different attempts to assassinate or depose him. In the US, the CIA believed that if he lost his famous beard, he would lose power, so they hatched a plan to dose his socks with thallium-tainted talcum powder to make his hair fall out. The plan failed.

Mercury
This toxic element has been used for thousands of years as a medicine. The ancient Greeks applied it as an ointment, and Chinese alchemists believed it would increase lifespan and vitality. Only recently did people realize just how toxic it is.

Poisonous
Abraham Lincoln took "little blue pills," the main ingredient of which was mercury. He found they made him cross and stopped taking them soon after his inauguration as president in 1861.

Polonium
The isotope polonium-210 is very dangerous, but it is also a radioactive material that is found naturally in the human body because it exist at low levels in our environment, and it is present in the food chain.

Alexander Litvinenko
In 2006, the former member of the Russian secret service, Alexander Litvinenko, was murdered in London when his tea was poisoned with a high dose of polonium.

LANTHANOIDS

Magnetic speed

On June 1, 2010, the first high-speed Maglev train started to operate in Shanghai, China. These trains use magnetic levitation to move at up to 375 miles per hour (600km/h) along the line between stations. The strong magnets are made from the lanthanoids, and scandium and yttrium.

Scientists puzzled over these elements for decades before they were understood. This is why they are also known as "rare earth metals," although many are not scarce at all. They are used in smart weapons, plasma screens, and hybrid cars.

All in a row
These 15 soft metal elements have their own special line, and share many properties because of their similarities in size and the way their electrons are arranged.

LANTHANOIDS TIMELINE

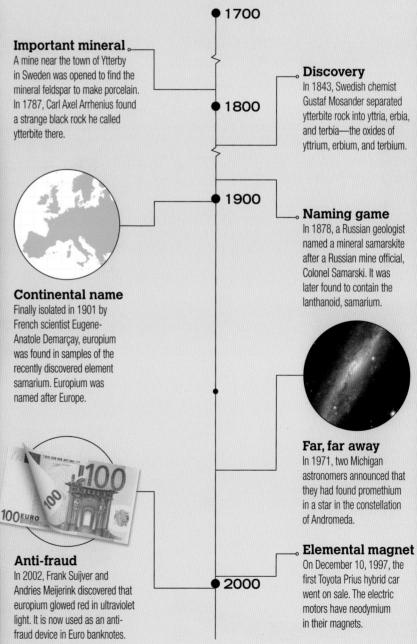

1700

Important mineral
A mine near the town of Ytterby in Sweden was opened to find the mineral feldspar to make porcelain. In 1787, Carl Axel Arrhenius found a strange black rock he called ytterbite there.

1800

Discovery
In 1843, Swedish chemist Gustaf Mosander separated ytterbite rock into yttria, erbia, and terbia—the oxides of yttrium, erbium, and terbium.

1900

Naming game
In 1878, a Russian geologist named a mineral samarskite after a Russian mine official, Colonel Samarski. It was later found to contain the lanthanoid, samarium.

Continental name
Finally isolated in 1901 by French scientist Eugene-Anatole Demarçay, europium was found in samples of the recently discovered element samarium. Europium was named after Europe.

Far, far away
In 1971, two Michigan astronomers announced that they had found promethium in a star in the constellation of Andromeda.

Anti-fraud
In 2002, Frank Suijver and Andries Meijerink discovered that europium glowed red in ultraviolet light. It is now used as an anti-fraud device in Euro banknotes.

2000

Elemental magnet
On December 10, 1997, the first Toyota Prius hybrid car went on sale. The electric motors have neodymium in their magnets.

LANTHANUM

LANTHANOID

57 **La** **138.905**

The lanthanoids are named after this silvery white element that forms a metal so soft that it can be cut with a knife. Lanthanum is never found in its pure form—only in two minerals, monazite and bastnäsite. It took scientists 100 years to work out how to purify it.

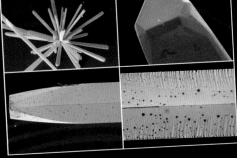

Atomic number: 57

Formula: La

Atomic weight: 138.9055

State at 68°F (20°C): solid

Boiling point: 6267°F (3464°C)

Melting point: 1688°F (920°C)

Uses: metal only for research; as an alloy: storage of hydrogen gas; batteries; studio lighting; movie projection; optical glasses; refining;

electron microscopy; medications

e57 | p57 | n82

Looking closer
Electron microscopes generate images by bombarding something with electrons and then changing this action into a high resolution image. Lanthanum hexaboride helps to control the electrons efficiently.

Power store
A lanthanum-nickel alloy is vital in the batteries of hybrid cars. The alloy also helps to store hydrogen gas for use in hydrogen-powered vehicles.

CERIUM

58 **Ce** **140.116**

LANTHANOID

Cerium, the most abundant of the lanthanoids, is a bit of a show-off. Shavings of it burst into flames as soon as they touch the air, so it is used for special effects in movies. It also coats the inside of self-cleaning ovens, because it oxidizes greasy cooking mess and turns it to ash that can be wiped away more easily.

Atomic number: 58

Formula: Ce

Atomic weight: 140.116

State at 68°F (20°C): solid

Boiling point: 6229°F (3443°C)

Melting point: 1470°F (799°C)

Uses: carbon arc lighting for streetlighting, movie sets, and projectors; flat-screen TVs; low-energy bulbs; floodlights; catalytic converters; self-cleaning ovens; flints;

incandescent gas mantles; glass-polishing agent

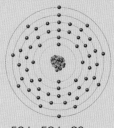

e58 | p58 | n82

Flash point
Run a knife along this soft metal and you get a shower of sparks. The only other element that does this is iron (see pp.60–61). Cerium is part of the material used to make flints for lighters.

Name in the stars
This gray-colored metal is named for the dwarf planet Ceres (left), which in turn was named after the Roman god of agriculture. It is commonly found in the minerals bastnäsite, monazite, and samarskite.

PRASEODYMIUM

59

Pr

140.908

LANTHANOID

Scientists love praseodymium because it has been used to slow the speed of light to a virtual standstill, and to get one thousandth of a degree from absolute zero, –460°F (–273.15°C), the closest we are likely to get.

Light shield
Until they were separated in 1885, praseodymium and neodymium were thought to be only one element called didymium. Today, praseodymium oxide and neodymium are used to coat goggles for welders and glassmakers, to filter out yellow light and infrared radiation.

Multi-source mineral
Monazite (below) is an important ore that contains many of the lanthanoids, including all four of the elements on these pages. It was also the only significant source of commercial mining for lanthanoids until the mid-1960s, when concern about the radioactivity of the group was raised.

Super metal
Alloyed with magnesium, praseodymium makes super-strong parts for aircraft engines. The element can be found in super magnets as an alternative to neodymium. And it is part of mischmetal, an alloy used to produce sparks in fire starters.

Atomic number: 59
Formula: Pr
Atomic weight: 140.908
State at 68°F (20°C): solid
Boiling point: 6368°F (3520°C)
Melting point: 1708°F (931°C)
Uses: protective goggles; permanent magnets; aircraft engines; yellow coloring for glass, enamel and glazes

e59 | p59 | n82

NEODYMIUM

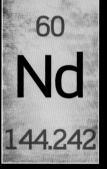

60

Nd

144.242

LANTHANOID

Neodymium's magnetism and other properties make it handy for earbuds, computer hard drives, cell phones, and wind turbines. Analyzing it also helps determine the ages of some rock types.

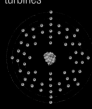

Super magnet
Neodymium makes the strongest magnets you can get, able to lift 1,000 times their own weight. They are also used to hold together dentures.

Atomic number: 60
Formula: Nd
Atomic weight: 144.242
State at 68°F (20°C): solid
Boiling point: 5565°F (3074°C)
Melting point: 1861°F (1016°C);
Uses: as a catalyst in chemical industry; lasers; tanning booths; protective goggles; permanent magnets for electronic devices, cars, and wind turbines

e60 | p60 | n84

PROMETHIUM

61 Pm [145]

LANTHANOID

Named for the Greek titan Prometheus, who stole fire from the gods and gave it to humankind, this is a very rare element. It decays quickly, but it can be put into tiny batteries where the energy that it releases powers guided missiles and heart pacemakers.

Atomic number: 61

Formula: Pm

Atomic weight: [145]

Boiling point: 5432°F (3000°C)

Melting point: 1908°F (1042°C)

Uses: in atomic batteries for heart pacemakers, guided missiles, watches, and radios; luminous paint; source of radioactivity and X-rays in measuring instruments; makes phosphor emit light that converts into electricity

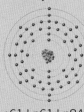

e61 | p61 | n84

Hard to find
Promethium is very rare indeed. It is thought that less than 2 lbs. (1 kg) exists on Earth and most of it is found in the mineral uraninite (left). The element decays so fast that a one million ton block would shrink to just 0.03 oz (1 g) in just over 700 years.

Multi-purpose
Many different lanthanoids combine to make hybrid cars work. Promethium, together with neodymium, terbium, and dysprosium, is used in the electronic motors and generators. Other lanthanoids are found in the glass, batteries, and catalytic converters.

By-product
Promethium was discovered by a group of scientists in 1944, but they did not announce it until 1946. They were analyzing the by-products of uranium fission in a nuclear reactor in Tennessee, at a place that is today called Oak Ridge National Laboratory.

SAMARIUM

62 Sm 150.36

LANTHANOID

Samarium can be alloyed with cobalt to make magnets that are 10,000 times more powerful than iron magnets, making them ideal for use in miniature devices and motors, such as inside electric guitar pickups and headphones. The element helps scientists to date rocks, and is used in the control rods of nuclear reactors, to mop up stray neutrons.

Atomic number: 62

Formula: Sm

Atomic weight: 150.36

State at 68°F (20°C): solid

Boiling point: 3261°F (1794°C)

Melting point: 1962°F (1072°C)

% in the Universe: 0.00000050

% in Earth's crust: 0.00060

% in Earth's oceans: 0.000000000045

% in humans: none

Uses: magnets for precision-guided weapons; optical lasers; glass; carbon arc lighting; as a neutron absorber in nuclear reactors; as an alloy in guitar pickups and motors; as a catalyst in chemical industries

Samarium-cobalt magnets

Electric guitar pickups

High performance
The samarium-cobalt magnets (left) are perfect for applications that operate at temperatures up to 500°F (260°C). They are resistant to corrosion and therefore used in high-end electric motors. The magnets are also found in pickups for electric guitars, speakers, and headphones.

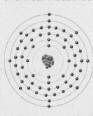

Silver metal
The element is found in the minerals samarskite (below), monazite, and gadolinite. It is a soft, silvery metal that ignites when it is heated to 300°F (150°C).

e62 | p62 | n88

EUROPIUM

63

Eu

151.964

LANTHANOID

Europium helps to catch criminals. It glows in ultraviolet light so works well as an anti-forgery measure. It can be easily molded and shaped, and helps energy-efficient lightbulbs produce a "warmer," more natural light.

Note marker
Europium glows red in ultraviolet light, making it ideal for adding to strips in the banknotes of the Euro. Forgeries can be detected by officials and bank tellers because they do not glow red.

Named for a continent
It took many years for scientists to isolate the lanthanoids from each other. In 1901, Eugene-Anatole Demarçay worked on samarium mangesium nitrate and discovered europium, named after Europe.

Atomic number: 63

Formula: Eu

Atomic weight: 151.964

State at 68°F (20°C): solid

Boiling point: 2784°F (1529°C)

Melting point: 1512°F (822°C)

Uses: euro banknotes; low-energy light bulbs; in nuclear reactors; as a laser material; superconducting alloys; as a red phosphor in color televisions

e63 | p63 | n89

GADOLINIUM

64

Gd

157.25

LANTHANOID

Gadolinium has a special skill—it absorbs neutrons produced by nuclear reactions, so is used in shielding and control rods in reactors. It is also injected into patients before an MRI scan, because its high magnetism makes the image clearer.

Silver element
Gadolinium is a soft, silvery-white metal that is very versatile. If as little as 1 percent of it is added to iron or chromium, it improves their workability and their resistance to high temperatures. It is ferromagnetic—strongly attracted by a magnet.

Lanthanoid source
Monazite is an important ore of thorium, lanthanum, and cerium, but it also contains samarium, europium, and gadolinium. The mineral occurs as small, brown, heavy crystals in rock, or in grains, called monazite sands, which become concentrated in the soils downslope from the main rock. Other heavy minerals and metals are found nearby, including gold, platinum, magnetite, rutile, and zircon.

Atomic number: 64

Formula: Gd

Atomic weight: 157.25

State at 68°F (20°C): solid

Boiling point: 5923°F (3273°C)

Melting point: 2395°F (1313°C)

Uses: magnets; data storage; electronic components; MRI scanners; nuclear reactors; color televisions; in microwave applications; as an intravenous agent for MRI scanning

e64 | p64 | n93

Lighting the set

In the 1890s, the carbon arc light, with its intense white light, was developed to light the streets at night. By the great age of black-and-white Hollywood movies, carbon arc lighting, which used various lanthanoids including samarium and cerium, became popular for use on set and in movie projectors. In the late 1920s, these early, and noisy, carbon arcs were replaced by other forms of lighting. However, by 1935, the carbon arc lamp had been redesigned for use in the new Technicolor films, and continued in use until 1950.

TERBIUM

65

Tb

158.925

LANTHANOID

Terbium is so rare that it costs four times as much as platinum, but it can make a lot of noise. Terbium alloys expand or contract in a magnetic field, causing vibrations that turn any surface into a loudspeaker. So, if you can hear a sound coming from your tabletop, it is due to terbium.

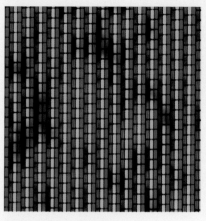

Atomic number: 65

Formula: Tb

Atomic weight: 158.9253

State at 68°F (20°C): solid

Boiling point: 5846°F (3230°C)

Melting point: 2478°F (1359°C)

Uses: low-energy lightbulbs; ships' sonar systems; in TV and X-ray screens; lasers; fuel cells; as a crystal stabilizer in solid-state devices; as an alloy in electric motors; as anti-fraud strips in euro banknotes

e65 | p65 | n94

Sonar on destroyers
Terbium is used in naval sonar systems. Sonar operates by sending out sound waves that bounce off nearby objects as echoes. Low frequency sounds travel farther in seawater, and a terbium alloy operates at such a low frequency that it can reach farther than other sonars.

Improving viewing
The most common use of terbium and its compounds is to make color television and X-ray screens clearer. The backs of the screens are coated with different phosphors, which give off light when hit by electrons. Phosphors that contain terbium bring bright green to a color screen. Europium (*see* p.133) phosphors help bring bright red. Because of their small particle size, screens that use these phosphors have higher definition.

DYSPROSIUM

66

Dy

162.5

LANTHANOID

The name means "hard to get" because the scientist who discovered it had to do so much work to separate it. Dysprosium corrodes so fast that it is useless as a pure metal, but it helps to make strong magnets and produce intense beams of white light.

Disk material
Computer hard drives read and record data on magnetic material. The magnetic storage is a platter that rotates at high speed, with the head (above right) reading and writing data. The surface coating of the platters includes dysprosium oxide.

The name comes from ***dysprositos***, Greek for **"difficult to get at."**

Silver
Soft, silvery dysprosium reacts with water and air, so it is hard to use. It is found in minerals such as monazite, xerontime, and fergusonite. It is in magnets for motors and generators, and as dysprosium iodide in halide discharge lamps, which give a very bright light. Dysprosium oxide-nickel is used in nuclear control rods.

Atomic number: 66

Formula: Dy

Atomic weight: 162.5

State at 68°F (20°C): solid

Boiling point: 4653°F (2567°C)

Melting point: 2574°F (1412°C)

Uses: data storage of compact discs and hard disks; magnets in motors and generators; halide lamps; neutron-absorbing nuclear control rods; lasers; speaker systems; sensors; transducers

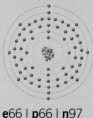

e66 | p66 | n97

HOLMIUM

Holmium is the Latin name for Stockholm, the city of this element's discoverer. It is not magnetic, but it boosts the magnetic field of other metals, making them more powerful. Added to yttrium iron garnets, it makes lasers for surgery.

67

Ho

164.93

Eye laser
Holmium: YAG lasers are very precise instruments. They allow the surgeon to cut very precisely with minimum damage to the surrounding tissue. These lasers are now employed in many different medical areas, including eye surgery, dentistry, and neurosurgery.

Atomic number: 67
Formula: Ho
Atomic weight: 164.93
State at 68°F (20°C): solid
Boiling point: 4892°F (2700°C)
Melting point: 2682°F (1472°C)
Uses: in nuclear reactor control rods; in alloys for magnets;

in medical lasers for noninvasive surgery; as yellow or red coloring for glass and cubic zirconia

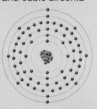

e67 | p67 | n98

Rare metal
In Uppsala, Sweden, in 1878, scientist Per Teodor Cleve was working with yttrium (*see p.74*), when he succeeded in separating holmium from erbium. Holmium is a soft, silver metal that is one of the rarest of the lanthanoids, but is found in minerals such as monazite and bastnaesite.

ERBIUM

68

Er

167.259

Erbium loves pink and helps speed up the Internet. It makes jewelry bright pink and is added to glass to make rose-tinted eyeglasses and goggles for glassmakers. It "boosts" light traveling along optical fibers, allowing data to move faster and helping the Internet to work more efficiently.

Atomic number: 68
Formula: Er
Atomic weight: 167.259
State at 68°F (20°C): solid
Boiling point: 5194°F (2868°C)
Melting point: 2784°F (1529°C)
Uses: as an alloy to reduce hardness; pink coloring agent

for glazes and glassware; safety goggles; amplifiers; medical lasers; photographic filters; fiber-optic cables

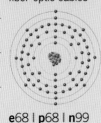

e68 | p68 | n99

Better transmission
Broadband signals carried by fiber-optic cables may use an erbium-doped fiber amplifier (EDFA). This increases the range of frequencies used to transmit a signal.

Easy working
Erbium is extracted from minerals such as monazite (right) and bastnaesite, and can be easily hammered into thin sheets. It is sometimes alloyed with vanadium because it reduces the metal's hardness and makes it easier to work with.

THULIUM

69

Tm

168.934

LANTHANOID

A very rare lanthanoid, hard to extract from its mineral ores, and with few uses, thulium is not without its difficulties. However, it can be useful for stage lighting, laser surgery, and X-rays. It is also used in personal radiation devices because it can help measure low exposure levels. In euro banknotes, its blue fluorescence helps to prevent fraud.

Atomic number: 69
Formula: Tm
Atomic weight: 168.934
State at 68°F (20°C): solid
Boiling point: 3542°F (1950°C)
Melting point: 2813°F (1545°C)
Uses: very few commercial uses, so mainly for research; stable thulium-169 as a radiation source for portable X-ray machines, to create medical lasers

e69 | p69 | n100

Gray metal
Mainly found in the minerals monazite, gadolinite, xenotime, and euxenite, thulium is an easily worked element that can be cut with a knife.

YTTERBIUM

70

Yb

173.04

LANTHANOID

Ytterbium's electrical conductivity varies as pressure increases. This unusual characteristic makes it handy in gauges to measure shock waves from nuclear explosions. It is also used to strengthen stainless steel, and in solar cells, lasers, and portable X-ray machines.

On the move
A small amount of ytterbium-169 acts just like a tiny X-ray machine. This means that commercially it can be used as a radiation source for portable X-ray machines that need no electricity. It also amplifies signals traveling along fiber-optic cables.

Atomic number: 70
Formula: Yb
Atomic weight: 173.045
State at 68°F (20°C): solid
Boiling point: 2185°F (1196°C)
Melting point: 1515°F (824°C)
Uses: for memory devices; tuneable lasers; industrial catalyst; as an alloy with stainless steel; in fiber-optic cable

e70 | p70 | n103

LUTETIUM

71

Lu

174.967

LANTHANOID

Lutetium is the most expensive metal in the world! It is also the hardest and densest of the lanthanoids. Lutetium is named for the Latin word for Paris, as it was discovered at the Sorbonne university there in 1907 by French scientist Georges Urbain.

Atomic number: 71
Formula: Lu
Atomic weight: 174.967
State at 68°F (20°C): solid
Boiling point: 6156°F (3402°C)
Melting point: 3025°F (1663°C)
Uses: very few commerical uses so mainly for research; as a catalyst to crack hydrocarbons in oil refineries; to date meteorites; in noninvasive medical scanning; in cancer therapy

e71 | p71 | n104

Dating meteorites
Some radioactive isotopes of the element, such as lutetium-176, are used as a way to date the age of meteorites relative to the age of Earth.

Experimental laser

In quantum optics laboratories today, research is being carried out on lanthanoids cooled to near absolute zero by lasers. The lanthanoids are made to collide. This coming together causes a reaction, the two moving objects exerting force on each other for a short time. How they behave and what happens after the collision helps scientists learn about lanthanoids and may lead to the development of commercial or scientific applications. The process also allows the scientists to trap lanthanoid atoms for further investigation.

ACTINOIDS

These 15 elements are mostly man-made and all of them are dangerously radioactive. Just watch out—you don't want them near you for too long! But some do important work that helps astronauts, doctors, and firefighters in their work.

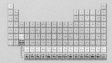

The bottom line

Two of these elements occur naturally in large quantities—uranium and thorium. Protactinium, actinium, neptunium, and thorium are made in nuclear reactors and particle accelerators.

ACTINOIDS TIMELINE

1700

First find
In 1789, uranium was the first of the actinoids discovered by the self-educated German chemist Martin Klaproth (1743–1817).

1800

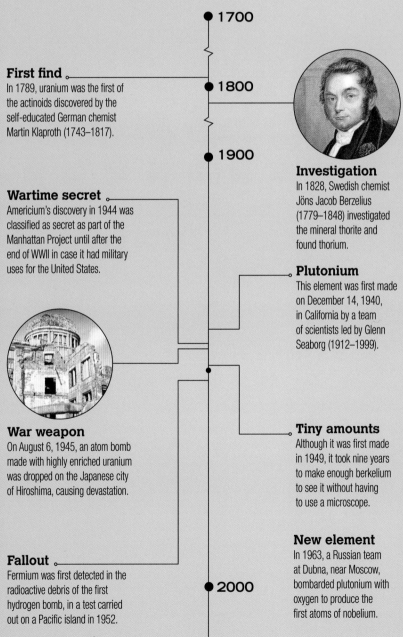

1900

Investigation
In 1828, Swedish chemist Jöns Jacob Berzelius (1779–1848) investigated the mineral thorite and found thorium.

Wartime secret
Americium's discovery in 1944 was classified as secret as part of the Manhattan Project until after the end of WWII in case it had military uses for the United States.

Plutonium
This element was first made on December 14, 1940, in California by a team of scientists led by Glenn Seaborg (1912–1999).

War weapon
On August 6, 1945, an atom bomb made with highly enriched uranium was dropped on the Japanese city of Hiroshima, causing devastation.

Tiny amounts
Although it was first made in 1949, it took nine years to make enough berkelium to see it without having to use a microscope.

New element
In 1963, a Russian team at Dubna, near Moscow, bombarded plutonium with oxygen to produce the first atoms of nobelium.

Fallout
Fermium was first detected in the radioactive debris of the first hydrogen bomb, in a test carried out on a Pacific island in 1952.

2000

ACTINIUM

ACTINOID

Actinium should be easy to spot at nighttime in the labs where it is made, because it glows pale blue in the dark. This is due to its intense radioactivity knocking electrons from the air atoms around it. Scientists produce actinium by bombarding radium with neutron particles.

Actinium is about **150 times** more **radioactive** than **radium**.

89 Ac [227]	

Atomic number: 89
Formula: Ac
Atomic weight: [227]
State at 68°F (20°C): solid
Boiling point: 5792°F (3200°C)
Melting point: 1922°F (1050°C)
% in the Universe: almost none
% in Earth's crust: almost none

% in Earth's oceans: almost none
% in humans: none
Half-life: 21.77 years
Uses: in research; neutron soil probes

e89 | p89 | n138

Soil probe
Scientists sometimes use neutron soil probes to establish how much water there is in soil, particularly in areas of drought. The probes use radioactive material such as actinium to emit high-energy neutrons that collide with hydrogen atoms in water and soil. Some neutrons are reflected back and counted by the beryllium neutron detector.

Finding the element
Traces of actinium are found in uranium ores such as uranitite (above). In 1899, French chemist André-Louis Debierne, who worked with Marie Curie in Paris, discovered actinium in uranium ore (then called pitchblende) when he was experimenting with new methods of separating lanthanoids.

Deep-sea science
Tracers such as actinium are used by scientists to track the effects of a constantly changing climate on the deep ocean. They take samples that allow them to track the path of the actinium as it moves through the ocean, and measure the amount of dilution. This helps them record and predict changes in the oceans.

THORIUM

90
Th
232.038

ACTINOID

Much of the internal heat of the Earth is thought to come from the radioactive decay of thorium. It is more abundant in Earth's crust than uranium (*see pp.*144–145) but, like uranium, it can be used to fuel a nuclear chain reaction.

Atomic number: 90
Formula: Th
Atomic weight: 232.038
State at 68°F (20°C): solid
Boiling point: 8645°F (4785°C)
Melting point: 3182°F (1750°C)

Uses: for aircraft and spacecraft parts; as an industrial catalyst; to coat tungsten wire in electronic goods and lightbulbs; in petroleum cracking; as thorium dioxide in laboratory crucibles, in camera lenses

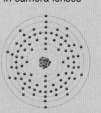

e90 | p90 | n142

Named for a god
This element is named for Thor, the Norse god of thunder. It was discovered by Swedish chemist Jöns Jacob Berzelius in 1828 in a sample of the mineral now called thorite. Thorium is also found in other minerals that include monazite, euxenite, and thorianite.

Aircraft parts
Thorium forms an alloy with magnesium that is used in engines and other parts for aircraft, missiles, tanks, and spacecraft. It gives the metal great strength and strong resistance to high temperatures, while being light in weight.

White glow
Combined with oxygen, thorium absorbs infrared heat energy and re-emits it as white light. It was used in gas lights until the danger was recognized.

PROTACTINIUM

91
Pa
231.036

ACTINOID

Atomic number: 91
Formula: Pa
Atomic weight: 231.036
State at 68°F (20°C): solid
Boiling point: 7232°F (4000°C)
Melting point: 2862°F (1572°C)
% in the Universe: almost none

% in Earth's crust: 0.00000000000099
% in Earth's oceans: almost none
% in humans: none
Uses: only research

e91 | p91 | n140

Scientific discovery
German physicists Lise Meitner (above) and Otto Hahn identified the isotope protactinium-231 in 1918.

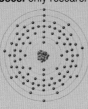

This is one of the rarest and most expensive elements. In 1961, the UK Atomic Energy Authority made a batch that was 99.9 percent pure. They extracted 4.4 oz (125 g) from 66 tons of spent uranium fuel, but spent $500,000 to do it. Protactinium is named after the Greek *proto*, which means "before," and the element actinium it becomes as it decays.

NEPTUNIUM

93
Np
[237]

ACTINOID

Neptunium is formed naturally as uranium decays, before it becomes plutonium. It is also a decay product of the radioactive element americium, which is used in household smoke detectors. Neptunium was discovered in 1940 by scientists in California.

Atomic number: 93
Formula: Np
Atomic weight: [237]
State at 68°F (20°C): solid
Boiling point: 7056°F (3902°C)
Melting point: 1191°F (644°C)
Half-life: 2,145,500 years

Uses: mainly for scientific research; neutron detectors; in spacecraft generators; in navigation beacons

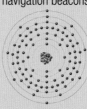

e93 | p93 | n144

Planets and gods
As the element next to uranium (named for the seventh planet in our solar system, Uranus), neptunium is named for the eighth planet and the god Neptune.

URANIUM

92

U

238.029

ACTINOID

Uranium is powerful, heavy, poisonous, and radioactive. In its most unstable, radioactive form, uranium-235, it creates huge amounts of heat when a neutron is fired into its nucleus, splitting it into two smaller nuclei. This heat makes the steam in nuclear power stations—2.2 lb (1 kg) of enriched uranium can produce as much energy as 15 tons of coal. Uranium is the explosive in atomic bombs and the metal in anti-tank ammunition.

Atomic number: 92

Formula: U

Atomic weight: 238.029

State at 68°F (20°C): solid

Boiling point: 7468°F (4131°C)

Melting point: 2075°F (1135°C)

Half-life: 700 million years

% in the Universe: 0.000000020

% in Earth's crust: 0.00018

% in Earth's oceans: 0.00000033

% in humans: 0.00000010

Uses: as a coloring agent for ceramic glazes and glass; in atomic bombs; in the nuclear power industry; in submarines and nuclear weapons; when depleted: ships' ballast; bullets; counterweights for aircraft; tank armor

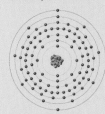

e92 | p92 | n146

Uranium ores

There are traces of uranium almost everywhere in Earth's crust, and vast quantities in the world's oceans, although in low concentrations. Uranium's main ore is uraninite (right), but it can be found in many other minerals, including carnotite, torbernite, and autunite. Uraninite, also known as pitchblende, can be as much as 80 percent uranium.

The **half-life** of uranium-235 is about **700 million years**.

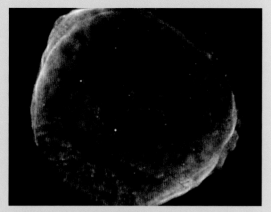

From space to Earth
Discovered on Earth in 1789 and named for the planet Uranus, uranium was carried to our planet as the result of one or more supernovae explosions. These catastrophic events happen when stars have burned up all their nuclear fuel and the cores collapse. Most of the material of the stars is thrown outward and travels through space. Minerals carrying uranium probably arrived on Earth on board iron meteorites.

General Leslie Groves and nuclear physicist Robert Oppenheimer

The "Little Boy" atomic bomb

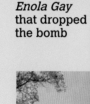

The bomber *Enola Gay* that dropped the bomb

World changer
In September 1942, US general Leslie Groves was put in charge of the research and development that became known as the Manhattan Project. He set up three sites, at Los Alamos in New Mexico, Oak Ridge in Tennessee, and Hanford in Washington. Groves personally chose the physicist Robert Oppenheimer to lead the Los Alamos laboratory and it was there that the atomic bomb was developed and tested. At 8.15 a.m. on August 6, 1945, an American B-29 bomber dropped the first atomic bomb deployed in war on the Japanese city of Hiroshima. It was an attempt to bring fighting to an end by the surrender of Japan. The bomb was mostly made from uranium-235.

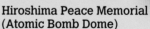

Hiroshima Peace Memorial (Atomic Bomb Dome)

Atomic mushroom cloud over Hiroshima

On the grid
Uranium plays an essential role in the modern world. Most countries use it to generate electricity inside nuclear power plants. Heat is given off inside the reactor by fission—the splitting of uranium-235 atoms in a controlled chain reaction. The heat is used to turn water into steam. The steam turns huge turbines that drive generators to produce the electricity to power our businesses and homes.

Elemental factory

A worker at the Novosibirsk Chemical Concentrates Plant, a nuclear fuel assembly factory in Russia, uses forceps to transfer highly dangerous pellets of uranium dioxide. He is wearing special protective clothing including gloves and a mask, but even that will not fully protect him against radiation, so the forceps are necessary. The fuel pellets are put into hollow metal tubes called fuel pins that are used in a nuclear power plant to start a controlled nuclear fission reaction. Millions of pellets are used for this purpose.

Inside a nuclear reactor

This radiation is being produced in the water that surrounds the core (center) of a nuclear reactor. Pieces of uranium are stacked up in metal tubes called rods and form the core. High-speed charged particles pass through the water to release the enormous energy needed to create power. The water keeps the reactor core cool.

POWER FROM ELEMENTS

Elements provide our fuel. The atoms of radioactive elements such as uranium and plutonium can be split in nuclear reactions to release massive amounts of energy that we turn into electricity. Hydrogen and carbon are inside the wood, coal, oil and gas that we burn to get heat or power. Other elements help us harness the massive power of the sunlight that hits Earth, and the forces of the waves and the wind.

Carbon fossil fuels

Fossil fuels, which contain high percentages of carbon, were formed in the distant past from the remains of dead plants and animals. Over hundreds of millions of years, heat and pressure in Earth's crust converted the remains into crude oil, coal, and natural gas. When we burn these fossil fuels, the stored carbon locked inside is released into the atmosphere as carbon dioxide. Fossil fuels are used all over the world to power everything from cars and industrial plants to the electric lights at home and in work.

Mined coal contains up to 90% carbon.

Oil and gas are hydrocarbons (hydrogen and carbon).

Biomass and energy

A renewable source of energy is something that can be used again and again. In the search for renewable energy, people today are exploring the use of biomass—natural material that stores sunlight as chemical energy. Biomass fuels can include wood, straw, manure, and waste products such as paper and cardboard. They also include the methane that is given off from trash and animal waste.

The crop sorghum can be used to burn directly and also to make ethanol as a fuel.

Geothermal power

Heat from deep inside Earth can be harnessed. Deep wells are drilled to reach hot rocks and cold water pumped in, returning to the surface as hot water and the steam of dissolved gases. This power is used to drive turbines and generators.

Geothermal power station in New Zealand

Captured power

By placing wind turbines in areas where there is regularly wind to turn the blades, their motion can be used to generate electricity. Tidal energy comes from the movement of water, H_2O, in the oceans. The flow of water created by the tides is used to generate electricity.

Neodymium magnets are used in wind turbines and to capture tidal power.

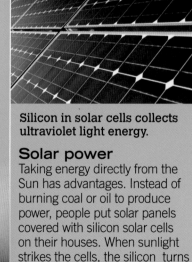

Silicon in solar cells collects ultraviolet light energy.

Solar power

Taking energy directly from the Sun has advantages. Instead of burning coal or oil to produce power, people put solar panels covered with silicon solar cells on their houses. When sunlight strikes the cells, the silicon turns some of it into electricity to channel for use in the home.

Nuclear power

It is not necessary to burn fuel to create nuclear energy so, unlike the fossil fuel industries, nuclear power plants do not release pollutants into the air. By splitting uranium atoms in a process called fission, heat is released that can be used to change water into steam, which turns huge turbines to drive generators to make electricity.

Nuclear reactor hall in a power plant

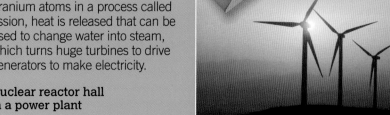

PLUTONIUM

ACTINOID

94

Pu

[244]

Plutonium releases radioactive alpha particles all the time, making it a great source of energy for spacecraft and the base for terrifyingly powerful bombs. Nearly all plutonium is man-made, created in a nuclear reactor when uranium atoms absorb neutrons. If you could touch it, the element would feel warm to the touch at all times because of this constant activity.

Atomic number: 94

Formula: Pu

Atomic weight: [244]

State at 68°F (20°C): solid

Boiling point: 5842°F (3228°C)

Melting point: 1184°F (640°C)

Half-life: of plutonium-238, 88 years

% in the Universe: none

% in Earth's crust: none

% in Earth's oceans: none

% in humans: none

Uses: to make nuclear weapons such as atomic bombs; in the nuclear industry; to make electricity for space probes, spacecraft and rovers; once used to power pacemaker batteries

e94 | p94 | n150

Power source in space
Plutonium was used to power devices in the Apollo 14 flight to the Moon in 1971. It also provided the power supply used by the two Voyager spacecraft in 1977.

War finisher
It took 132 lbs (60 kg) of uranium to make the first atomic bomb, dropped on Hiroshima, Japan, in 1945. It only took 13.7 lbs (6.2 kg) for a piece of plutonium the size of an orange to make an even more powerful blast a few days later, when another bomb was dropped on the city of Nagasaki (left).

Fast reactor
Fast breeder reactors are designed to produce power and new fuel at the same time. The uranium that powers the reactor converts into plutonium, which can be separated out for use elsewhere. It is possible that this type of reactor may provide a longer-lasting fuel supply. However, extracting the plutonium is not without its dangers and some breeder reactors, like this one in Japan, have been shut down.

Glowing with energy
This pellet of plutonium is illuminated by the red glow of its own radioactivity. Plutonium does not occur in nature except as minute quantities from the decay of uranium-238. All the isotopes of plutonium are radioactive and it is highly toxic.

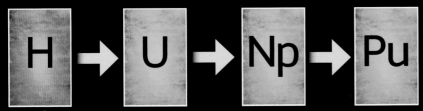

Hydrogen isotope deuterium

Isotope Uranium-238

Isotope Neptunium-238

Plutonium-238

Making plutonium

Plutonium was discovered in 1940 by Glenn Seaborg and a team of scientists working at Berkeley, California. They bombarded uranium-238 with deuterium to create neptunium-238, which then decayed into plutonium-238. The Manhattan Project produced enough plutonium for the Nagasaki bomb.

Plutonium's most **stable isotope**, **plutonium-244**, has a **half-life** of more than **80 million years**.

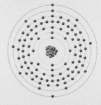

CURIUM

ACTINOID

96

Cm

[247]

This synthetic element is made inside nuclear reactors by bombarding plutonium with alpha particles. Curium is highly radioactive and it glows red in the dark.

Atomic number: 96

Formula: Cm

Atomic weight: [247]

State at 68°F (20°C: solid

Boiling point: unknown

Melting point: 2453°F (1345°C)

% in the Universe: none

% in Earth's crust: none

% in Earth's oceans: none

% in humans: none

Uses: primarily in research; to provide power on space missions

e96 | p96 | n151

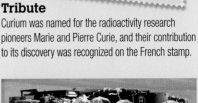

Tribute

Curium was named for the radioactivity research pioneers Marie and Pierre Curie, and their contribution to its discovery was recognized on the French stamp.

APXS at work on Mars

Curium has been used to provide power for electrical equpiment on space missions. The Alpha Particle X-Ray Spectrometer (center in the picture) is fitted to the Mars rover Curiosity to work out the concentrations of chemical elements in the planet's rocks and soils.

Smashing atoms

Glenn Seaborg and his team of scientists discovered curium in 1944 by using the 60-inch cyclotron at the University of California Lawrence Radiation Laboratory (below). They had already found plutonium (left) in the cyclotron early in 1941.

Curiosity explores Mars

Exploration rovers on Mars cannot get enough energy from solar panels alone. To power movement and the instruments they carry onboard, their power systems convert heat from the natural radioactive decay of plutonium-238 into electricity. The same plutonium isotope is used in the power systems of NASA spacecraft. The Curiosity Rover, which is currently exploring the surface of Mars, uses about 9 lbs. (4 kg) of plutonium to produce about 110 watts of power in its Multi-Mission Radioisotope Thermoelectric Generator (MMRTG).

AMERICIUM

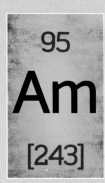

95

Am

[243]

ACTINOID

Americium's discovery was kept secret during WWII in case it proved to have military uses. It did not, but this synthetic element is in almost every home, potentially saving lives in smoke alarms. A tiny sliver of foil gives off alpha particles, and if smoke gets in, the soot absorbs some of these ions, triggering the alarm. Less than 0.04 oz (1 g) of americium is enough to fuel three million detectors.

Atomic number: 95
Formula: Am
Atomic weight: [243]
State at 68°F (20°C): solid
Boiling point: 3652°F (2011°C)
Melting point: 2149°F (1176°C)
Half-life: 7,370 years for Am-243

Uses: in smoke detectors; to analyze materials in X-ray fluorescence spectroscopy, for portable X-rays machines)

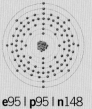

e95 | p95 | n148

BERKELIUM

Atomic number: 97
Formula: Bk
Atomic weight: [247]
State at 68°F (20°C): solid
Boiling point: unknown
Melting point: 1807°F (986°C)

Half-life: 1,380 years for BK-247
Uses: only in scientific research

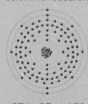

e97 | p97 | n150

97

Bk

[247]

ACTINOID

Berkelium was first made in 1949. It took five years to collect enough americium to do the experiment, and another nine years to make an amount of berkelium big enough to be seen without a microscope.

Creating the element
The element was created by Glenn Seaborg, Albert Ghiorso, and Stanley Thompson in a laboratory in Berkeley, California, for which it was named. It was made by bombarding americium with helium ions.

CALIFORNIUM

98

Cf

[251]

ACTINOID

Californium is a synthetic element whose powerful radioactive rays can find out what elements are hidden inside something. It is valuable in hunting for gold and oil, and in scanning baggage for explosives.

Atomic number: 98
Formula: Cf
Atomic weight: [251]
State at 68°F (20°C): solid
Boiling point: unknown
Melting point: 1652°F (900°C)

Half-life: 900 years for isotope Cf-251
Uses: in metal detectors; oil well industry; in medicine

e98 | p98 | n153

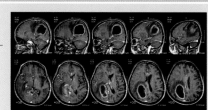

Medical insight
Californium is used medically as well. It acts as a contrast agent to enhance the contrast between, and so the visibility of, structures in MRI scanning.

From the debris
Fermium was discovered in the fallout from Ivy Mike, a thermonuclear explosion test carried out by the United States on a Pacific atoll on November 1, 1952.

Atomic number: 100
Formula: Fm
Atomic weight: [257]
State at 68°F (20°C): solid
Boiling point: unknown
Melting point: 2781°F (1527°C)

Half-life: 100.5 days for Fm-257
Uses: only for research

e100 | p100 | n157

FERMIUM

100

Fm

[257]

ACTINOID

It is hard work making fermium, and hard to do since most of it decays very fast. It was discovered in 1952 by a team of scientists led by Albert Ghiorso.

By 1961, only **10 millionths** of **0.04 oz (1 g)** of Einsteinium had been **made**.

Atomic number: 99

Formula: Es

Atomic weight: [252]

State at 68°F (20°C): solid

Boiling point: unknown

Melting point: 1580°F (860°C)

Half-life: 1.29 years for Es-252

Uses: no uses other than scientific research

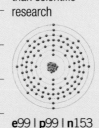

e99 | p99 | n153

EINSTEINIUM

99

Es

[252]

ACTINOID

This element is named for the pioneering German physicist Albert Einstein, and was first found in the debris from the Ivy Mike bomb test in 1952 (below left). It was once made naturally inside planet Earth, but is now manufactured only in nuclear reactors.

MENDELEVIUM

101

Md

[258]

ACTINOID

Only miniscule amounts of this element have been made, a few atoms at a time inside reactors, so no one has ever seen it. The first 17 atoms were made in 1955 by Albert Ghiorso and his team, who bombarded einsteinium with helium ions.

Named for...
Albert Ghiorso (above) named this element for the creator of the periodic table, Dmitri Mendeleev.

Atomic number: 101

Formula: Md

Atomic weight: [258]

State at 68°F (20°C): solid

Boiling point: unknown

Melting point: 1521°F (827°C)

Half-life: 51.5 days for isotope Md-258

Uses: no uses outside research

e101 | p101 | n157

Atomic number: 102

Formula: No

Atomic weight: [259]

State at 68°F (20°C): solid

Boiling point: unknown

Melting point: 1521°F (827°C)

Half-life: 58 minutes for No-259

Uses: none outside scientific research

e102 | p102 | n157

102

No

[259]

NOBELIUM

ACTINOID

Many scientists tried to make element 102, starting in the 1950s, and it took 40 years of debates between Russia and the United States to decide who discovered it—in the end, it was decided for Russia. It is named for Swedish chemist and inventor of dynamite Alfred Nobel, who set up the Nobel Prizes for work in the sciences and toward world peace.

LAWRENCIUM

103

Lr

[262]

ACTINOID

Element 103 is named after Ernest Lawrence, who built the first powerful particle accelerators where synthetic elements are made. Only a few atoms have been created, by bombarding californium with boron nuclei.

Atomic number: 103

Formula: Lr

Atomic weight: [262]

State at 68°F (20°C): solid

Boiling point: unknown

Melting point: 2961°F (1627°C)

% in the Universe: none

% in Earth's crust: none

% in Earth's oceans: none

% in humans: none

Half-life: 10 hours for Lr-266

Uses: research only

e103 | p103 | n159

NONMETA

LS & GASES

LIFE AND COLOR

We have reached the right-hand side of the periodic table, where some of the elements are less reactive than their relatives, but make up for this lack of sparkle by being vital for life on Earth. On these pages you will find the nonmetals (the key to life on Earth), the noble gases (headed up on the table by helium, the second most common gas in the Universe), and the halogens, which are eager to find just one more electron. . .

COFFEE

Neon

Jet (carbon)

Helium

Diamond
(carbon)

Diamond
(carbon)

Kelp
(iodine)

Turquoise
(phosphorus)

Rock salt (chlorine)

Sulfur

Iron pyrite
(sulfur)

Coal
(carbon)

Rust (oxygen)

Opal (oxygen)

Ice (oxygen)

Fluorite (fluorine)

Urea (nitrogen)

Topaz (fluorine)

Variscite (phosphorus)

Copper sulfate (sulfur)

Graphite (carbon)

A select bunch
The nonmetals include gases and solids that vary greatly in their chemistry. Group 17 is home to the six reactive halogens, while the seven rare noble gases occupy Group 18 of the table.

NONMETALS
These elements are hard to pin down— literally, as they can be gas, solid, or liquid. Most nonmetals are brittle when solid, and mostly look dull rather than shiny. There are only a few of them, compared with the 84 metals in the periodic table, but nonmetal elements make up most of the Earth, especially its crust.

HALOGENS
Halogens need only one more electron to complete their outer shells. This makes them eager to combine with other elements, especially those on the left-hand side of the periodic table, which have one electron that they like to donate.

NOBLE GASES
Noble gases are the only elements that are monatomic, which means that their molecules exist as a single atom at standard temperature and pressure. They were once called "inert gases" because scientists did not think they reacted chemically at all, but in fact some can form compounds, so their name was changed to "noble gases."

Galena (sulfur)

NONMETALS & GASES

Life in the oceans

We live in a world of water, with oceans and seas covering 71 percent of the planet's surface. The dissolved nonmetal gases oxygen, nitrogen, and carbon dioxide are absorbed by these waters, and used by an ecosystem of marine plants and animals that depend on one another to survive. Together with other ecosystems on land, the oceans help to maintain a balance in Earth's atmosphere. It is a delicate balance and is in danger from both natural disasters such as earthquakes or storms, and man-made disasters, such as oil spills and the dumping of waste materials.

Nonmetals are hard to pin down: they can be gas, solid, or liquid. These are elements without the strengths of metals, but they include elements vital to life, such as oxygen and carbon, and are far more common than metals.

Mixed bunch
This small group numbers only seven. These elements have significantly lower melting and boiling points than the metals and are poor conductors of heat and electricity.

NONMETALS TIMELINE

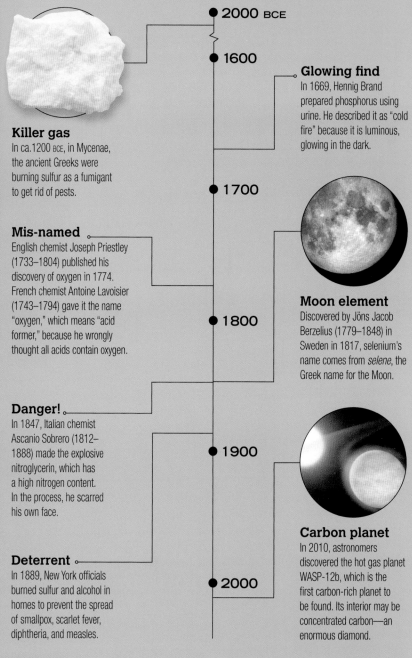

● 2000 BCE

● 1600

● 1700

● 1800

● 1900

● 2000

Killer gas
In ca.1200 BCE, in Mycenae, the ancient Greeks were burning sulfur as a fumigant to get rid of pests.

Glowing find
In 1669, Hennig Brand prepared phosphorus using urine. He described it as "cold fire" because it is luminous, glowing in the dark.

Mis-named
English chemist Joseph Priestley (1733–1804) published his discovery of oxygen in 1774. French chemist Antoine Lavoisier (1743–1794) gave it the name "oxygen," which means "acid former," because he wrongly thought all acids contain oxygen.

Moon element
Discovered by Jöns Jacob Berzelius (1779–1848) in Sweden in 1817, selenium's name comes from *selene*, the Greek name for the Moon.

Danger!
In 1847, Italian chemist Ascanio Sobrero (1812–1888) made the explosive nitroglycerin, which has a high nitrogen content. In the process, he scarred his own face.

Deterrent
In 1889, New York officials burned sulfur and alcohol in homes to prevent the spread of smallpox, scarlet fever, diphtheria, and measles.

Carbon planet
In 2010, astronomers discovered the hot gas planet WASP-12b, which is the first carbon-rich planet to be found. Its interior may be concentrated carbon—an enormous diamond.

CARBON

NONMETAL

Carbon is very often called the "king of the elements." It does a lot of work. It's key to our human bodies—the second most abundant element inside us—and the food we eat. In combination with hydrogen, carbon is the fuel that powers our world. In its diamond allotrope, carbon is the hardest known substance in nature, plus it has the highest thermal conductivity of any element. Another form, graphite, is one of the softest of all materials.

6

C

12.011

Atomic number: 6

Formula: C

Atomic weight: 12.011

State at 68°F (20°C): solid

Boiling point: 8720°F (4827°C)

Melting point: 6332°F (3500°C)

% in the Universe: 0.50

% in Earth's crust: 0.18

% in Earth's oceans: 0.0028

% in humans: 18.5

Uses: as hydrocarbons in coal, oil, natural gas fuels; in petrochemical industries that produce polymers, fibers, paints, solvents, plastics; as charcoal; as graphite for pencils; in metal smelting in the iron and steel industries; as carbon fiber; as diamonds to cut rocks and drilling, as jewelry; in nanotechnology

e6 | p6 | n6

Hard as ...
Diamonds are pure carbon. They are created deep in the heat and pressure of the planet, 100 miles (160 km) down. They can cut anything, but only other diamonds can mark them.

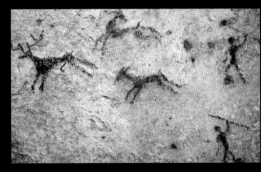

First art
Some of the earliest cave paintings dating from prehistoric times were drawn with charcoal. Almost pure carbon, charcoal is made by burning wood in the absence of air. Carbon even gets its name from the Latin word *carbo*, which means charcoal or coal.

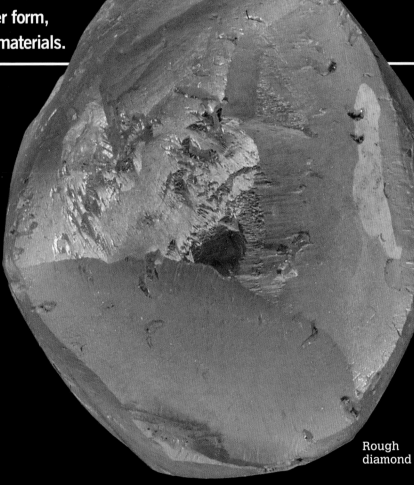

Rough diamond

Nearly **nine million compounds** of carbon have been **discovered**.

OTHER FORMS

Shungite

Coal

Carbon is the **fourth** most abundant element in the universe, after **hydrogen, helium,** and **oxygen**.

Nodding donkey drills in an oil field

Oil refinery

Refined oil distributed to gas stations

Gasoline burned in cars is released as CO_2

CO_2 molecules

Carbon for life
Carbon atoms have a unique ability to make a great variety of strong and stable bonds. They're vital in forming the complicated molecules of life on Earth. Carbon is the primary ingredient in proteins, fats, carbohydrates, and nucleic acids such as DNA cells, which contain the instructions used in the development and functioning of all living things.

Food supply
Our supplies of carbon get used up as we go about our ordinary, everyday lives. Our diet of carbohydrates, fats, and protein supplies us with all the replacement carbon that we need. Virtually everything we eat contains carbon.

Graphite

Carbon variety
There are hundreds of carbon-bearing minerals on Earth, possibly more than 500. The element occurs naturally in different forms, or allotropes, that look and behave very differently. Diamonds are very hard and, when polished, they are transparent. Graphite on the other hand is soft and a dense black-gray.

Runaway heating
The atmosphere of the planet Venus is made up almost completely of carbon dioxide, with some nitrogen and sulfuric acid. These gases trap heat from the Sun like a greenhouse, making Venus the hottest planet in our solar system.

From ground to air
Hydrogen and carbon compounds, hydrocarbons, are the main component of fossil fuels including oil, natural gas, and coal. These are formed over millions of years from the fossilized, carbon-rich remains of plants and animals. They are dug up and burned to power our world, a byproduct of which is carbon dioxide. Over the past 100 years we have burned so much fossil fuel that the percentage of CO_2 in our atmosphere has risen to levels that may mean the Earth is heating up. Replacing these fuels will take millions of years. A great effort is now being made to find more renewable sources of energy.

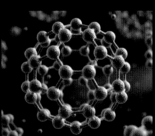

New forms
One allotrope of carbon is the fullerenes, cages and tubes with different numbers of carbon atoms. Nanotubes are fullerenes that are very strong and very light. They can be used to reinforce graphite, for example in tennis rackets and for drug delivery in the body. And scientists are trying to figure out ways to use carbon nanotubes in electronics as semiconductors.

Graph: CO₂ level (parts per million) vs Year, showing values from 250 to 400 on y-axis and 1700 to 2000 on x-axis

Eating machine

This hungry caterpillar will eat hundreds or even thousands of times its own body weight. It acquires the carbon stored in plant tissues for all its life processes, and gives off carbon dioxide in respiration (*see* page opposite). If the caterpillar is eaten, the carbon will pass on to its predator. If it dies, the carbon will be released as it decays.

THE CARBON CYCLE

Carbon is the essential ingredient of life and governs how we live it. We are made of carbon, we eat carbon, and our civilization is powered by it. The carbon cycle allows living things to reuse carbon again and again, while keeping our planet's carbon reserves in balance. But human activity may be distorting that balance, with far-reaching and potentially disastrous consequences.

Cycle step 1—photosynthesis

Carbon exists in Earth's atmosphere in the compound carbon dioxide. Plants, and some algae, capture carbon dioxide in their leaves and take up water through their roots. Light energy from the Sun transfers electrons from water (H_2O) to carbon dioxide (CO_2), which produces carbohydrates and oxygen in a process called photosynthesis. The carbohydrates are simple sugars used by the plant as food and to make cells. Animals get their carbon by eating plants, or other animals that have eaten plants.

Green chlorophyll in leaves captures sunlight

Animals such as koala bears eat the plants

Human damage

Greenhouse gases such as carbon dioxide act like a blanket, trapping heat from the Sun near Earth's surface and raising the temperature to keep us warm. We add carbon dioxide to the atmosphere every time we burn fossil fuels—coal, oil, and gas. We are adding it faster than plants or the ocean can reabsorb it. The blanket is thickening and temperatures on Earth are rising. This climate change may bring extreme weather and terrible flooding in the future.

Burning fossil fuels

Step 2—respiration

Every living thing respires. When this happens in the presence of oxygen it is called aerobic respiration. In this process sugar molecules react with oxygen molecules to release energy. Water and carbon dioxide are produced as waste products which are excreted from the body. In this way, carbon is returned to the atmosphere.

Carbon dioxide in

Oxygen out

Photosynthesis

Oxygen in

Carbon dioxide out

Respiration

Step 3—decomposition

A great deal of carbon is returned to the atmosphere as carbon dioxide by decomposers. These bacteria, fungi, and some of the larger animals feed on the rotting remains and waste products of plants and animals, returning carbon dioxide to the atmosphere through respiration.

Acid ocean

The oceans cannot dissolve more and more carbon dioxide without damage. The gas reacts in water, releasing hydrogen ions and making the water more acidic. This means less calcium carbonate in ocean water, which interferes in the way that animals produce shells. Coral reefs are especially affected.

Coral reef

Geological carbon cycle

Living things play a role in one carbon cycle, rocks and minerals in another. The geological carbon cycle takes many, many millions of years. The remains of plants and animals, especially marine animals, become rock, such as limestone, at the bottom of the ocean. Chemical processes, including weathering, erosion, and volcanic eruptions, release carbon from limestone back into the atmosphere.

Limestone with shellfish fossils

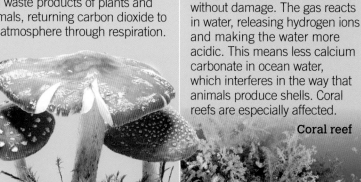

Fungi are the best decomposers in forests

Carbon and the planet

Many scientists describe life as "carbon-based" and a whole branch of chemistry is devoted to the study of matter that contains carbon atoms: organic chemistry. Carbon is a relatively small atom. But the four electrons in its outer shell means it can form all kinds of bonds, single, double, or triple bonds, chains, branches, rings some millions of atoms long. This versatility allows it to shape the incredibly diverse kinds of life on Earth, life seen at its most contrasting and simply stunning in Earth's tropical rainforests.

NITROGEN

NONMETAL AND GAS

It makes up 78 percent of our air, but nitrogen is no softie. The bond between nitrogen's two atoms is strong and stable, and making it releases huge amounts of energy, so nitrogen is used in explosives. This gas provides the raw material for the nitrites, nitrates, and ammonia that plants need for growth, and as a liquid coolant, at –320°F (–196°C) it freezes almost everything.

7

N

14.007

Atomic number: 7

Formula: N

Atomic weight: 14.0067

State at 68°F (20°C): gas

Boiling point: –320.431°F (–195.795°C)

Melting point: –346°F (–210°C)

% in the Universe: 0.10

% in Earth's crust: 0.0020

% in Earth's oceans: 0.000050

% in humans: 3.2

Uses: fertilizers; nylon; dyes; explosives; plastics; textiles; refrigerant gas; cleaners; freezing and transport of food; coolant for computers and superconductors; as a freezing mist in modern cookery; as a power source for paintball; to fill aircraft and vehicle tires; in steel production

e7 | p7 | n7

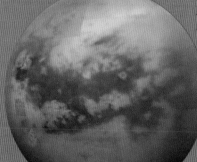

Nitrogen moon
The largest of Saturn's known moons, Titan, is locked in a deep-freeze. When the probe Huygens landed there in 2005, it sent back data that scientists are still analyzing. Titan's atmosphere is mainly nitrogen—up to 90 percent—and the temperature is –288°F (–178°C). It rains liquid methane onto the frozen surface of this large moon.

In 1772, chemist **Daniel Rutherford** discovered what he called **"noxious air,"** air that turned out to be **nitrogen gas**.

Food preserver
Manufacturers of many food products use nitrogen gas to expel oxygen from a package before it is sealed. If oxygen remained inside, it would allow bacteria to grow more easily and spoil the food. Nitrogen also creates a pressurized atmosphere in which the packaging does not collapse, so potato chips, for example, will not be crushed.

Freezer storage
Nitrogen is used regularly in the laboratory, for example to preserve blood until it is needed for research or transfusions. Liquid nitrogen provides a temperature of –320°F (–196°C) for this purpose.

Explosive substances
When compounds containing nitrogen combust or decompose, the nitrogen turns back into a gas, releasing a lot of heat. The rapidly expanding gas results in explosions. Invented in 1847 by Italian chemist Ascanio Sobrero, nitroglycerine is one of these compounds. It is used to make dynamite, employed for demolition on construction sites and elsewhere. In its pure form, it is very dangerous to transport or use, as the slightest jolt can cause it to detonate.

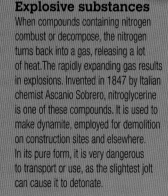

The nitrogen cycle

All living things need nitrogen to produce amino acids that allow them to live and grow. However, only bacteria can use nitrogen as a gas, so the nitrogen cycle allows the gas to be processed and used. Bacteria in the soil absorbs nitrogen and converts it into nitrates. The nitrates are taken up by the roots of plants, which in turn are eaten by animals. When living things die, their nitrogen is returned to the atmosphere and the cycle begins again.

Other gases in the atmosphere 22%

Nitrogen in the atmosphere 78%

Roots of the matter

Nitrogen is "fixed" (forms a chemical compound) when it is combined with oxygen to form nitrates. Some nitrates are formed when lightning flashes and triggers a chemical reaction. Many more are created by bacteria, some of which cause special swellings called nodules on the roots of plants. Nitrogen is also added to the soil by farmers because the nitrates enrich the soil and encourage growth. However, too much may mean that the nitrogen contaminates local water sources.

Nitrogen-fixing nodules on roots

Applying nitrogen-rich fertilizer

Boiling cold

Liquid nitrogen's boiling point is an amazing −320°F (−196°C). At this temperature, it is used as a coolant for computers, to freeze materials, in medicine to remove warts, and as a way of creating clouds of fog to make a dramatic effect when serving food in restaurants! It has to be handled only when wearing safety gear because it can cause severe frostbite if it splashes on skin.

Poisonous waters

This satellite image shows harmful algal bloom in the Great Lakes of North America. The algae produce toxins that can kill animals and people. They are caused by the agricultural run-off of fertilizers containing nitrogen.

The light of discovery

Phosphorus is found in compounds in at least 200 different minerals including apatite (right). It was discovered in 1669 by the merchant and alchemist Hennig Brand in Hamburg, Germany. He boiled urine, gold-colored, believing he could distil gold. Instead, he isolated a white, waxy substance that he called phosphorus, from the Greek *phosphoros,* meaning "bringer of light," because it glowed in the dark.

15	
P	
30.974	

PHOSPHORUS

NONMETAL

Phosphorus has been called "the devil's element" because it is poisonous, and white phosphorus burns readily in the air and even in water. However, this element is vital to life. It is part of our DNA, and in our bones and teeth. When you drink a can of soda, clean your teeth, or even strike a match, you are using phosphates, the compounds in which phosphorus appears in nature. It even helps crops grow as a fertilizer.

Atomic number: 15

Formula: P

Atomic weight: 30.9737

State at 68°F (20°C): solid

Boiling point: 536.9°F (280.5°C)

Melting point: 111.47°F (44.15°C)

% in Universe: 0.00070

% in Earth's crust: 0.099

% in Earth's oceans: 0.0000070

% in humans: 1

Uses: white phosphorus in flares and incendiary devices; flame-retardants; strike-anywhere matches; fertilizers; steel production; detergents; in toothpastes and shampoos; glassware and china production; in pesticides; in high-temperature lubricants; to coat metals; in water treatments

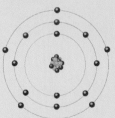

e15 | p15 | n16

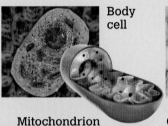

Body cell

Mitochondrion

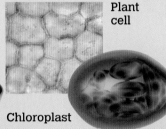

Plant cell

Chloroplast

Cell power
In humans, mitochondria in our body cells take food and make energy for us to use. Chloroplasts convert light energy from the Sun into sugars to be used by plant cells. Phosphorus plays an important role in both kinds of energy transfer, as well as helping in the repair and growth of the cells and tissues.

FOUND IN

Phosphorite

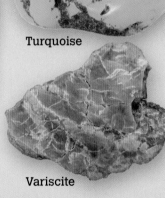

Turquoise

Variscite

Arrival on Earth
Meteorites that crashed into our planet four billion or so years ago, now known as Gibeon meteorites, are believed to have carried phosphorus in a mineral called schreibersite. This mineral is an alloy of iron, phosphorus, and nickel.

Reactive
This highly reactive element is only found in minerals in nature. It comes in different colored forms, including white, red, violet, and black. The white form is very reactive and unstable. The red form is made by heating the white, and is more stable.

Good match
In 1830, a French chemist invented the first phosphorus-based match, which used white phosphorus. But long-term use of the matches caused an illness called "phossy jaw," with toothache and eventual brain damage. Modern safety matches are struck on red phosphorus on the side of the matchbox. The red phosphorus turns to white and ignites.

Collecting guano

For more than a century people called *guaneros*, who live on the Ballestas Islands off the coast of Peru, have collected precious bird droppings, known as guano, from dangerous cliff edges. The first visitors to the islands found some of the guano piled up over 165 ft (50 m) high! Here, the guano is being bagged up, ready to be shipped to the mainland and sold. There is a thriving market for both seabird and cave-dwelling bat guano, which make excellent fertilizers due to their high levels of phosphorus and nitrogen.

OXYGEN

NONMETAL AND GAS

8
O
15.999

Most life on Earth needs oxygen. It is in the air we breathe and the water we drink. There was only a mere trace of it when the planet formed, but it increased as a by-product of photosynthesis, which is how plants turn sunlight into food. Oxygen is not flammable on its own, but the flames of candles and forest fires burn hotter and faster because of it.

Atomic number: 8

Formula: O

Atomic weight: 15.999

State at 68°F (20°C): gas

Boiling point: −297.332°F (−182.962°C)

Melting point: −361.82°F (−218.79°C)

% in the Universe: 1.00

% in Earth's crust: 46

% in Earth's oceans: 86

% in humans: 65

Uses: steel industry; for the manufacture of chemicals; antifreeze; welding and cutting of metals; treatment of sewage and effluent; treatment of respiratory diseases; for respiration in submarines, aircraft, spacesuits, and spacecraft; liquid oxygen is an oxidizer in rocket fuel systems; medical oxygen therapy

e8 | p8 | n8

Ozone molecule

Oxygen molecule

Dynamic oxygen
Oxygen makes things happen. At standard temperature and pressure it is an odorless, colorless, and tasteless gas. It is in all the molecules of every living thing on Earth. Its two linked atoms combine easily with other substances to release the energy that living things need. Ozone, the gas in the upper atmosphere that protects us from the Sun's ultraviolet rays, has three linked oxygen atoms.

Oxygen for life
The air we breathe drives the chemical processes in our bodies. The oxygen in the air is carried through our nose or mouth to millions of little air sacs called alveoli in the lungs. The alveoli pass oxygen to our blood and dispose of waste gases in the form of carbon dioxide and water vapor. Our body cells break down glucose by combining it with the delivered oxygen and this releases the energy to the different parts of the body that need it to function. At this moment, hundreds of thousands of reactions taking place in our bodies rely on oxygen.

Oxygen is the **third most abundant** element in the **Universe**.

Corroding metal
Iron, and metals that contain iron such as steel, rust when they are exposed to and react with oxygen and water from the air, rain, or seawater. Rust is iron oxide, and it is created on the outside of the metal object because iron combines very easily with oxygen.

Life from the oceans

Dissolved in water, oxygen covers most of our planet's surface. From around 2.5 billion years ago, the oxygen in Earth's atmosphere began to build up. It came from bacteria in the oceans, which produced the gas by photosynthesis (*see below right*). It created the right conditions for life in its many different forms to develop. Today, marine organisms produce over half of the oxygen that animals need.

Oxygen in the stars

It has long been known that oxygen is an important part of the interstellar material from which new stars and planets develop. In 2016, a team of Brazilian astronomers announced that they had found a white dwarf, nicknamed Dox, that has an outer layer made up of 99.9 percent pure oxygen. This may have been caused by binary stars interacting.

Multi-tasker

Various industries use oxygen for cutting, welding, and melting metals. Because it can generate temperatures of up to 5400°F (3000°C), it can be used for oxyacetylene blowtorches. As liquid oxygen, it burns fuel for spacecraft, and in spacesuits astronauts breathe almost pure oxygen almost pure oxygen. Oxygen also helps people who have breathing difficulties, as well as scuba divers and mountaineers.

Steel production **Cutting and welding metal** **Healthcare**

Sunlight brings energy

Oxygen released as a by-product

Carbon dioxide (CO_2) enters through leaves

CO_2 and glucose make sugars for energy and growth

Photosynthesis

This process takes place in chloroplasts inside the cells of green plants. These structures use the energy in sunlight to make food in the form of glucose from molecules of carbon dioxide and water. Oxygen is formed as a by-product. The plants use the glucose for growth, to make starch to store energy, and to make cellulose, which is needed to build cell walls.

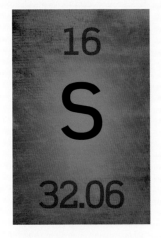

16	
S	
32.06	

SULFUR

NONMETAL

Sulfur oozes as a red liquid from active volcanoes, and was once known as brimstone. When it meets oxygen and heat, it burns bright red, and is a key ingredient in gunpowder and still used in firecrackers. Sulfur is in the proteins and enzymes of our bodies, where it is also vital for forming bones and fats. The element is very useful in making fertilizers, detergents, rubber tires, and even sweeteners for drinks.

Atomic number: 16

Formula: S

Atomic weight: 32.065

State at 68°F (20°C): solid

Boiling point: 832.3°F (444.61°C)

Melting point: 239.38°F (115.21°C)

% in the Universe: 0.050

% in Earth's crust: 0.042

% in Earth's oceans: 0.093

% in humans: 0.30

Uses: to produce sulfuric acid for use in chemical industries; in fertilizers; for vulcanization to strengthen black rubber; in fungicides; in insecticides; for black gunpowder; as a bleach; in preservatives for foodstuffs; cement and plaster; in paint production and batteries; in personal care products; in cosmetics; water treatment

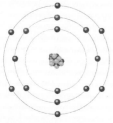

e16 | p16 | n16

Sulfur is in **keratin**, the **protein** that **makes** your **hair** and **nails**.

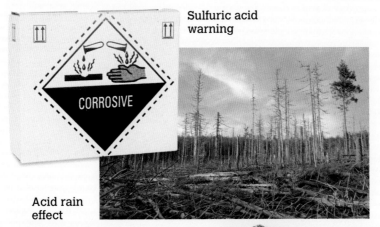

Sulfuric acid warning

Acid rain effect

Acid makers

Polluting gases such as sulfur dioxide (created when fuels containing sulfur are burned) are released into the atmosphere from cars, factories, and airplanes. The gases combine with water in clouds, falling to earth as a rain of sulfuric acid or in sleet and snow. The destructive mix erodes stone, corrodes metals, peels paints, and destroys whole forests.

Soothing spring

Many natural hot springs flow with warm sulfuric water. One of Italy's best-known hot springs is at Saturnia in Tuscany. It is said that the god Saturn lost his temper with warring men and sent a lightning bolt that split the earth. Out of the crack flowed the spring, now part of a spa.

Poisonous compound

In the past, some of the most dangerous substances in regular use were made from sulfur compounds. Realgar is an orange-red, arsenic sulfide mineral. It has been used as a pigment, a dye, and a medicine, as well as to create the white in fireworks. However, realgar is highly poisonous and most of the world's arsenic (see pp.124–125) is extracted from it.

Sulfur invention

In 1844, an American engineer, Charles Goodyear, accidentally dropped some Indian rubber mixed with sulfur onto a hot stove. He found that when the liquid rubber was heated with sulfur, it increased the elasticity and strength of the rubber ten-fold. Goodyear immediately applied for a patent but unfortunately he did not profit from his discovery, dying in debt.

Yellow element

Pure sulfur is an unmistakable bright yellow. It was isolated in 1809 by the French chemists Joseph Louis Gay-Lussac and Louis-Jacques Thénard. Today, sulfur is mainly used by chemical industries to manufacture sulfuric acid, which is used to make fertilizers, batteries, and cleaners.

A really bad smell!

Pure sulfur is almost odorless. However, when the element combines with hydrogen, it makes a smell of rotten eggs that people hate. Hydrogen sulfide is also what frightens off predators when a skunk sprays to protect itself. According to recent research, all mammals have odor receptors in their noses that contain copper, and this is really sensitive to the smell of sulfur.

34

Se

78.971

Atomic number: 34

Formula: Se

Atomic weight: 78.971

State at 68°F (20°C): solid

Boiling points: 1265°F (685°C)

Melting point: 429.4°F (220.8°C)

% in the Universe: 0.0000030

% in Earth's crust: 0.0000050

% in Earth's oceans: 0.000000045

% in humans: 0.0000050

Uses: as an additive to glass to de-color or color; pigments for ceramics, paint, and plastics; photoelectric cells; solar cells; photocopiers; anti-dandruff shampoo; additive to make stainless steel; semiconductors; light meters

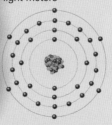

e34 | p34 | n45

SELENIUM

NONMETAL

Selenium cannot make up its mind. It comes in two forms (allotropes)—a red nonmetal, and a gray metalloid that lets electricity pass through it better in the light than the dark, so it has been used in photocells. Every cell in our bodies contains more than a million atoms of it, but too much would poison us. Compounds are added to glass to make it clear, or color it red.

Warning smell

Selenium also gives off a strong smell when it is heated, but unlike sulfur, the smell is of radishes and more attractive! Trace quantities are needed for healthy joints, heart, and eyes, and we absorb them through the food we eat.

Heat collector

In 2010 it was found that a relatively small amount of selenium, embedded in zinc oxide, significantly increases the efficiency of solar panels.

Red glass

Glass colored by selenium is one of the most brilliant reds known. Ruby red selenium is also used in the preparation of ceramic glazes.

Variety of form

There are different allotropes, or structural forms, of selenium. The most stable is a metallic gray (below), which is the only one that conducts electricity. There are also bright red and black allotropes.

Dangerous work

Sulfur, like all the other atmospheric gases, is released by volcanic eruptions. Its acrid, foul-smelling fumes pour out of many active volcanoes around the world. The sulfur solidifies in the open air and for many centuries has been dug out and collected for use. Here, at Ijen volcano in East Java, Indonesia, men, with covered faces to keep out the fumes, load sulfur by hand into paniers to carry more than 650 ft (200 m) down the mountain. They sell the sulfur to factories, where most of it is converted into sulfuric acid for use in fertilizers.

What volcanoes reveal

We can find out about the elements inside our planet by looking at the different materials that come up from deep inside Earth when a volcano erupts. And the way the volcano erupts tells us about the gas content of the magma. A large release of pent-up gas bubbles in the magma will make the explosion more violent.

EARTH'S ELEMENTS

Elements are everywhere on and inside Earth. They float in its atmosphere, form its crust, dissolve in the oceans, and swirl as molten rock in the mantle and core. Heat forces up the rocks until they cool and sink, causing the tectonic plates of the crust to move at the speed your fingernails grow! Amazingly, around 90 percent of our planet is made up of only four elements—iron, oxygen, silicon, and magnesium.

Elemental Earth

We live on the outer layer of our planet, the crust, surrounded by the mixture of gases that make up the atmosphere. Under our feet is the interior of the planet made up of solid and liquid layers—a thin silicate crust, a thick iron and magnesium silicate mantle, and a thick metallic core.

Atmosphere
This is where the gas elements—mostly nitrogen and oxygen—are found.

Crust
At 3–44 miles (5–70km) deep, the crust is the source of all the metals and raw materials we use.

Mantle
This middle layer is 1,800 miles (2,900 km) deep and made up of oxygen, silicon, and magnesium.

Outer core
At 1,429 miles (2,300 km) deep, there is mainly molten iron, with nickel and sulfur.

Inner core
A solid core 745 miles (1,200 km) across is mostly iron and nickel.

Composition of Earth

Most of Earth's oxygen is locked up in minerals in Earth's crust, oxygen-based compounds form the mantle, and the heavy and dense elements iron and nickel occupy the core.

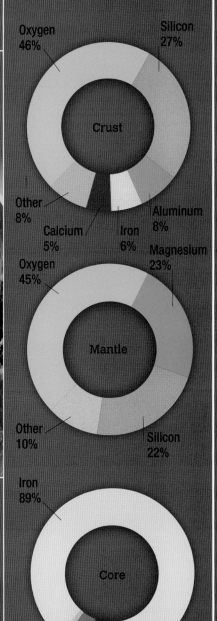

Crust
- Oxygen 46%
- Silicon 27%
- Other 8%
- Calcium 5%
- Iron 6%
- Aluminum 8%

Mantle
- Oxygen 45%
- Magnesium 23%
- Other 10%
- Silicon 22%

Core
- Iron 89%
- Other 1%
- Sulfur 4.5%
- Nickel 5.5%

Heat source

Some 44 trillion watts of heat continually flow from Earth's interior into space—vital heat that maintains life on our planet. Around 50 percent of this comes from the decay of radioactive elements such as uranium, potassium and thorium in the mantle. Uranium-238 and thorium-232 alone generate some 20 trillion watts.

Potassium metal

Melted crust

When large meteorites impacted the surface of early Earth, they blasted the crust, forming new materials such as glassy tektites, which are mainly silicon dioxide.

Tektites

HALOGENS

Halogen line-up

The five toxic halogens have distinctive colors. Iodine is a dark-gray crystalline solid, which when heated, gives off a purple vapor (left). Bromine is a dark red liquid that becomes an orange-brown vapor (center). Fluorine (right) is a pale yellow gas, and chlorine is a very pale green gas. Astatine is almost black and a solid, becoming a dark-colored vapor when it is heated.

These elements are very keen to combine with other elements, especially those on the left of the periodic table. They react vigorously with alkali metals and form strongly acidic compounds with hydrogen, from which simple salts can be made.

Mixed bunch

Elements in the halogen group have seven electrons in their outer shells. Iodine and astatine are solids, while bromine is liquid, and fluorine and chlorine are gases.

HALOGENS TIMELINE

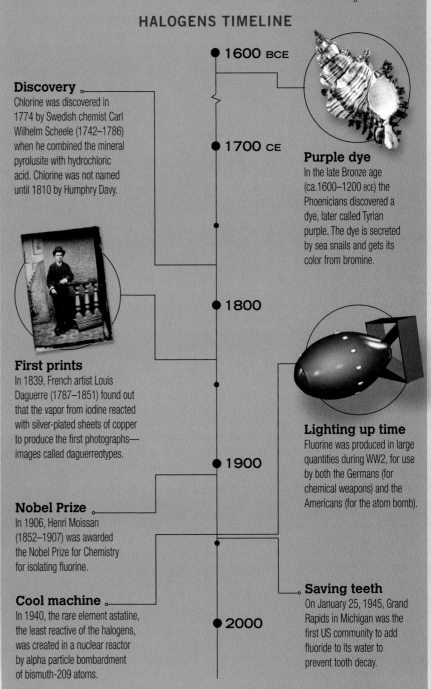

● 1600 BCE

● 1700 CE

● 1800

● 1900

● 2000

Discovery

Chlorine was discovered in 1774 by Swedish chemist Carl Wilhelm Scheele (1742–1786) when he combined the mineral pyrolusite with hydrochloric acid. Chlorine was not named until 1810 by Humphry Davy.

Purple dye

In the late Bronze age (ca.1600–1200 BCE) the Phoenicians discovered a dye, later called Tyrian purple. The dye is secreted by sea snails and gets its color from bromine.

First prints

In 1839, French artist Louis Daguerre (1787–1851) found out that the vapor from iodine reacted with silver-plated sheets of copper to produce the first photographs—images called daguerreotypes.

Lighting up time

Fluorine was produced in large quantities during WW2, for use by both the Germans (for chemical weapons) and the Americans (for the atom bomb).

Nobel Prize

In 1906, Henri Moissan (1852–1907) was awarded the Nobel Prize for Chemistry for isolating fluorine.

Cool machine

In 1940, the rare element astatine, the least reactive of the halogens, was created in a nuclear reactor by alpha particle bombardment of bismuth-209 atoms.

Saving teeth

On January 25, 1945, Grand Rapids in Michigan was the first US community to add fluoride to its water to prevent tooth decay.

FLUORINE

HALOGEN

9
F
18.998

This light yellow gas is so toxic that several chemists died trying to isolate it. It is also so reactive that metals can catch fire in it, and it explodes when mixed with hydrogen. It will take an electron from nearly any atom or molecule, which is why it forms so many compounds and is useful in medicine, plastics, and to create non-stick coatings. It is added to military combat uniforms and other clothing to repel water.

Atomic number: 9

Formula: F

Atomic weight: 18.998

State at 68°F (20°C): gas

Boiling point: −306.6°F (−188.11°C)

Melting point: −363.41°F (−219.67°C)

% in the Universe: 0.000040

% in Earth's crust: 0.054

% in Earth's oceans: 0.00013

% in humans: 0.0037

Uses: non-stick pans; plumber's tape; waterproof clothing and shoes; welding; etching and frosting glass; in the nuclear industry to refine uranium; toothpastes; added to drinking water; in refrigerators; industrial coolants and propellants; in rocket fuels

e9 | p9 | n10

Fluorine minerals
The main ore of fluorine is fluorite, although it is also extracted from other minerals including apatite and cryolite. Fluorite (above) is known for its incredible variety of colors from purple through blue, green, yellow, and pink to black and orange.

Glow in the dark
Many fluorite crystals glow violet-blue under ultraviolet light. This is because of the presence of europium ions. Others glow yellow because of the presence of yttrium.

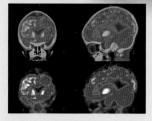

Tracking
Fluorine-18 is used in PET scans, which show how the body works. Fluorine-18 is a radioactive isotope that is added to the sugar molecules of glucose. When it is injected, it goes to the places where glucose is used for energy.

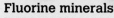

Strengthening teeth
Fluoride helps to prevent tooth decay, making teeth resistant to acid attacks from bacteria and sugar. It is added to many toothpastes and in many countries it is also added to the drinking water.

Toothpaste contains **fluorine** to protect **teeth** and **prevent decay**.

Non-stick
Your favorite frying pan is probably coated in polytetrafluoroethylene (PTFE), better know as Teflon. Compounds containing fluorine repel any other atoms that come near, so these pans become non-stick.

CHLORINE

HALOGEN

Chlorine gas is greenish yellow and smells like bleach. It is often used to keep swimming pools clean and safe by killing bacteria, germs, and algae. The element is very reactive and so is not found in its free form in nature as it quickly forms compounds with other elements— for example salt (sodium chloride). Our bodies need chlorine to help us digest food, move our muscles, and fight off germs.

Atomic number:	17
Formula:	Cl
Atomic weight:	35.453
State at 68°F (20°C):	gas
Boiling point:	−29.27°F (−34.04°C)
Melting point:	−150.7°F (−101.5°C)
% in the Universe:	0.00010
% in Earth's crust:	0.017
% in Earth's oceans:	2.0
% in humans:	0.2

Uses: in the past as chloroform and chemical weapons; as a disinfectant and sterilizer; to make PVC; as table salt; for dating ice and rock samples; bleaching; to fight infection and bacteria; medicine; textile, paints, and plastic manufacture; paper production; in the chemical industry

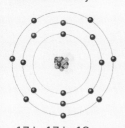

e17 I p17 I n18

Pure salt
Himalayan Pink Salt is much sought after because people believe it is the purest salt on Earth, although there is no proof of this. It is rock salt mined in the Punjab region of Pakistan, and is made up of more than 95 percent sodium chloride, but has larger crystals than table salt.

Clean water
Anyone who visits a swimming pool knows the familiar smell of chlorine in the water. It is used in swimming pools around the world to kill bacteria. And chlorine is added to many household cleaning products, such as bleaches and disinfectants.

Soothing frog
One of the poison dart frogs, *Epipedobates tricolor,* has a chlorine compound in its skin that acts as a very strong painkiller. The structure of the compound closely resembles nicotine, a natural compound with pain relief properties.

Plastic fantastic
One compound of chlorine is polyvinyl chloride, or PVC. This lightweight and strong plastic is widely used for many everyday things including window frames, car interiors, water pipes, and blood bags.

Yellow death
Chlorine gas is dangerous and very poisonous. On April 22, 1915, during the Second Battle of Ypres, the Germans fired 150 tons of chlorine gas at French, Canadian, and Algerian troops. Because it is heavier than air, the gas filled the foxholes and trenches, turning water in the soldiers' lungs to hydrochloric acid and causing over 1,000 deaths and many more casualties.

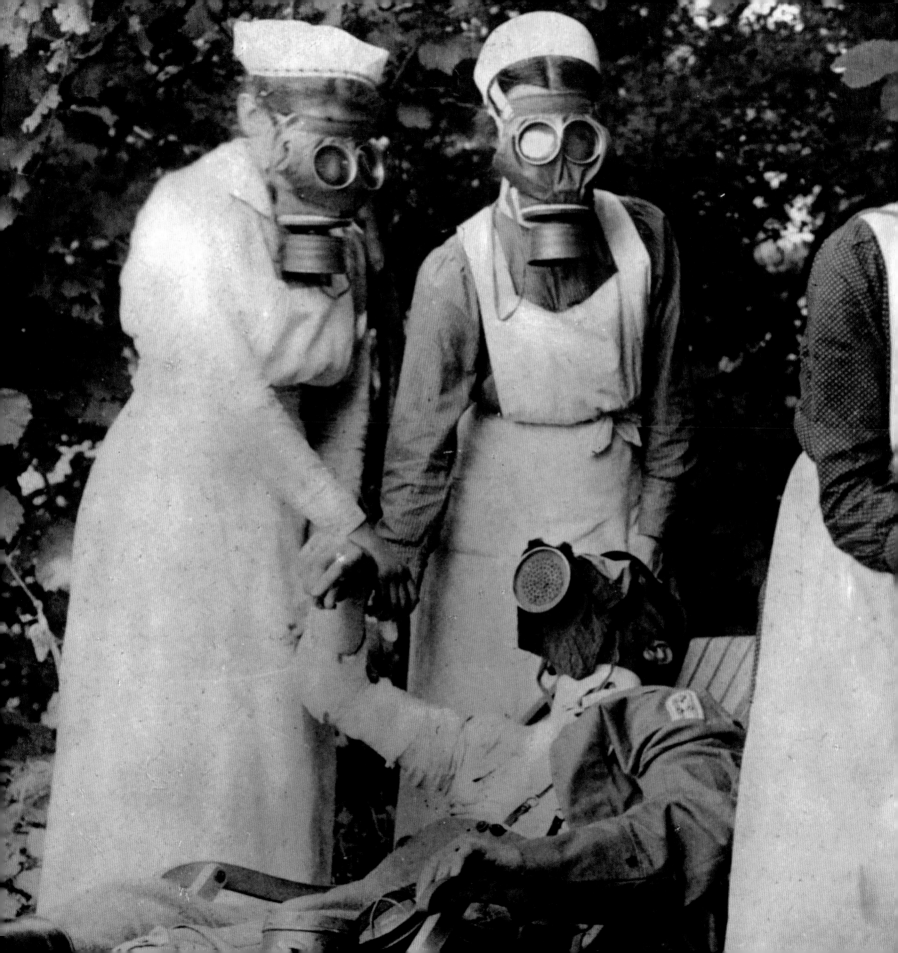

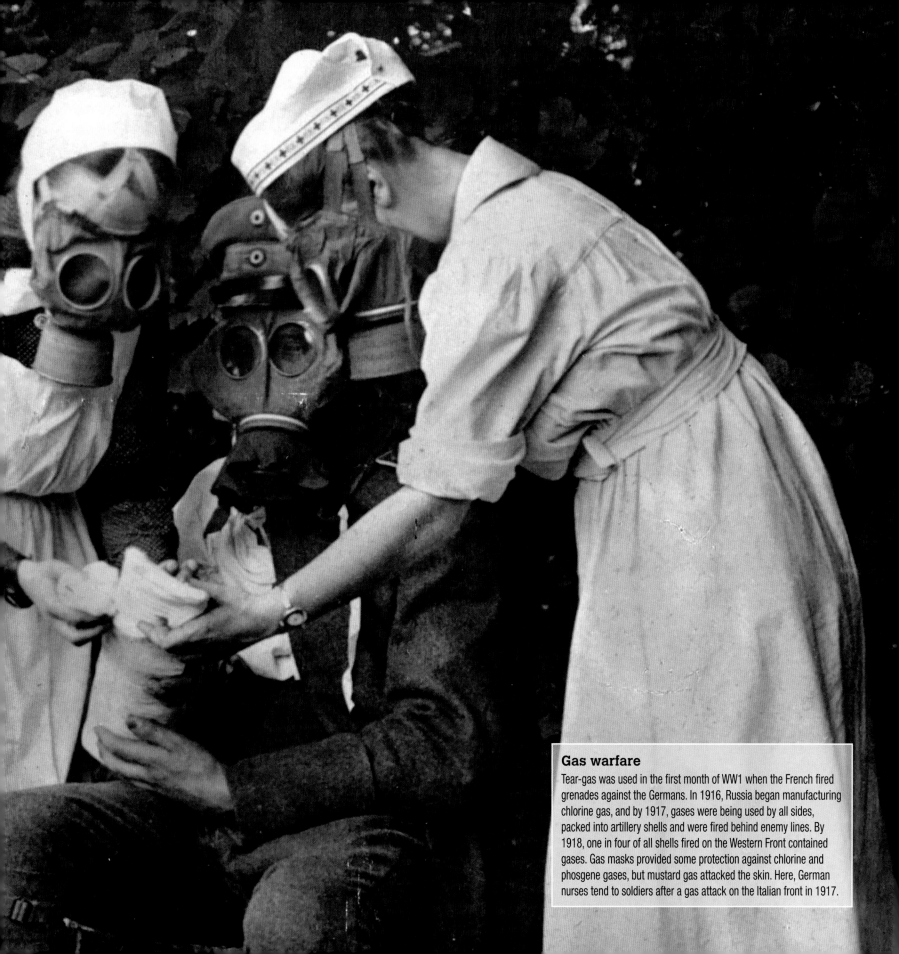

Gas warfare

Tear-gas was used in the first month of WW1 when the French fired grenades against the Germans. In 1916, Russia began manufacturing chlorine gas, and by 1917, gases were being used by all sides, packed into artillery shells and were fired behind enemy lines. By 1918, one in four of all shells fired on the Western Front contained gases. Gas masks provided some protection against chlorine and phosgene gases, but mustard gas attacked the skin. Here, German nurses tend to soldiers after a gas attack on the Italian front in 1917.

35
Br
79.904

BROMINE

What is that horrible smell? It could be bromine, named after the Greek *bromos*, meaning "stench." We are rarely far from it, for it dissolves easily in water and so is found in oceans, lakes, and springs. Once vital to make purple dye for rich Romans, it has been a disinfectant and fire limiter, but is used less and less today because it damages the ozone layer in the atmosphere, which protects Earth by absorbing most of the ultraviolet radiation of the Sun.

Atomic number:	35

Formula: Br

Atomic weight: 79.904

State at 68°F (20°C): solid

Boiling point: 137.8°F (58.8°C)

Melting point: 19°F (−7.2°C)

% in the Universe: 0.00000070

% in Earth's crust: 0.00030

% in Earth's oceans: 0.0067

% in humans: 0.00029

Uses: agricultural chemicals; insecticides; pharmaceuticals; flame retardants; furniture foam; gasoline; plastic casings for electronics; halon fire extinguishers (now not used in some countries); dyes; film photography; to purify water; in medicines; in sanitizers

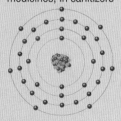

e35 | p35 | n45

The **oceans** contain more than **one trillion tons** of the **toxic** and **oily** element **bromine**.

Dead Sea source
Today, the element is extracted from bromine-rich salts in seawater. The Dead Sea in the Middle East has the highest concentration of bromine in the world. Seawater is drawn off into an enormous network of evaporation ponds (above), before being put through a chemical process to extract the bromine.

Early find
Bromine turns seaweed red. In 1978, 24 species of red and green seaweeds from the Sea of Japan were tested by scientists. They determined that a brilliant green color is a result of the iodine content, while the red seaweeds were shown to be rich in bromine.

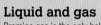

Liquid and gas
Bromine gas is the only halogen that becomes liquid at room temperature. In fact, the only other element that does this is mercury *(see pp.96–97)*. Here, the gas form coexists with its liquid form at the bottom. The gas is toxic, and the liquid can cause serious burns. The liquid is used for fumigants and photographic chemicals.

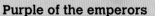

Purple of the emperors
Tyrian purple was the color used for the togas of the imperial family in ancient Rome. It is a natural dye extracted from murex sea snails. They collected the snails by the thousands and boiled them for days in lead-lined vats. It was not until the early 1900s that scientists discovered that the color was caused by bromine.

IODINE

HALOGEN

Iodine is a shiny black solid at room temperature, but when heated will change to a purplish gas, and it is named after the Greek word, *iodes*, for this color. We need it to help control growth and body temperature. It is a powerful disinfectant—on open wounds it kills bacteria.

Atomic number: 53

Formula: I

Atomic weight: 126.904

State at 68°F (20°C): solid

Boiling point: 363.9°F (184.4°C)

Melting point: 236.7°F (113.7°C)

Uses: disinfectants; laundry starches; printing inks and dyes; catalysts; feed supplements; photographic chemicals; acetic acid manufacturing; polarizing filters for LCDs; medical uses; table salt

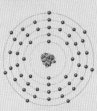

e53 | p53 | n74

Taken by mouth
In 1829, a French doctor developed Lugol's Solution, or Lugol's Iodine, as a medication and disinfectant that is still sold today.

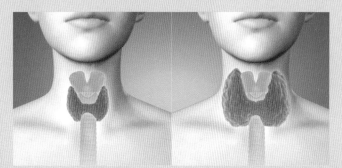

Making hormones
Iodine is vital to all of us. The element is channelled to the thyroid gland where it is stored until it is needed for the production of hormones, which are necessary for all the cells in the body to work. If there is not enough iodine in someone's diet, this can lead to an enlarged thyroid (above right).

Early prints
Daguerreotypes, an early photographic process, were introduced to the world in 1839 by their inventor, Louis Daguerre. A silver plate was polished and then exposed to the vapors of iodine and bromine. The silver bromide and silver iodide reacted to light and turned black.

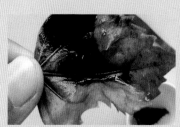

Starch test
Iodine is used to test for starch, and will turn something blue-black in color if there is starch present. Plants store glucose, which includes starch, fats, and oils. Wheat, rice, corn, oats, barley, and potatoes are particularly rich in starch.

Atomic number: 85

Formula: At

Atomic weight: [210]

State at 68°F (20°C): solid

Boiling point: 662°F (350°C)

Melting point: 572°F (300°C)

% anywhere: none

Half-life: 8.1 hours

Uses: only in research

e85 | p85 | n125

ASTATINE

HALOGEN

Highly radioactive astatine, isolated in 1940 after a very long search, is one of the rarest elements on Earth. It gets its name from the Greek *astatos*, for "unstable," and occurs as a decay product of heavier elements.

TENNESSINE

HALOGEN

On April 5, 2010, scientists in Russia and the United States announced the creation of tennessine. They bombarded atoms of berkelium with ions of calcium until a few atoms of the new element were produced.

Atomic number: 117

Formula: Ts

Atomic weight: [294]

State at 68°F (20°C): solid

Boiling point: unknown

Melting point: unknown

% anywhere: none

Uses: only in research

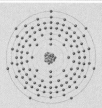

e117 | p117 | n177

NOBLE GASES

Bright lights
Used in advertising signs, neon glows in a shaped tube that has electrodes at either end. When the power is switched on, some of the atoms lose electrons to become positively charge ions. The charged ions and electrons carry the current between the tube's electrodes, giving off photons of bright light. Different colors are made by painting the glass with chemicals.

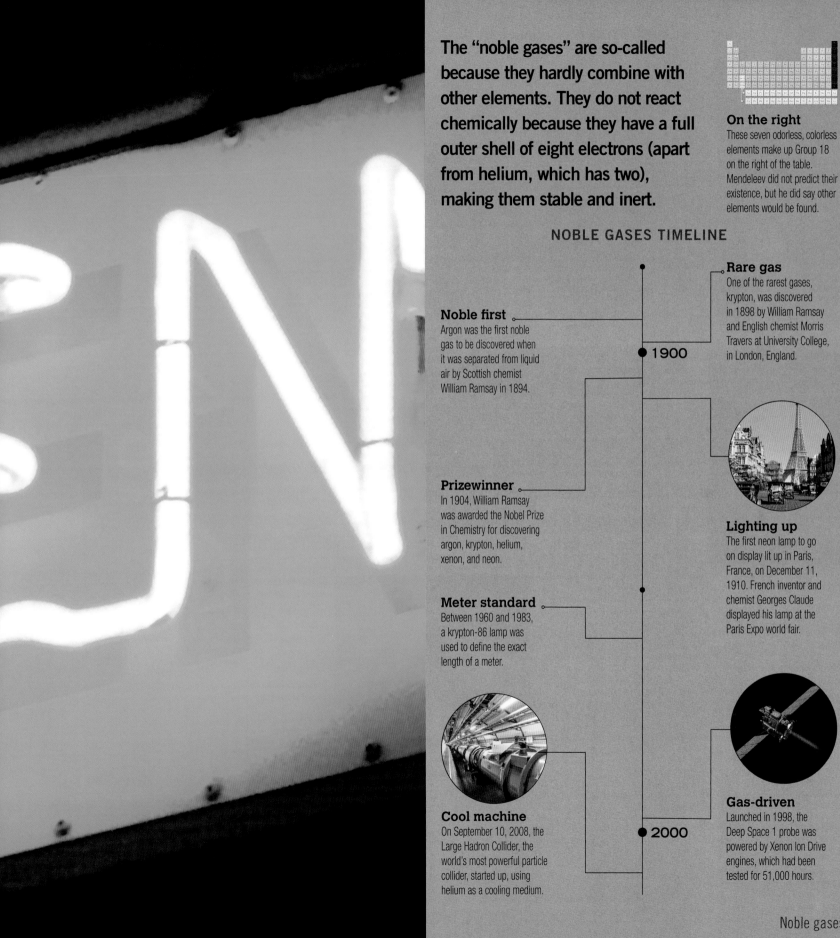

The "noble gases" are so-called because they hardly combine with other elements. They do not react chemically because they have a full outer shell of eight electrons (apart from helium, which has two), making them stable and inert.

On the right
These seven odorless, colorless elements make up Group 18 on the right of the table. Mendeleev did not predict their existence, but he did say other elements would be found.

NOBLE GASES TIMELINE

Rare gas
One of the rarest gases, krypton, was discovered in 1898 by William Ramsay and English chemist Morris Travers at University College, in London, England.

Noble first
Argon was the first noble gas to be discovered when it was separated from liquid air by Scottish chemist William Ramsay in 1894.

● 1900

Prizewinner
In 1904, William Ramsay was awarded the Nobel Prize in Chemistry for discovering argon, krypton, helium, xenon, and neon.

Lighting up
The first neon lamp to go on display lit up in Paris, France, on December 11, 1910. French inventor and chemist Georges Claude displayed his lamp at the Paris Expo world fair.

Meter standard
Between 1960 and 1983, a krypton-86 lamp was used to define the exact length of a meter.

Cool machine
On September 10, 2008, the Large Hadron Collider, the world's most powerful particle collider, started up, using helium as a cooling medium.

● 2000

Gas-driven
Launched in 1998, the Deep Space 1 probe was powered by Xenon Ion Drive engines, which had been tested for 51,000 hours.

HELIUM

NOBLE GAS

Helium keeps party balloons up and inhaling this gas makes your voice sound squeaky, but its main use is more serious. Liquid helium at −516°F (−269°C) cools superconducting magnets in MRI scanners to help doctors look inside our bodies. Weirdly, scientists knew helium was in the Sun before they realized it was also here on Earth!

High flier
Helium is the second lightest element in the Universe and lighter than air, so helps balloons and airships to rise. Half the world's reserves are stored in a disused gasfield near Amarillo in Texas.

Atomic number: 2

Formula: He

Atomic weight: 4.002602

State at 68°F (20°C): gas

Boiling point: −452.07°F (−268.928°C)

Melting point: unknown

% in the Universe: 23

% in Earth's crust: 0.00000055

% in Earth's oceans: 0.00000000072

% in humans: none

Uses: as a cooling medium for the Large Hadron Collider, in MRI scanners, and in satellites, and spacecraft; to fill balloons and airships; in the manufacture of fiber-optics and semiconductors; deep-sea diving apparatus; lasers; microscopes; for electric arc welding

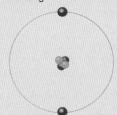

e2 | p2 | n2

Inert atmosphere
Helium is inert, it does not react with anything. This makes it perfect to help create a safe atmosphere for welding. In all electric arc welding, the electrode, the molten metal, and any other heat-affected metal parts must be protected from oxygen in the surrounding air.

Sun observation
Helium's name comes from the Greek *helios*, which means "Sun." This is apt because the gas was identified by a yellow line in the solar spectrum observed in 1868 by astronomer Pierre Janssen.

Deep-sea diving
The usual mixture of air for divers is oxygen and nitrogen. However, for deep dives, helium is added to reduce both the amount of oxygen (to avoid oxygen toxicity), and the amount of nitrogen (to avoid nitrogen narcosis). The deeper the dive the more helium is used, and the less oxygen and nitrogen.

Helium was first **found** on **Earth** in **gases** leaking from **Mount Vesuvius**.

NEON

NOBLE GAS

The scientists who isolated neon knew they had succeeded when they saw "a blaze of crimson light from the tube," which is why neon tubes are mostly used for brightly lit street signs and advertisements. Neon is the fifth most common element in the Universe, but it is quite rare on Earth. It has many different uses, however, including in televisions, and helium-neon lasers. And bright red aircraft beams that penetrate fog are neon lights.

10
Ne
20.180

Atomic number: 10

Formula: Ne

Atomic weight: 20.1797

State at 68°F (20°C): gas

Boiling point: −410.883°F (−246.046°C)

Melting point: −415.46°F (−248.59°C)

% in the Universe: 0.13

% in Earth's crust: 0.00000030

% in Earth's oceans: 0.000000012

% in humans: none

Uses: fluorescent tubes; lightning arrestors for protection; switching gear; lightning protection; deep-sea diving; helium-neon lasers; television tubes; plasma tubes and balls; wave meter tubes; aircraft and aircraft beacons for fogs

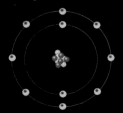

e10 | p10 | n10

True color
We call all lit-up street signs "neon," but only the bright red or reddish-orange signs are true neon. The other colors are made by different noble gases, or the tubes have been coated with a different color.

Bright name
Neon is so much part of our vocabulary that a freshwater fish, *Paracheirodon innesi*, is called the neon tetra. It gets this name because of its iridescent metallic blue and red stripes.

AVOID EXPOSURE
LASER LIGHT IS EMITTED
FROM THIS APERTURE

Twin-gas laser
Helium-neon lasers are the most common and inexpensive of all the lasers. They are used among other things for barcode scanners in supermarkets and shops, to align tools, and to analyze blood.

Noble dome
The fascinating dancing lights of a plasma ball are created by arcs of light trying to make their way from the center to the edge. The clear glass ball is full of a mixture of noble gases, often including neon, and there is a high-voltage electrode at its center. When you put your hand on the glass, the plasma will snake toward it because you are creating a discharge path that has less resistance than the gases and glass.

Neon **does not** form **compounds** with **other elements** or **react** **to** any **other substance**.

ARGON

NOBLE GAS

Argon is named for the Greek for "lazy" because it is so inactive. This makes it handy, like helium, for creating an inert and safe atmosphere for arc welding, where oxygen would explode. It is also used in lightbulbs, inside double-glazed window units because it conducts heat badly, and in laser eye surgery.

Atomic number: 18

Formula: Ar

Atomic weight: 39.948

State at 68°F (20°C): gas

Boiling point: −302.526°F (−185.848°C)

Melting point: −308.81°F (−189.34°C)

Uses: welding; lightbulbs and

fluorescent tubes; double-glazing; steel manufacture; dating minerals

e18 | p18 | n22

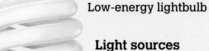

Low-energy lightbulb

Light sources
Argon is used in all types of lightbulb. It is inert and so will not oxidize even at high temperatures. It stops the oxygen in the lightbulbs from corroding the hot tungsten filament, which means that the lightbulbs last longer.

Fluorescent lightbulb

Dating rocks
Archeologists and geologists use potassium-argon dating (K-Ar dating) to find out about very old rocks. Potassium-40 decays to argon-40. By comparing the K-40 with the Ar-40 in a rock sample, and knowing the rate of decay, they can work out the date.

Argon and steel-making
Argon is an important industrial gas that is used in particular for the manufacture of steel in foundries. It is blown through the molten metal to purify it, and also helps prevent oxidation of the hot metals.

KRYPTON

NOBLE GAS

When William Ramsay and Morris William Travers spotted orange and green lines in the slowly evaporating purified liquid argon they were studying, they knew they had isolated a new element. Its name is Greek for "hidden," as it had been so hard to find.

Atomic number: 36

Formula: Kr

Atomic weight: 83.798

State at 68°F (20°C): gas

Boiling point: −244.147°F (−153.415°C)

Melting point: −251.27°F (−157.37°C)

Uses: fluorescent

lights; flash lamps for cameras; lasers; to date ice cores and groundwater; in flashing lights on airport runways

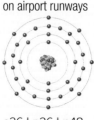

e36 | p36 | n48

Nuclear monitor
The isotope krypton-85 can be used to monitor for other radioactive elements such as plutonium. It was used by Western powers during the Cold War (1945–1990) to estimate Soviet nuclear production. Here, in 1963, a rocket is paraded through Moscow's Red Square.

Fictional planet
Krypton inspired the name "kryptonite" for the made-up material that weakens Superman. The reason Superman arrives on Earth is that his home planet Krypton has been destroyed. Krypton the element is actually a bit of a hero because it is in the powerful flashing runway lights that guide planes back to earth, even in fog.

Standard measure
Between 1960 and 1983, the meter measurement was officially defined by the wavelength of krypton-86. The definition was 1,650,763.73 wavelengths of orange-red light in a vacuum produced by burning the element.

XENON

54

Xe

131.293

NOBLE GAS

Xenon is an unusual noble gas because it will make chemical compounds. Its uses vary from being a very safe anesthetic, and giving car headlights a blue glow, to helping push spacecraft and satellites into position.

Atomic number: 54

Formula: Xe

Atomic weight: 131.293

State at 68°F (20°C): gas

Boiling point: −162.578°F (−108.099°C)

Melting point: −169.15°F (−111.75°C)

Uses: flash bulbs; sunbed lamps; food processing; ruby lasers; to etch microprocessors; in satellites; in nuclear energy; in cancer treatment

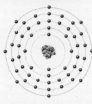

e54 | p54 | n77

Space power
Xenon is the best propellant for ion thrusters, the engines that are used to keep satellites in their correct orbit and spacecraft into the correct place. Here, NASA's NSTAR ion thruster is being tested for the Deep Space 1 probe which was launched in 1998.

Bright light
Xenon's bright light comes in useful in many ways. It is found in high-speed flashbulbs employed by professional photographers, in sunbed lamps, and in bactericidal lamps that are used in food preparation and processing.

Hidden store?
Recent research has suggested that there may be xenon trapped beneath our feet. Scientists have proved that xenon is capable of binding with other materials, and may have been absorbed by minerals such as perovskite.

Practical use
Xenon is used in a variety of ways. It is in high-pressure arc lamps that provide ultraviolet light for tanning beds (above). It is used as an anesthetic and for medical images, as well as to sterilize surfaces, for example in laboratories.

RADON

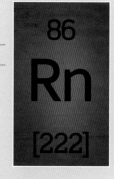

86

Rn

[222]

NOBLE GAS

Radioactive radon is produced as a result of the decay of uranium and thorium. As it is such a heavy gas, it can gather dangerously in low-lying areas such as basements. If it is cooled beyond its freezing point of −96°F (−71°C), it glows yellow, turning orange if chilled further.

Atomic number: 86

Formula: Rn

Atomic weight: [222]

Boiling point: −79.1°F (61.7°C)

Melting point: −96°F (−71°C)

% in the Universe: almost none

% in Earth's crust: none

% in Earth's oceans: almost none

% in humans: none

Half-life: 14.6 hours

Uses: research

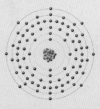

e86 | p86 | n136

Everywhere in nature
Radon is formed by the radioactive decay of uranium-238. The uranium is found naturally in soils, rocks, and underground water sources, particularly in areas that are rich in granite. In the open air, radon does not cause problems.

OGANESSON

118

Og

[294]

NOBLE GAS

This synthetic element is made in a particle accelerator where heavy ions are crashed together for months, eventually creating a few atoms that rapidly decay. It is thought to be a noble gas, similar to radon.

Atomic number: 118

Formula: Og

Atomic weight: [294]

Boiling point: unknown

Melting point: unknown

% in the Universe: none

% in Earth's crust: none

% in Earth's oceans: none

% in humans: none

Half-life: 9 seconds

Uses: research

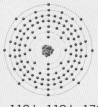

e118 | p118 | n176

The colors of night

Cities all over the world are lit up at night, but few are more colorful than Kowloon, Hong Kong, famous for signs made with red and orange neon, yellow helium, blue mercury, and a myriad of other chemical colors. Hong Kong is known as a city that never sleeps, and this area of the city is as bright as day right through the night. Many craftsmen are kept busy creating the neon signs on the shopfronts that are surrounded by dazzling light displays and changing colors on the skyscrapers and other tall structures that tower above.

acid
A chemical that is corrosive and is soluble in water, turning blue litmus paper red. Acids neutralize alkalis.

algae
Plantlike organisms that usually grow in water, and have no roots, stems, or leaves.

alkali
A substance that dissolves in water and neutralizes acids; the chemical opposite of an acid.

allotrope
One of two or more distinct forms of the same element that have different properties but are the same state of matter (solid, liquid, or gas). Diamond and graphite are solid allotropes of carbon.

alloy
A mixture of metals, or a mixture of a metal with an element.

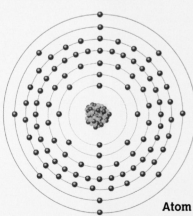

Atom

atmosphere
The layer of mixed gases that surround a planet, star, or moon.

atom
The basic part of an element. Atoms are made up of smaller particles: electrons, protons, and neutrons.

atomic number
The number of protons in the nucleus of an atom.

bacteria
Single-celled organisms, some of which cause diseases. Most bacteria can only be seen with a microscope.

base
The chemical opposite of acid. Bases react with acids to form salts.

catalyst
A substance that increases the rate of a chemical reaction without itself undergoing any permanent chemical change.

cell
The basic unit of all living things except viruses.

chain reaction
A nuclear reaction that splits the nucleus of an atom, releasing neutrons that then split the nuclei of other atoms.

cholorphyll
The green chemical in plants that absorbs the energy from sunlight and gives the leaves their green color.

compound
A substance made of two or more elements that are bonded, or linked, together chemically.

conductivity
The ability or power of a material that allows heat or electricity to pass through it.

corrosion
The chemical breakdown of the surface of a metal.

crystal
A clear, transparent mineral; a solid body that has a regular shape in which plane faces intersect at definite angles, due to the regular internal structure of its atoms, ions, or molecules.

DNA
The double spiral-shaped molecule found in the nucleus of every one of the cells in a living body. It contains all the genetic instructions the body needs to grow and develop. DNA stands for *deoxyribonucleic acid*.

ecosystem
A community of plants and animals that live in a particular place, and

Diatomic element

depend on each other for survival. In an ecosystem each organism has a part to play.

electron
A negatively charged particle that orbits the nucleus of an atom.

electromagnet
A coil of wire, usuallly with a metal core and commonly made of soft iron, which becomes magnetic when an electric current flows through the coil.

electronics
Relating to electrons. A scientific investigation of how electrons move through materials; electronic devices or equipment.

element
A substance which is made of only one type of atom.

enzyme
Any chemical from a living thing which changes the speed of a chemical reaction without being used up itself.

evaporate

To change from liquid into a gas or vapor.

fertilizer

A manure or chemical that is added to the soil to help the growth of plants.

fission

The splitting of heavy atomic nuclei to form two lighter ones. Energy is released in the process.

fluorescence

The giving off of colored light by an object when it is viewed in ultraviolet light.

fossil fuel

Fuel such as coal, crude oil, or natural gas, that are made from the remains of dead plants and animals. When fossil fuels burn completely, they combine with oxygen and release stored carbon as carbon dioxide gas.

fusion

The combining of very light atomic nuclei to form a heavier nucleus. Energy is released in the process.

gas

A state of matter in which the atoms are free to move around, enabling the substance to fill any container in which it is placed.

generator

An engine that converts mechanical energy into electrical energy.

glucose

The simplest form of sugar. Glucose in food is broken down in the body of living things to release energy.

gravity

The force that pulls everything toward the center of Earth, making objects fall and giving them weight.

half-life

The time it takes for half of the atoms in a sample of a radioactive element to decay; the time taken for the count-rate from a radioactive sample to halve.

hemoglobin

An oxygen-carrying, iron-containing protein found in red blood cells.

hydrocarbon

A compound containing only carbon and hydrogen atoms. Most are found in crude oil.

inert

Describes an element that does not tend to react with other elements to form a compound.

infrared

Relating to low-frequency waves of electromagnetic energy. Infrared radiation is felt as heat.

Carbon (coal)

GLOSSARY

Halogen (iodine)

ion
An atom that has either lost or gained at least one electron so that it is positively (+) or negatively (–) charged.

iridescent
Describes when something reflects light, producing a rainbowlike display of colors; varying in color when seen in different lights or from different angles.

isotope
Different versions of the atoms of one element. They have the same numbers of electrons and protons, but different numbers of neutrons.

laser
An intense, focused beam of light used for welding, surgery, astronomy, and much more. Laser stands for *Light Amplification by Stimulated Emission of Radiation*.

light-year
The distance traveled by light in one Earth year. One light-year is equivalent to 5.9 million million miles (9.5 million million km).

liquid
A state of matter between solid and gas. A liquid can flow, and it will always take the shape of its container.

magnet
A substance or object that attracts iron, cobalt, nickel, gadolinium, and their alloys.

magnetism
Having the power to attract objects made or iron or steel, or force them away. A magnet does not have to touch an object to pull it.

magnetosphere
An area of space surrounding a planet or star that is dominated by the planet or star's magnetic field.

meteorite
A fragment of rock from outer space that reaches Earth's surface instead of completely burning up in the atmosphere.

microchip
A collection of microscopic electronic circuits on a small piece of semiconductor material such as silicon.

microscope
An optical instrument that has a magnifying lens or combination of lenses to see objects that are too small to be seen clearly with the naked eye.

mineral
A naturally occurring solid compound whose atoms are ordered in crystal patterns. Many rocks are made of minerals.

mitochondria
The part of a cell in which energy is released from the cell in order to carry out chemical reactions.

molecule
A group of atoms bonded together so that they act as a single particle. The number of atoms in a molecule can be from as few as two to many thousands.

MRI scanner
A machine that provides detailed images of sections of the human body that are used for medical diagnosis. MRI stands for *Magnetic Resonance Imaging*.

nanotechnology
Technology that manipulated individual molecules and atoms to create microscopic devices.

native element
A mineral that consists of a single chemical element that is not combined with other substances.

nebula
A cloud of gas and dust in space.

neutron
A particle that has no electrical charge, slightly bigger than a proton. There are neutrons in the nuclei of all atoms except those of hydrogen.

non-reactive
Unlikely or unable to react chemically.

nuclear
Relating to the nucleus, or core, of an atom.

nuclear reaction
A nuclear reaction is caused when the structure of an atomic nucleus is altered through the release of energy or by being broken apart.

nucleus
The positively charged central area of an atom, composed of neutrons and protons, and most of the mass.

ore
A metal-bearing mineral or rock that can be mined.

organism
Any living thing; for example, an animal, plant, or microbe.

oxidation
The combination of a substance with oxygen; the removal of hydrogen from a substance; the loss of electrons from an atom.

ozone
A colorless gas that is an unstable, poisonous allotrope of oxygen.

particle
A tiny part, such as an atom or molecule, that makes up matter.

particle accelerator
A machine that uses magnets to accelerate particles around a track. Collisions between the particles release huge amounts of energy and sometimes create new particles or elements.

photoelectric cells
An electronic device that is used to detect light in cameras and night-vision apparatus, and to generate electrical power in solar cells.

photosynthesis
The process by which plants use the energy in sunlight to make food (glucose sugar) from carbon dioxide and water. Oxygen is released as a by-product.

pigment
A coloring matter or substance.

Organic molecule (vitamin B8)

Pyrite crystals (iron sulfide)

GLOSSARY

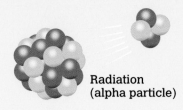

Radiation
(alpha particle)

pollution
The introduction of harmful substances into the environment.

properties
The characteristic qualities of a material or substance.

protein
Substances used in building the bodies of all living things. They have chainlike molecules formed from carbon, hydrogen, oxygen, and nitrogen, and often sulfur as well.

proton
A positively charge particle found in the nucleus of an atom.

radiation
Anything that radiates from its source. It could be waves, such as light or sound, or it could be a beam of invisible particles, such as neutrons.

radioactive decay
The natural breakup of atomic nuclei in radioactive elements.

radioactivity
The emission of nuclear radiation.

reactive
Describes an element or compound that combines chemically with another element or compound.

recycle
To treat or process waste material to make it suitable for reuse.

rust
A type of corrosion that happens when iron comes into contact with oxygen and water.

semiconductor
A material whose electrical conductivity is between that of a metal and a nonmetal. Semiconductors are often made of metalloid compounds.

smelting
Extracting metal from its ore by heating the ore in a furnace.

solar cell
A photoelectric cell that converts sunlight into electrical energy.

solid
A state of matter in which the particles are packed tightly together so they are unable to move about very much.

Tin

sonar
A device for locating objects underwater by echolocation, the use of reflected sound waves.

supernova
A huge explosion that takes place when a star has used up all of its fuel and collapses.

synthetic
Describes an element that is created artificially—made inside nuclear reactors and particle accelerators.

tissue
A collection of living cells inside the body of a living thing.

ultraviolet radiation
Invisible electromagnetic waves with wavelengths that are shorter than wavelengths of visible light and longer than those of X-rays.

X-ray
A high-frequency wave of electromagnetic energy that is absorbed by body tissues, so is used in medicine to produce images of the inside of the body.

GLOSSARY

A

Aluminum can

B

(continued)

C

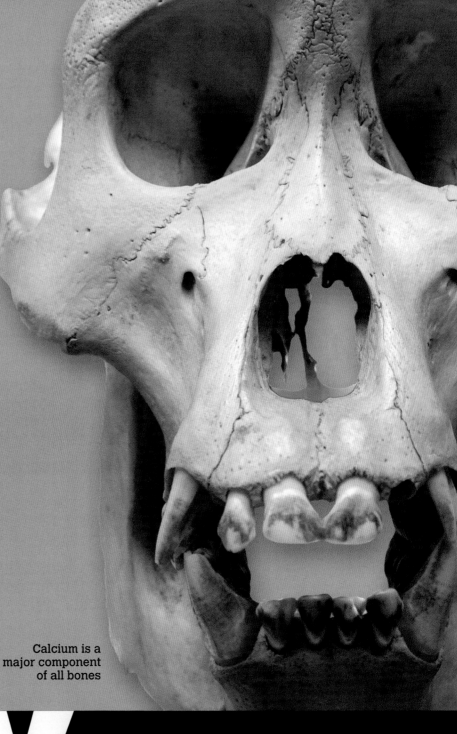

**Calcium is a
major component
of all bones**

INDEX

Humphry Davy

Meteorite

**Magnetite,
an ore of iron**

INDEX

Phosphorite

**Uraninite
(uranium ore)**

Zinc nugget

INDEX

ACKNOWLEDGMENTS

Photos ©: 123RF: 98 center right (antvlk), 104 center right (Borislav Marinic), 12 bottom center (vadim0001), 98 bottom left (gors4730), 143 center bottom left (mikewaters), 110 bottom center (Moreno Soppelsa), 189 center bottom right (Panu Puaktungyai), 111 top right (Petr Levicek), 203 right (Ruslan Gilmanshin), 23 bottom left (sergiitrofymchuk), 118 bottom center (Tom Grundy); Åke Dahllöf: 74 center left top; Alamy Images: 186-187 (akg-images), 156-157 (Buiten-Beeld), back cover jar of chlorine (By Ian Miles-Flashpoint Pictures), 38-39 (Chronicle), 93 bottom center left bottom (Cindy Hopkins), 70 center right (Danita Delimont), 94-95 (Danita Delimont), 91 left (dpa picture alliance), 75 bottom center (GL Archive), 145 top right (INTERFOTO), 100 (ITAR-TASS Photo Agency), 134-135 (Jamie Pham), 92 (Niels Poulsen mus), 93 bottom center left top (Pictorial Press Ltd), 8-9 background (robertharding), 61 center left (Sabena Jane Blackbird), 115 (Science History Images), 182-183 (sciencephotos); American Bicycle Group/Dan Henry: 55 center left; AP Images: 127 bottom right (Alistair Fuller), 140-141 background (Kyodo), 194 bottom left; Bapty: 50-51 helmet, 118 top center right; Bigstock/vvoevale: 53 right; CERN: 64-65; Denis Skov: 11 lithium and throughout, 75 center right, 181 bottom left; Dreamstime: 66 top right (Alisonh29), 50 top center right (Andra Cerar), 54 center left bottom (Anton Starikov), 192 bottom (Bbbar), 125 bottom right (Belliot), 74 bottom left, 123 center left, 142 center right (Björn Wylezich), 138 center left (Chrisp543), 33 center (Christian Weiß), 113 center left (Chuyu), 113 bottom center (Dekanaryas), 71 center (dgstudio), 87 top right (Dr Ajay Kumar Singh), 50 center right (Farbled), 107 top right (Fibobjects), 141 center right (Georgios Kollidas), 83 center bottom (Grafphotogpaher), 128-129 background (Hungchungchih), 76 center left (Ihsan Gercelman), 96 center top (Iosif Yurlov), 48-49 (Ivanru), 12 bottom center right, 103 top right (Izanbar), back cover molten metal (Jatuporn79), 28 bottom (Ken Backer), 104 center left (Krishnadas Chandrasekharan), back cover DNA (Kts), cover bottom center right (Luciano Mortula), 136 bottom left (Mylightscapes), 113 bottom right (Nomadsoul1), 113 top left (Paul Cowan), back cover Hindenburg, 21 top left (Picturemakerslc), 159 center bottom right (Rainer Walter Schmied), 176 center left (Richard Lammerts), 67 bottom center left (Richie Lomba), 41 center (Rizami Annuar), 45 bottom (Steve Allen), 84 bottom left (Steve Mann), 33 bottom left (Steven Corton), cover spine shell (Tentenenn), 61 center (Thomas Langlands), back cover beans (Tvk888), 77 top center (Typhoonski), 42 (Vesna Njagulj), 67 bottom center right (Vladyslav Danilin), 124-125 rock (Wlad74), 70 bottom (Xing Wang), 158 center bottom (Yinghua), 200 left (Yury Shirokov); Energy.gov/ORNL: 132 bottom left; Fotolia: 131 top left (aerostato), 50 top center left (aleks-p), 85 center (alinamd), 83 bottom center (andrea lehmkuhl), 83 bottom left (antiksu), 175 center (arhendrix), 59 bottom right (aterrom), 171 center right (bennyartist), 18 center right, 104 bottom, 109 bottom left (Björn Wylezich), 113 center top (Carolina K Smith MD), 171 top center left (crevis), 136 center left (dechevm), 171 top center right (Dmitry Knorre), 50 bottom left, 67 center left bottom, 96 center bottom (Eduardo Estellez), 55 center top (edwardolive), 33 center right bottom (enskanto), 50 center top right (epitavi), 185 bottom left (Eric Isselée), 191 center right (Ericus), 113 center right (euthymia), 51 center top, 67 bottom left (farbled_01), 176 bottom (forcdan), 176-177 (Foto-Ruhrgebiet), 83 center left bottom (Freely), 27 center right top, 76 bottom right (Georgios Kollidas), 12 bottom right (Glevalex), 113 bottom left (goldpix), 174-175 bottom spread (hammann1982), 53 top (Herschel Hoffmeyer), 89 top left (ikonacolor), 159 bottom left (isavira), 19 bottom, 26 bottom (isoarska), 18 top right (jonnysek), 149 bottom left (josefkubes), 35 bottom right (Juulijs), 192 center (Kadmy), 54 center left top (magnaphotography), 33 top right (maksim_e), 19 top center, 158 bottom center (marcel), 66 bottom right (Margrit Hirsch), 25 right (Marina), 150 bottom left (masakato11), 13 center left (McCarthys_PhotoWorks), 18 center (merial), 137 center (michaelvaulin), 169 top right (Miyuki Satake), 106 bottom right (MR), 131 bottom right (nikolayn), 12 bottom center left inset (nspooner), 27 center left bottom (Only Fabrizio), 27 center right bottom (orion_eff), 12 bottom center left background (Pecold), 130-131 stone (Reload Studio), 54 center right bottom (Rob Byron), 12 top right (robertharding), 71 center right bottom (seagames50), 27 bottom right (Sergiy Serdyuk), 51 center (sumire8), 86-87 lightbulb (trekandphoto), 18 bottom center left (udonsook), 50 center bottom right (Uros Petrovic), 51 center bottom, 59 center right (uw images), back cover chrome nugget (uwimages), 109 top right (Velizar Gordeev), 71 bottom right (Vidady), 18 center top, 18 bottom center right, 33 center right top, 35 center top, 50 center, 55 center bottom (vvoe), 71 top right (yongkiet), cover top center left (zole4); Getty Images: 80-81 (Miguel Sotomayor), 172-173 (Tui De Roy/Minden Pictures), 102-103 background (Westend61); Harvard Library/NASA/CXC/Rutgers/J.Hughes et al.: 145 top left; HI4PI/Benjamin Winkel: 20-21 background; IC International: 142 center left; iStockphoto: 125 bottom left (13160449), 28 center top (4X-image), 171 center right top, 206 left (A_Pobedimskiy), 90 center right (AarreRinne), 144 bottom, 206 right (abadonian), 165 center right (acilo), 89 bottom right (Adam88xx), 27 center left top (adamkaz), 149 center left (AdShooter), 61 top left, 195 bottom left (adventtr), 109 center top (akova), cover bolt, 84 center left (alacatr), 93 bottom left bottom, 143 center top (Alan_Lagadu), 109 top center (Alessandro2802), 83 bottom right (allou), 11 top right (AltoClassic), 103 top left (AmandaLewis), 174 top left (AMR Image), 175 top left (AndamanSE), 63 bottom center right (Andrea Izzotti), 40 center (AndreaAstes), 163 bottom right (Andrey Prokhorov), 171 center left (andyKRAKOVSKI), 76 top right (AniphaeS), 168 center right (annedde), 165 bottom center right (Antagain), 50 bottom center left (antoniotruzzi), 105 bottom right (aoldman), 107 center (apletfx), 110 center top right (April30), 93 bottom left top (assalve), 50 bottom center, 207 (bagi1998), 143 center top left (Beeldbewerking), 163 top right (benjaminalbiach), 93 top left (bereta), 43 top left (BlackJack3D), cover bottom center left (blueringmedia), 165 center (Bobtokyoharris), 171 bottom left (Bosca78), cover center right (brainmaster), 84 bottom right (breckeni), 194 center bottom right (BrendanHunter), 70 center left top (BruceBlock), 159 center top left (ChaoticMind75), 188 top right (chiggs), 177 center right (chinasong), 34-35 background (ClaudioVentrella), 47 bottom left (clu), 149 bottom center left (coddy), 66 bottom left (CTRPhotos), 83 center left, 149 center right (Dazman), 129 bottom left (dem10), 85 top right (DieterMeyrl), 193 top right (Dimos), 176 center bottom (dja65), 72-73 (Dmitry_Chulov), 87 center (dobok), 13 top left alchemy, 93 center, 110 center bottom, 183 center (duncan1890), 192 top (DustyPixel), 108 center left (edoneil), 79 center left (eldadcarin), 166-167 (ErikaKirky), 13 right servers (ersinkisacik), 26 center (ewg3D), 183 top right (eZeePics Studio), 168 bottom right (Falcor), cover bottom left (fatmayilmaz), 74 center bottom (federicocimino), 163 bottom center (felixR), 194 center top right (Fertnig), 119 bottom center (filonmar), 93 bottom right (FlamingPumpkin), 184 bottom left (Floortje), 83 center left top (FokinOl), 169 center right (fotokostic), 76 bottom center (franckreporter), 84 center right top (FrankvandenBergh), 91 center right (Freder), 11 top center right (Frozenmost), 136 top right (Geo-grafika), 141 center left (georgeclerk), 137 bottom center (gerenme), cover center left top (ginosphotos), 177 top left (GlobalP), 90 center left bottom (gmutlu), 195 center left (grybaz), 181 top left (Heiko119), cover center left (hh5800), 122 center left bottom (huettenhoelscher), 129 center left (iconeer), 143 bottom right (ilbusca), 143 center top right (Innerflux), 10 top (intst), 158 bottom right (ithinksky), 79 top center, 79 top right (ivan-96), cover spine red blood cell, 61 center right (Ivcandy), 51 bottom left (Ivorr), 70 center top (J_GriffithPhotography), 19 center (jakkapan21), 183 bottom right (jamesbenet), 124 bottom left (javi_martin), 85 bottom right (JaysonPhotography), 45 top right (jewhyte), 189 center left (jfmdesign), 93 center center right bottom (joecicak), 132 center left bottom (joel-t), 93 bottom center (Joesboy), 55 center right (jondpatton), 87 center right (Jordanlye), 13 top right (JunotPhotography), 123 top right (kadmy), 193 left (Kallen061), 63 center right top, 113 top right, 119 center left (Kerrick), 208 (Kerrick), 108 bottom, 202 right (kodachrome25), 116-117 background (Krasyuk), 62 (krissanapongw), 163 center top (lagereek), 58 bottom (Lalocracio), 189 center top right (Lars Neumann), 77 bottom right, 130 bottom center, 203 left (Lebazele), 158 top right (LiuNian), 127 top left (lolon), 132 center right bottom (Lorerock81), 63 bottom right (lpkoe), 110 center top left (lucentius), 158 center top (luismmolina), 123 bottom center right (macky_ch), 193 bottom right (madsci), 185 center top left (magnetcreative), 63 center left (malerapaso), cover bottom right, 1, 13 top left gold, 55 bottom right, 93 center right bottom right, 159 center bottom left (MarcelC), 28 center left (MarkFGD), 119 bottom left (MarVal), 136 center right (Maxiphoto), 32 (maxsol7), 194 center left (mgkaya), 145 bottom (MichaelUtech), 54 bottom right (mikulas1), 163 center bottom (milehightraveler), 149 bottom center right (Mimadeo), 193 center right (Mirko_Rosenau), 165 bottom left (mmac72), 114 center right (Mordolff), 131 top center (mustafagull), 171 center right bottom (MVorobiev), 177 top right (Natikka), 77 center left (Nexxtus), 70 center bottom (Nickbeer), 40 bottom left (Nickos), 13 right chip (nicodemis), 110 bottom left (nicoolay), 122 center (nightman1965), 16-17 (Nikada), 89 bottom center (nikamata), 85 center right (nikkytok), 37 bottom right, 171 top center, 189 top right (NNehring), 119 bottom right (objectifphoto), 37 bottom left (OK-Photography), 108 center (OliverChilds), 130 top center (omada), 165 center left (ooyoo), 164 (ouchi_iro), 106 center right, 127 center bottom right (papovaphoto), 12 bottom left inset background (PaulGregg), 149 right (pelicankate), 63 bottom center left (PetarAn), 163 top left (Pgiam), 83 top left (photocatjb), 190-191 (PhotographerOlympus), 151 top right (PictureLake), 86 center (Pillon), 145 center bottom (PocholoCalapre), 12-13 top background (poplasen), back cover center right (Pradit_Ph), 44 center left (praisaeng), 192 center right (primeimages), 30-31 (quangpraha), 13 Marie Curie (raclro), 105 bottom left (rebius), 74 center top, 176 center (RelaxFoto.de), 195 center right (Ridofranz), 71 center right top (rightdx), 163 center right (robynmac), 97 top right (ROMAOSLO), 93 bottom center right top (rtguest), 105 top right (RudyBalasko), 6-7 (rypson), 67 center right top (SabirBabayev), 178-179 (saiko3p), 127 center bottom left (sasimoto), scratchy background texture and throughout (Savushkin), 123 top center right (schlol), 93 center right bottom left (scottbeard), 52-53 background, 175 center left (sdlgzps), 119 center right (sebastianosecondi), 97 top center (sedmak), 26 right (SeppFriedhuber), 19 center top (SERGZEL), 82 (sezer66), back cover brooch, 74 center right (shutterman99), 195 bottom right (simonbradfield), 63 top left (Sitade), 75 center top (skynesher), 175 center right (SoumenNath), 108 top right (Spauln), 28 center (Starcevic), 165 bottom right (strmko), 185 center bottom left (Studio1One), cover spine gold coin, 168 center left bottom (studiocasper), 109 center left (studionobra), 162 center left bottom (subtik), 113 center bottom (SunChan), 171 bottom right (Sunnybeach), 154 center right bottom (Sutthaburawonk), 122 center left top (swedewah), 149 top left (swyz), 176 center right (Tanaphong), 165 bottom center left top, 175 bottom right (temmuz can arsiray), 180 (theartist312), cover top right, cover spine molecule, 83 center top, 174 center, 174 center right, 198 right, 200 right (theasis), 88 center (THEGIFT777), 177 center (tiler84), 51 top center (tilzit), 123 top center left (TomasSereda), 21 center right (Tramino), 88 bottom left, 204 left (traveler1116), 118 top center left (travellinglight), cover center right bottom (tussik13), 133 top right (typhoonski), 149 bottom right (VioNet), 149 center bottom (vkp-australia), 139 (vladimir_n), 133 center (vojtechvlk), cover center left bottom, 18 center right top, 18 bottom right, 75 bottom left, 86 bottom, 109 center bottom, 161 center left, 162 bottom left, 185 center right, 199 (VvoeVale), 188 center (vvvita), 163 center left (WendellandCarolyn), 184 center bottom (wenht), 97 bottom right (whitemay), 171 top left (wir0man), 117 center top (wonry), 184 bottom right (wragg), 165 top left (wwing), 127 bottom left (wynnter), 13 bottom right, 63 bottom left (xenotar), 191 bottom center (xenotar), 188 bottom right (yongkiet), 130 top right (yurazaga), 126 (zdo9), 112 (zhudifeng), 194 bottom center (Zoran Kolundzija); Library of Congress: 97 bottom center (Andreas Feininger), 90 center left top (B.L. Singley), 53 bottom (Carol M. Highsmith), 79 top left (Detroit Photographic Co.), 108 center right (Herbert George Ponting), 103 bottom right (Keystone View Company), 59 top right, 83 center right (Russell Lee), 61 bottom right (Underwood & Underwood), 127 center bottom (WPA Federal Art Project), 46, 68-69, 110 top right, 145 center right, 150 center right, 151 bottom right; Courtesy of LLNL: 114 bottom left; NASA: 74 center left bottom (ESA), 22 (H. Ford (JHU), G. Illingworth (USCS/LO), M. Clampin (STScI), G. Hartig (STScI), the ACS Science Team, and ESA), cover, back cover Mercury (Johns Hopkins University Applied Physics Laboratory/Carnegie Institution of Washington), 61 top right (JPL), back cover bottom right, 36 bottom right (JPL-Caltech), 85 bottom left (Virgil L. Sharpton, University of Alaska, Fairbanks), 10-11 background, 18-19 sun, 21 top right, 21 bottom right, 23 top left, 23 planets, 63 center, 87 bottom right, 91 bottom right, 105 center left, 106 top right, 117 bottom right, 118 bottom left, 122 top right, 129 center right, 130 bottom left, 150 center left, 151 center right, 152-153, 161 right, 163 bottom left, 168 center left top, 169 bottom right, 175 top right, 191 center right, 195 top; Science Source: back cover bottom left (Alexandre Dotta), 24, 25 left (Alexandre Dotta), 33 bottom right, 185 right (Andrew Lambert Photography), 120, 121 (Andrew Syred), 60 bottom left (Biophoto Associates), 41 center left, 169 left, 188 left (Charles D. Winters), 12 bottom background, 13 bottom background (Clive Streeter/Dorling Kindersley/Science Museum, London), 132 center top left (De Agostini Picture Library), 63 center right bottom, 75 top right, 84 center right bottom, 88 right, 89 left, 93 center right top left, 133 left (Dirk Wiersma), 9 top (Dr. Mitsuo Ohtsuki), 18 center left, 184 top right (Gary Ombler/Dorling Kindersley), 45 left, 132 bottom right, 137 bottom right (Harry Taylor/Dorling Kindersley), 97 top left (Harry Taylor/Dorling Kindersley/Natural History Museum, London), 159 center (M. I. Walker), 77 top right (Manfred Kage), 44 top center (Martyn F. Chillmaid), 160, 161 background (Michael Szoenyi), 89 top right (National Physical Laboratory/Crown Copyright), 148 (Patrick Landmann), 36 top right, 106 bottom left, 107 bottom (Phil Degginger), 56, 57 (Philippe Psaila), 146, 147 (RIA Novosti), 18 center bottom, 37 center, 44 center, 50 center top left, 58 center bottom, 66 bottom center, 118 top right, 122 center right, 133 bottom, 136 bottom center, 137 top left, 138 top right, 171 center, 177 bottom right (SPL), 12 bottom left inset (Steve Gorton), 87 top left (Steve Gschmeissner), 58 right, 59 left (Ted Kinsman), 43 top right (Thierry Berrod, Mona Lisa Production), 151 left (U.S. Department of Energy), 43 bottom right, 47 center, 47 bottom center, 124 center left, 127 center top right, 145 top center left; Shutterstock: back cover zinc ingots, 67 bottom right (Bjoern Wylezich), 196-197 (ESB Professional), 127 center top (Everett Historical), 28 center right (farbled), 45 right (Ivan Cholakov), 79 bottom (Katarzyna Wolska Pociask), 40 right, 41 left (Natali_ua), 111 top left (Stephen Chung), 132 center right top (tam_odin), 23 center (Todd Dalton), 5 (V. Kuntsman); The Bowes Museum: 79 center right; The University of British Columbia/Paul Hickson: 97 bottom left; Thinkstock/delb0y: cover top center; USGS/NOAA: 142 background; Wellcome Images: 13 Dmitri Mendeleev, 25 center top, 25 center bottom, 35 center, 35 center bottom, 117 center bottom, 123 bottom center left, 124 bottom right; Wikimedia: back cover coin (Bank CCCP), 27 right (Dnn87), 155 center right (Lawrence Berkeley Laboratory), 154 center right top (Lawrence Berkeley National Laboratory), 13 Glenn Seaborg (NARA), 44 top right (Peter Van den Bossche), 93 center right top right (US Mint), 123 bottom left (War Department), 118 bottom right, 145 top center, 154 bottom left.

All other images © Scholastic Inc.

The publisher would like to give particular thanks to the following people for their help: Dawn Bates, Tory Gordon-Harris, Ali Scrivens, John Goldsmid, Marybeth Kavanagh, Debbie Kurosz, and Ed Kasche; Jane Whittaker and Claire Jordan of The Bowes Museum, Co. Durham, England; Denis Skov; Tony Watts, Bapty & Co.; Ake Dahilof; Professor Paul Hickson, University of British Columbia; Kate Hunts, Lawrence Livermore National Laboratory; University College Museums and Collections, London; Steetley Minerals, Nottinghamshire, England; Holts, London.

Silicon metal